Reading Opera between the Lines

A characteristic feature of Wagnerian and post-Wagnerian opera is the tendency to link scenes with numerous and often surprisingly lengthy orchestral interludes, frequently performed with the curtain closed. Often taken for granted or treated as a filler by audiences and critics, these interludes may in fact take on very prominent roles, representing dream sequences, journeys or sexual encounters, and in some cases becoming a highlight of the opera. Christopher Morris investigates the implications of these important but strangely overlooked passages. Combining close readings of individual musical texts with an investigation of the critical discourse surrounding the operas, Morris shows how the interludes shed light not only on the representational and narrative capacities of the orchestra, but also on the supposed 'absolute' realm of instrumental music, a concept to which many critics appealed when they associated the interludes with 'purely musical' and 'symphonic' qualities.

CHRISTOPHER MORRIS is Lecturer in Music at University College Cork. His articles have appeared in the *Journal of Musicological Research*, *Musical Quarterly* and the *Journal of the Royal Musical Society*.

New perspectives in music history and criticism

GENERAL EDITORS
JEFFREY KALLBERG, ANTHONY NEWCOMB AND RUTH SOLIE

This series explores the conceptual frameworks that shape or have shaped the ways in which we understand music and its history, and aims to elaborate structures of explanation, interpretation, commentary, and criticism which make music intelligible and which provide a basis for argument about judgements of value. The intellectual scope of the series is broad. Some investigations will treat, for example, historiographical topics, others will apply cross-disciplinary methods to the criticism of music, and there will also be studies which consider music in its relation to society, culture, and politics. Overall, the series hopes to create a greater presence for music in the ongoing discourse among the human sciences.

PUBLISHED TITLES

Leslie C. Dunn and Nancy A. Jones (eds.), *Embodied Voices: Representing Female Vocality in Western Culture*

Downing A. Thomas, *Music and the Origins of Language: Theories from the French Enlightenment*

Thomas S. Grey, *Wagner's Musical Prose*

Daniel K. L. Chua, *Absolute Music and the Construction of Meaning*

Adam Krims, *Rap Music and the Poetics of Identity*

Annette Richards, *The Free Fantasia and the Musical Picturesque*

Richard Will, *The Characteristic Symphony in the Age of Haydn and Beethoven*

Christopher Morris, *Reading Opera between the Lines: Orchestral Interludes and Cultural Meaning from Wagner to Berg*

Reading Opera between the Lines

Orchestral Interludes and Cultural Meaning from Wagner to Berg

CHRISTOPHER MORRIS

CAMBRIDGE
UNIVERSITY PRESS

PUBLISHED BY THE PRESS SYNDICATE OF THE UNIVERSITY OF CAMBRIDGE
The Pitt Building, Trumpington Street, Cambridge, United Kingdom

CAMBRIDGE UNIVERSITY PRESS
The Edinburgh Building, Cambridge CB2 2RU, UK
40 West 20th Street, New York, NY 10011-4211, USA
477 Williamstown Road, Port Melbourne, VIC 3207, Australia
Ruiz de Alarcón 13, 28014 Madrid, Spain
Dock House, The Waterfront, Cape Town 8001, South Africa

http://www.cambridge.org

First published 2002

Printed in the United Kingdom at the University Press, Cambridge

Typeface Palatino 10/12 pt.   *System* LATEX 2$_\varepsilon$ [TB]

A catalogue record for this book is available from the British Library

Library of Congress Cataloguing in Publication data

Morris, Christopher 1966–
Reading opera between the lines : orchestral interludes and cultural meaning from
Wagner to Berg / Christopher Morris.
        p.   cm. – (New perspectives in music history and criticism)
Includes bibliographical references (p.) and index.
ISBN 0 521 80738 7
1. Music – Philosophy and aesthetics.   2. Entr'acte music – History and criticism.
3. Opera.   I. Title.   II. Series.
ML3845 .M87   2002   784.18′93 – dc21   2001043313

ISBN 0 521 80738 7 hardback

For Cindy

CONTENTS

ACKNOWLEDGEMENTS

This project would never have got off the ground without the encouraging words of Gaynor Jones, who convinced me that these in-between orchestral passages might merit scholarly investigation. I am particularly grateful to David and Vivienne Foster and to Norman and Gwen Zelmer for their support. Rachel Segal has been an invaluable ally, forcing me to rethink issues with her spot-on questions, and Julian Rushton was supportive of my work from the very beginning. My thanks also to James Parakilas for some helpful suggestions, and to Julie Hubbert for reading a draft chapter at very short notice. As both doctoral supervisor and friend, Peter Franklin has stimulated my thinking again and again, but, more than that, he has encouraged me to think about music in new and more meaningful ways. For that I am in his debt. To Cindy I owe a great deal. This book is dedicated to her.

I would like to express my gratitude to the Committee of Vice-Chancellors and Principals of the Universities of the United Kingdom for an Overseas Research Studentship, to the University of Leeds for a Tetley and Lupton Scholarship and Lord Snowden Award, and to the Social Sciences and Humanities Research Council of Canada for a Doctoral Fellowship. My thanks also to University College Cork for its support of my research through travel grants and an Arts Faculty Research Grant.

Grateful thanks are due to the copyright holders for permission to include excerpts from the following scores: *Feuersnot*, Copyright 1901, 1910 by Adolph Förstner. US Copyright renewed. Copyright assigned 1943 to Hawkes & Son (London) Ltd (a Boosey & Hawkes Company) for the world excluding Germany, Italy, Portugal and the former territories of the USSR (excluding Estonia, Latvia and Lithuania). Reproduced by permission of Boosey & Hawkes Music Publishers Ltd; *Die Rose vom Liebesgarten*, Copyright 1901, 1905 by Max Brockhaus Musikverlag; *A Village Romeo and Juliet*, Copyright 1910 by Hawkes & Son (London) Ltd. Reproduced by permission of Boosey & Hawkes Music Publishers Ltd; *Der Schatzgräber*, Copyright 1919 by Universal Edition. Reproduced by permission of Alfred A. Kalmus Ltd; *Wozzeck*, Copyright 1926 by Universal Edition A.G., Vienna. Reproduced by permission of Alfred A. Kalmus Ltd.

Acknowledgments

A portion of chapter 2 originally appeared as 'What the Conductor Saw: Sex, Fantasy, and the Orchestra in Strauss's *Feuersnot*', *Journal of Musicological Research* 16/2 (1996). It is reproduced here with permission of Taylor and Francis Ltd. Chapter 4 is a revised version of ' "Sympathy with Death": Nostalgia and Narcissism in the Post-Wagnerian Orchestra', which appeared in the *Musical Quarterly* 85/1 (2001). It is reproduced here with kind permission of Oxford University Press.

Introduction

Video productions of opera stagings are occasionally confronted with the awkward problem of what to do during the recurring and often lengthy orchestral interludes in the Wagnerian and post-Wagnerian repertoire. The standard solution is to film the conductor in the pit, with perhaps occasional shots of the orchestra. While the theatre audience sits in darkness, we peer into that usually invisible space as Claudio Abbado and the Vienna Philharmonic perform Berg's *Wozzeck* or James Levine and the Metropolitan Opera Orchestra interpret Wagner's *Ring*. In the celebrated Chéreau–Boulez centenary *Ring* from Bayreuth, opera video producer Brian Large resorts to a combination of prerecorded footage (a journey up the hill to the Festspielhaus) and slowly zooming shots of the vacated stage. Other solutions include freeze-frame images from the staged action or panning shots of the score in an operatic version of the 'follow the bouncing ball' technique once popular in television.

All seem to obey that unwritten rule of film and video, that the screen should never go dark, that there should always be an image. It is a rule that stands at odds with the kind of experience that these operas celebrate, for although the interludes are occasionally accompanied by a scenic transformation or pantomime, they tend most often to be performed in front of a closed curtain or obscured stage. They are part of a musico-theatrical experience, partly inspired by Wagner's experiments at Bayreuth, that depends on a heavily darkened auditorium and a concealed or partially concealed orchestra pit. The result is a carefully manipulated environment based precisely on the withdrawal of the visual. The effect of this contrast is lost when translated to the more visual media of film and television, where the interludes really do seem to serve nothing more than that 'in between' function that their name implies, whether *interlude, Zwischenspiel, entr'acte* or *intermezzo*.

Orchestral interludes of this kind can prove as problematic for audiences as for producers. The closing of a curtain or the onset of a scenic transformation can serve as a cue to relax and lower attentiveness until the beginning of the next scene, a tendency that manifests itself in the form of a general audience 'buzz' and the rustling of programmes as spectators strain in the feeble light to make out a plot synopsis.

1

Sir Thomas Beecham once berated English audiences for their inability to maintain silence during interludes, adding:

What the public does not see it takes no interest in, and I would advise all young composers, if they wish their music to be heard, never to lower the curtain for one second during the course of the act.[1]

The difficulty is compounded by the fact that a scenic change, with its potentially disruptive noise, will often be taking place behind the curtain during the interlude. Siegfried Wagner illustrated the problem in the score of his opera *Der Heidenkönig* (1914), when he prefaced an orchestral interlude with the following instruction:

During the interlude great care should taken to ensure that the piece, which the composer values highly, is not ruined by the noise of the scene change.[2]

Concerns such as these testify to a conflict between an understanding of music theatre as a concentrated, unbroken 'aesthetic' experience in which the orchestral role is integral, and more traditionally 'operatic' conceptions that tend to centre to a greater degree on voice and stage action.

Origins

As *entr'actes* and *sinfonie*, orchestral interludes had formed a traditional component of operatic form from its very beginnings in the seventeenth century. Within the context of the overall operatic experience, though, their function was (perhaps quite naturally) peripheral to the dramatic, vocal, and visual appeals of the staged scenes. They might have offered musical contrast or set a mood in the broadest sense, but they were equally likely to provide an opportunity to converse, to socialise, to gaze at that other operatic spectacle: the audience. In this capacity the orchestral interlude played a passive role, although one that had come to define part of what attending the opera meant. One of the recurring features of the history of opera, though, is the self-conscious attempt to reform and refine the genre, and in the late eighteenth century the question of the orchestra's role and the nature of the *entr'acte* came under scrutiny. In his famous dedication of *Alceste* (1769) Gluck articulated a desire that composers pay more attention to the dramatic potential of the orchestra:

I considered that the sinfonia [overture] should inform the spectators of the subject that is to be enacted, and constitute, as it were, the argument... that

---

[1] Thomas Beecham, *A Mingled Chime* (New York: G. P. Putnam's Sons, 1943), p. 144.
[2] Piano-vocal score (Bayreuth: Carl Giessel, 1913).

[the orchestra] should not break up a sentence non-sensically, nor interrupt the force and heat of the action inappropriately.[3]

Gluck's statement, itself heir to a long tradition of reformist thought in France and Italy, is a call to rethink a tradition of orchestral music that has little relevance to the dramatic aim, that hampers the goal of a 'beautiful simplicity', and that fails to contribute to a unity of 'expression'.[4] David Charlton has chronicled the experiments with the role of the *entr'acte* in the *opéras comiques* of Grétry during the 1780s and 1790s, experiments that included orchestral rearrangements of earlier vocal numbers, anticipation of an aria to be sung when the curtain opens, and musical representations of action imagined to be taking place between the acts.[5] Anxious to stress the implications of these developments for operatic reform, Grétry declared proudly in his 1797 *Mémoires*:

I was the first to suppress the orchestral piece known as the *entr'acte*, in order to substitute another which would have greater connection with the preceding or succeeding action of the drama.[6]

In fact, as Charlton points out, Grétry's experiments followed earlier explorations of dramatically relevant *entr'actes*, such as those in Philidor's *Tom Jones* (1765) and Gossec's *Les pêcheurs* (1766). By the 1790s thematic quotations from the main body of the opera were common features of overtures, and the idea of a programmatic anticipation of the plot, already demonstrated in Gluck's *Iphigénie en Aulide* (1774), seems to have been further encouraged by – and to have in turn demanded – technical refinements of wind instruments and the expansion of opera orchestras, particularly in *opéra comique* of the Revolutionary period.[7] In Méhul's *Mélidore et Phrosine* (1794), with its vivid built-in *entr'acte* to the third act, we can already see the outlines of nineteenth-century preludes in

---

[3] Patricia Howard (ed. and trans.), *Gluck: An Eighteenth-Century Portrait in Letters and Documents* (Oxford: Oxford University Press, 1995), p. 85.

[4] Much of the dedication addresses itself to Italian opera and its vocal biases, but the remarks on the orchestra suggest French opera, and particularly the *tragédies lyriques* of Rameau, as both target and model: 'target' in the sense that the copious *symphonies de danse* and other forms of *divertissement* in Rameau's operas exemplify Gluck's charge of 'inappropriate' orchestral music, and 'model' in the sense that his descriptive symphonies (storms, battle scenes) and programmatic overtures (such as the overture to *Zoroastre* of 1749) demonstrate how the orchestra might be drawn into a very direct dramatic role.

[5] David Charlton, *Grétry and the Growth of Opéra-Comique* (Cambridge: Cambridge University Press, 1990), pp. 308–10.

[6] A.-E.-M. Grétry, *Mémoires*, vol. III (Brussels: Publication of Belgian Govt., 1925), p. 191, trans. in Charlton, *Grétry and the Growth of Opéra-Comique*, p. 29.

[7] A particularly vivid programmatic overture is to be found in Méhul's *Le jeune Henri* (1797). The rejected overture to *Fidelio* (*Leonore* Overture No. 3) has often been performed as an *entr'acte* before the third act.

which the ensuing act's plot developments and dramatic mood could be established musically. In other words, it is not only in the extent but in the nature of the orchestra's dramatic involvement that this repertoire seems to anticipate nineteenth-century practice. Summarising theoretical and critical responses to the opera orchestra in France in the late eighteenth century, Charlton concludes:

[T]here is evidently a public acceptance that orchestras and instruments embodied narrative capacity, even within instrumental movements; and an expectation that the interior life of operatic figures would be completely symbolised by orchestral means ... to the extent that their consciousness, inner contradictions and imaginations might be depicted from moment to moment so clearly that we might envision them as separable characters.[8]

So there was a shared understanding not only that the non-vocal musical discourse might participate dramatically with the voices, but also that the unstaged, textless orchestra might have access to 'interiority', a quality central to the nineteenth-century understanding of the opera orchestra.

One manifestation of these perceptions of the orchestra as dramatic agent was an increasing use of recurring motifs and themes that carry specific dramatic associations.[9] Usually heard at pivotal moments of the drama, these so-called 'reminiscence motifs' arguably form too skeletal a musical framework across the opera as a whole to be considered in relation to the (instrumentally centred) concepts of musical unity and organicism then beginning to emerge. What they do imply is a more thorough *dramatic* integration of the orchestral discourse, an integration that reflects the conscious drive towards a general aesthetic cohesiveness and wholeness in opera. Earlier eighteenth-century opera had thoroughly demonstrated the capacity of the orchestra to contribute to drama without reminiscence motifs, but the self-advertising quality of the motifs could perhaps be seen to have focused awareness on the potential of the orchestra as a medium that extended the drama's representational and narrative means while pulling its musical and theatrical components closer together in ways that contributed to the opera's perceived integrity.

These developments and the reformist views of Gluck and Grétry have nevertheless to be weighed against the realities of the theatrical environment. Repeatedly, the drive towards opera as 'legitimate', unified drama (based on appeals to classical ideals) had conflicted with

---

[8] David Charlton, ' "Envoicing" the Orchestra: Enlightenment Metaphors in Theory and Practice', in *French Opera 1730–1830: Meaning and Media* (Aldershot: Ashgate, 2000), p. 31.

[9] A feature of many turn-of-the-century *opéras comiques* (Grétry's *Guillaume Tell* of 1791 is a notable example), the technique was in a sense codified by Louis Spohr when he prefaced his *Faust* (1813) with an explanation of his method and intentions.

a conception of opera, reinforced by theatrical tradition, that unapologetically embraced its appeals to social occasion and spectacle. It was a conflict that the nineteenth century would inherit and further problematise. Accounts of audience behaviour in early nineteenth-century Paris tell a story of a struggle between the demand from some for silence and sustained concentration and the tendency for audiences to tailor their attentiveness, as they had done in the eighteenth century, to what were considered musical and dramatic highlights. The result was noise and activity that competed with the musico-dramatic spectacle and that represented either its natural complement or a disturbance, depending on the point of view. Judging by the reaction of one English visitor to the Opéra in 1815, the norms of audience behaviour in European theatres were far from universal: he was surprised to see members of the audience leaving and arriving throughout the performance, to hear doors slamming and people 'talking, laughing, and exchanging compliments' over the music.[10] But Parisian audience behaviour was changing, as reflected in the critical and anecdotal accounts of operatic performance in the 1830s. James H. Johnson has shown how silence and constant attention (or at least its appearance) were increasingly becoming the norm, as new definitions of musical experience and meaning gained currency in Parisian cultural life. Shaped in part by the changing social make-up of opera audiences and bound up with the Parisian reception of Beethoven's music and the ideas it generated, the new attitudes would gradually transform the identity of the operatic experience there, as they would in other parts of Europe.[11]

By seeking to exclude what were considered trappings, decoration, and distraction from the properly 'aesthetic' core of the musico-dramatic experience, these new definitions of music theatre marked a shift away from opera defined in terms of practices, settings, and occasion towards a concept of the 'work' that implies a form independent of its actual theatrical realisation. Critical to that notion was the impression of completeness and unity, implying a cohesive identity that would assert itself over the circumstances of performance rather than submitting to or depending on them. In this way the 'work' would draw the audience 'into' its coherent and always meaningful space rather than catering to the fragmenting effects of momentary and variable audience appeal. Writing in 1817, Weber declared that this would have to become the defining feature of German opera:

---

[10] Anon., *Memorandums of a Residence in France, in the Winter of 1815–16* (London: Longman, Hurst, Rees, Orme, and Brown, 1816), p. 289, cited in James H. Johnson, *Listening in Paris: A Cultural History* (Berkeley and Los Angeles: University of California Press, 1995), p. 170.

[11] Johnson, *Listening in Paris*.

Whereas other nations concern themselves with the sensual pleasure [*Sinnenlust*] of isolated moments, [the German] demands a self-sufficient work of art, in which all the parts make up a beautiful and unified whole.[12]

One of the sensual pleasures to which Weber undoubtedly alludes is the role of the voice in opera, an issue that pitted the new operatic ideals against the supposedly debased practices of Italian opera. Here opera's reliance on vocal music turns on the distinction between the sublime dignity of instrumental music and the all too earthly basis of the voice. Berlioz exemplifies this attitude when he characterises 'modern Italian cantilena' in terms of a 'voluptuous sensation' and contrasts it with the extraordinary effects of the instrumental music of Beethoven and Weber:

These are not at all what one experiences in the theatre: there one is in the presence of humanity and its emotions; here a new world is opened up to view, one is raised into a higher ideal region, one senses that the sublime life dreamed of by poets is becoming a reality.[13]

It is against the background of this polarisation of the vocal and instrumental that the orchestral role in opera expanded, a development that ultimately assumed the character of a redemption of theatre from its materiality.

Answering the call

Weber's appeal to the concept of a 'self-sufficient work of art' constitutes a challenge to German artists to uphold a national ideal of art and to realise it in operatic form. His article was addressed to the 'art-loving' citizens of Dresden on the occasion of his appointment as court Kapellmeister, and it was one of those citizens who would ultimately present himself as answering the call. Wagner not only inherited but further intensified Weber's nationalistic operatic idealism, and a through-composed orchestral discourse was to become central to his response. In the operas up to and including *Lohengrin* we encounter a whole range of issues surrounding the orchestra's role in opera: Wagner writes programmatic overtures and extended preludes and takes full advantage of the possibilities of reminiscence motifs. He also intensifies a long-standing tension between closed numbers and large, continuous scenes, between traditional forms and a tendency to blend those

---

[12] Carl Maria von Weber, 'An die kunstliebenden Bewohner Dresdens', *Dresden Abend-Zeitung*, 26 January 1817, in Georg Kaiser (ed.), *Sämtliche Schriften von Carl Maria von Weber* (Berlin and Leipzig: Schuster and Loeffler, 1908), p. 277. All translations are mine unless otherwise indicated.

[13] Hector Berlioz, article in *Le Correspondant*, 22 October 1832, trans. in Julian Rushton, *Berlioz: 'Roméo et Juliette'* (Cambridge: Cambridge University Press, 1994), p. 90.

numbers into longer through-composed structures against a continuous orchestral backdrop. It is a tendency already evident in the finales of late eighteenth-century opera, but it reaches an unprecedented scale in the chains of scenes in Revolutionary *opéra comique* (linked by recurring motivic material and orchestral sonority), in the grand, orchestrally centred scenes in the operas of Spontini, and in early German through-composed operas such as Weber's *Euryanthe* and Spohr's *Jessonda*, both premiered in 1823.

For all the blurring of divisions between individual numbers and the gradual abandonment of spoken dialogue in the comic genres, *caesurae* nevertheless remain common in these scores, both between numbers and between scenes. Writing shortly after the premiere of *Der fliegende Holländer* in 1843, Wagner acknowledged the prevalence of these operatic traditions in order to distinguish his own achievement: 'From the outset I had to abandon the modern arrangement of dividing the work into arias, duets, finales, etc., and instead relate the legend in a single breath.'[14] For all the self-promotion evident here, Wagner's claim cannot be dismissed entirely as hot air. *Holländer* does indeed seem to be marked by an extraordinary and sustained effort to elide numbers and scenes. Particularly striking is the opera's original version (1841), for not only do numbers and scenes tend to follow one another without a break, but the three acts are linked with orchestral interludes. When in 1901 Cosima Wagner presented *Holländer* at Bayreuth for the first time, she revived this version, no doubt hoping to emphasise its historical and stylistic links with the later music dramas. Wagner, however, had developed this continuous form from a draft scenario in one act submitted to the Paris Opéra as a possible curtain-raiser to a ballet. When the Opéra rejected the proposal, Wagner expanded the design, composing the music in the form of three linked acts. But for the Dresden premiere in 1843 he abandoned this plan and divided the opera into three discrete acts (the interludes were converted into act endings and introductions). The continuous version was less a first step in the unfolding of an as yet unconscious artistic destiny (as Bayreuth and Wagner himself later liked to imply) than an intermediary stage in the opera's transformation from curtain-raiser to main bill, and *Holländer* was not performed or published in this form during Wagner's lifetime. Even so, the temptation to interpret this early version as a taste of things to come is strong.

Looking at the form of *Der Ring des Nibelungen*, it becomes yet more difficult to challenge Wagner's self-styled image as radical reformer of

---

[14] Wagner, letter to Ferdinand Heine, August 1843, in Werner Breig, 'The Musical Works', trans. Paul Knight and Horst Loeschmann, in Ulrich Müller and Peter Wapnewski (eds.), *Wagner Handbook*, translation edited by John Deathridge (Cambridge, Mass.: Harvard University Press, 1992), p. 416.

opera. Although traces of the closed number tradition are still evident in the poetic text of the *Ring*, any impression of gaps is smoothed over with act-long spans of continuous music sustained by the orchestra, any jarring contrasts being subordinated to what Wagner proudly called his 'art of transition'.[15] In *Zukunftsmusik* (1860) Wagner complains of the 'painful' effects of the contrasts in number opera:

[After the recitative] the full orchestra strikes in with its inevitable ritornello to announce the aria, the same ritornello that the same master has used elsewhere as a connecting or transitional passage so meaningful that we had accorded it an articulate beauty all of its own. Then it had given us the most telling insight into the heart of the situation, but what if one of these gems of art is now immediately followed by a number aimed at the most base artistic tastes?[16]

Ostensibly, the role of the orchestral interludes in music drama is to maintain musical continuity during scene changes, to mobilise the art of transition by dovetailing one scene into the next. But in so doing they take on a narrative-interpretative function that is reinforced by the expansion of reminiscence motifs to what Wagner called a 'tissue of principal themes'[17] (the leitmotif technique), and they can in fact assume pivotal, even climactic roles both musically and dramatically (the *Trauermarsch* in *Götterdämmerung* certainly fits this description). The result is a conflict between music that represents a stop-gap measure (literally and figuratively) and the prominent position to which it is assigned.

Drawing on years of conducting experience, familiarity with the latest refinements of orchestral instruments, and the orchestration of six operas, Wagner was well prepared to create impressive orchestral effects. But, as we shall see, nineteenth-century ears, from Hanslick's to Nietzsche's, were in no way prepared for what was felt to be the utterly overwhelming effect of his orchestra. Imbued with Wagner's musical affinity for impressions of sublimity, exaltation, and emotional intensity, it proved to be the most effective weapon in the arsenal of music drama, unleashed from the very beginning with the impressive preludes. Not content to offer the orchestra a new and augmented role, Wagner had to declare himself heir to the symphonic tradition of Beethoven, a tradition he interprets in terms of the primacy of thematic/motivic manipulation and development. From this perspective every aspect of the motivically laden orchestral discourse represents an organic component in a

[15] Richard Wagner, letter to Mathilde Wesendonck, 29 October 1859, in Hanjo Kesting (ed.), *Richard Wagner Briefe* (Munich and Zurich: Piper Verlag, 1983), p. 405.
[16] Richard Wagner, *Zukunftsmusik* (1860), in Richard Sternfeld and Hans von Wolzogen (eds.), *Richard Wagner: Sämtliche Schriften und Dichtungen* (hereafter abbreviated as *SSD*), vol. VII (Leipzig: Breitkopf und Härtel, 1916), p. 134.
[17] Richard Wagner, *Eine Mitteilung an meiner Freunde* (1851), *SSD*, vol. IV, p. 322.

symphonic argument, which, applied to the interludes, would seem to elevate them even further from their *entr'acte* origins.

To the extent that Wagner's symphonic claim forms another layer in the propaganda with which he surrounded music drama, we might treat it with some caution. And yet, when Wagner sought to reform the ways in which musical theatre would actually be presented and received, and built the Festspielhaus at Bayreuth to demonstrate his ideas, the symphonic claim – or rather, the lofty musical idealism associated with the symphony – found a place. This is where the darkened auditorium takes on such importance, as a means of minimising the distracting sight of the audience, of declaring the importance of every moment of music drama, including interludes. As for the invisible orchestra, it would eliminate what for Wagner was the most deflating aspect of the concert hall: the sight of musicians performing. In a darkened environment Wagner envisions the audience entering a dream-like state that he associates above all with the contrast between the ideal nature of sound and the all too mundane reality of the visual.[18] It is an attitude that is summed up in a comment quoted by Cosima Wagner in her diary: 'Having created the invisible orchestra, I now feel like inventing the invisible theatre!'[19]

The shadow of Bayreuth

Wagner's goal of an audience utterly transported by his invisible orchestra realised itself not only literally, as early critical reactions suggest, but in a broader sense, through his extraordinary cultural and historical impact. For the orchestral practices of music drama proved a dominating, indeed overpowering influence on German and French opera into the twentieth century. It was enough that Wagner's handling of the orchestra seemed so unprecedented, so 'modern'; that Wagner's symphonic idealism addressed a sense of crisis over the identity of music with a persuasive rereading of the Romantic metaphysics of instrumental music; but all this was reinforced with the experience of Bayreuth, an experience that leading conductors such as Mahler were soon trying to duplicate as they experimented with techniques such as the thoroughly darkened auditorium, then still a novelty almost everywhere but Bayreuth. As one characteristic feature of music drama and of the Bayreuth experience,

---

[18] Richard Wagner, *Beethoven* (1870), *SSD*, vol. IX, pp. 75–9. Daniel Chua shows how the emphasis on music's invisibility emerged in Romantic aesthetics as a correlate to new constructions of subjectivity as autonomous and beyond the phenomenal world. See *Absolute Music and the Construction of Meaning* (Cambridge: Cambridge University Press, 1999), pp. 191–8.

[19] Diary entry for 23 September 1878, in Martin Gregor-Dellin and Dietrich Mack (eds.), *Cosima Wagner's Diaries: An Abridgement*, trans. Geoffrey Skelton (New Haven: Yale University Press, 1994), p. 324.

the Wagnerian concept of orchestral interludes was widely adopted in musical drama from the last decades of the nineteenth century to the interwar years, a span that embraces the height of Wagnerism at the end of the nineteenth century, a prewar period characterised by an increasing problematisation of the Wagner question and (not always successful) attempts to break free from the shadow of Bayreuth, and the subsequent decline of Wagnerian influence through the 1920s as a conscious resistance to what was now considered a moribund legacy of the nineteenth century took hold.

Typical of the first phase are operas such as Felix Weingartner's *Sakuntala* (1884) and Ernest Chausson's *Le roi Arthus* (composed 1885–95, first performed 1903), in which a thoroughly Wagnerian approach to the orchestra is mirrored by Wagnerian subjects and imagery in the poetic text. Here the interludes often recall specific passages in Wagnerian music drama: the interlude in Act I of *Le roi Arthus* recalls all too clearly the prelude to Act III of *Tristan und Isolde*, while the Act III interlude suggests the transformation music in *Parsifal*. Ernest Bloch's *Macbeth* (1910) and Max von Schillings's *Mona Lisa* (1915) exemplify a freer response to the Wagnerian legacy, both musically and dramatically. Although still laden with leitmotifs in the Wagnerian manner, the interludes prove adaptable to new contexts, in Bloch's case symphonic poems of proportions far in excess of anything Wagner imagined, and in *Mona Lisa* a *verismo*-like shock climax intended to represent the tortured visions of divine judgement haunting the title figure, who has just murdered her husband.[20] By the time of Richard Strauss's *Die Frau ohne Schatten* (1919) the very obvious allusion to the *Ring* in the spectacular, supernatural appeal of the interludes seems to possess an ironic, retrospective value, while in the operas of Alban Berg the sense of continuity and smooth transition that the interludes had promoted in music drama is forced into an uneasy alliance with the very sort of closed forms they had once displaced. Reflective of the cultural trends of the 1920s are the interludes of Strauss's *Intermezzo* (1924). Here the fragmentary, cinematic quality of the numerous brief scenes casts the interludes in a

---

[20] Prominent *intermezzi* are characteristic features of the *verismo* tradition at the turn of the century. They suggest less the Wagnerian and post-Wagnerian interlude, however, than the *entr'acte* tradition. Although often musically connected with the surrounding opera through thematic quotation and dramatically integral to the operas, these interludes nevertheless resemble 'arias without words', intensely lyrical orchestral numbers, usually with a central impassioned climax that fades toward a peaceful conclusion. In this sense they have a self-contained quality, offering islands of reflection and calm amidst violent melodrama. See, for example, the *intermezzi* in Mascagni's *Cavalleria rusticana* (1890) and *L'amico Fritz* (1891), Leoncavallo's *Pagliacci* (1892), d'Albert's *Tiefland* (1903), and Puccini's *Manon Lescaut* (1893), which, though not strictly a *verismo* opera, shares many of the features of the style.

role not unlike that of a film score, while the displacement of myth and legend for domesticity and a *Zeitoper*-like contemporary setting robs them of that irrational, magical, metaphysical dimension that was so central to their role in music drama. As a musico-theatrical device, the orchestral interlude ultimately outlived post-Wagnerian opera, adapting itself to the form of a foxtrot in Krenek's *Der Sprung über den Schatten* (1924), returning to its closed-number, *entr'acte* roots in Milhaud's *Esther de Carpentras* (1925), and playing a role in operas as diverse as those of Janáček, Shostakovich, Poulenc, and Britten. But that sense of seamless symphonic totality, of overwhelming effect, of magic and transportation that music drama invested in the orchestra is something that faded when the Bayreuth spell seemed to become mere smoke and mirrors.

'Post-Wagnerian' opera is defined here in terms not so much of a crude musical and dramatic influence (although there is enough evidence of that) as of a debate on the nature of opera that positions music drama as its point of reference. Wagner's achievement may be characterised as something to live up to, to extend, to redefine, to circumnavigate, but it remains *the* question, and the terms of the debate, even when they seem to present the 'Wagner question' as the 'Wagner problem', tend to remain within a Wagnerian orbit, taking their bearing from parameters established by his theory and compositional practice. Central among them is a musical idealism that pits the purer, metaphysical experience of music against the sensual reality of theatre with its words and images. Writing in 1924, Ernest Newman envisaged a new form of drama that would extend the principles of Bayreuth:

Can we not imagine something like the second act of *Tristan* with silent and only dimly visible actors, the music, helped by their gestures, telling us all that is in their souls, while they are too remote from us for the crude personality of the actors and the theatrical artificiality of the stage setting to jar upon us as they would do at present . . . Or, to go a step further, cannot we dispense altogether with the stage and the visible actor, such external coherence in the music being afforded by the impersonal voices floating through a darkened auditorium?[21]

In his *Musik in der Weltkrise* of 1922, Adolf Weissmann reflected on the 'symphonic orchestra' and its relationship to the stage:

In Germany there has always been a peculiar resistance to realism in dramatic action. The symphonic orchestra was an attempt to go beyond the objectivity of the stage. This is a tendency, in fact, that can now be seen not only in Germany, but in all established musical cultures. Everywhere the objectivity of the stage is being overcome by the spirituality of music.[22]

---

[21] Ernest Newman, *Wagner as Man and Artist* (New York: Alfred A. Knopf, 1924), p. 439.
[22] Adolf Weissmann, *Musik in der Weltkrise* (Stuttgart and Berlin: Deutsche Verlags-Anstalt, 1922), p. 242.

Thirteen years earlier, Rudolf Louis had wondered if the future of opera lay in a 'symphonic' conception of drama centred not on theatrical but on musical principles. Citing Friedrich Klose's 'dramatische Symphonie', *Ilsebill* (1903), as a possible model, he praises what he sees as a 'musical composition . . . complemented and illustrated by a kind of theatrically represented "programme" '.[23] And in the same year, in an article entitled 'L'opéra symphonique', French critic Camille Bellaigue praised Wagner as

one of the great masters of psychological music or of musical psychology. By transferring to theatre music, to applied music, the genius of the symphony, of pure music, he created figures that, if not necessarily more human or alive, do reveal more forcefully the complexity, or even the contradiction, in humanity, in the soul, and in life.[24]

Different perspectives, but they share a view of the orchestra as bearer of a music that transcends the possibilities of staged action. For Weissmann, the 'spirituality' of the orchestra rests on its resistance not simply to the stage, but to the voice:

The human voice is the strongest obstacle to the absolute spiritualization of opera. Bound to the body and its limitations, the voice is a perpetual advocate of the sensual.[25]

Here Weissmann drives a wedge between a sensual, embodied voice and a 'spiritualising' orchestra. But it is a distinction that often threatens to collapse, and this raises a question that will form an important focus of this study. To what extent is the interludes' resistance to the performing body – the absence of the singers and the concealment of the orchestra – reflected in or contradicted by the orchestral music, by the body in the music? As musical 'islands' in a theatrical setting, the interludes can be seen to reflect, at times quite self-consciously, on the identity of music itself, and this construction of music will often turn on the conflict between metaphysical aspirations and a musical language that is all too clearly rooted in the sensual. A consistent preoccupation of the period is an anxiety over the perceived decline of music, a decline attributed to a cultural decadence rooted in an unhealthy sensuality, nervousness and hypersensitivity. Its musical symptoms were detected in features such as overly chromatic voice leading, a lack of rhythmic distinctness, harmonic vagueness, and the primacy of colour. Often characterised in

---

[23] Rudolf Louis, *Die Deutsche Musik der Gegenwart* (Munich and Leipzig: Georg Müller, 1909), p. 125.

[24] Camille Bellaigue, 'L'opéra symphonique', *Revue des Deux Mondes* 103 (June 1909), 183.

[25] Weissmann, *Musik in der Weltkrise*, p. 243.

the critical discourse with terms such as 'impressionistic',[26] it was a tendency detected not only in the supposed reliance on atmosphere and colour in the music of Debussy and Delius, but also in the orchestral virtuosity of the leading figure of the New German School, Richard Strauss. Putting this view alongside Weissmann's 'spiritualising' orchestra, the interludes potentially represent critical battlegrounds in which the perception of musical decline confronts the metaphysics of music and the legacy of a symphonic tradition which is supposed to have been preserved in opera.

Further complicating the issue is the orchestra's perceived interiority, the sense that it concerns itself not with external events, but with an inner reality centred on subjective experience, emotion, desire, and the unconscious. This is a quality observed again and again in the Wagnerian orchestra. For Thomas Mann it represents 'the realm of subliminal knowledge, unknown to the word above',[27] while Bellaigue characterises Wagner's 'symphony' as 'more eloquent than the voice':

> It speaks for those who hold their silence, for those whom an excess of feeling or emotion – weariness, surprise, love, sadness or joy – overwhelms and renders silent.[28]

This, for Bellaigue, is one manifestation of the capacity of the Wagnerian orchestra to reflect that 'complexity' of the 'soul' to which he refers in the passage quoted earlier. His description perfectly captures one of the apparent roles of the orchestral interludes in post-Wagnerian opera, but it also raises the possibility of a conflict in which the orchestra can be seen to gravitate toward the very kinds of 'inner', spiritual experiences that the sensual appeal of post-Wagnerian musical language is said to neglect. Again the problem turns on the relationship of music and the body: if the critical concerns over modern music point to a polarisation of body and spirit and music's (mis)alignment with the former, might the interludes question this configuration and assert the material and corporeal foundation of music even when it is supposed to be at its most 'interior' and 'spiritual'?

Nor can there be any mistaking the gendered overtones of these confrontations: the degeneration of music is also the feminisation of music,

---

[26] For critic Walter Niemann, impressionism represented a purely external appeal to the senses and a betrayal of music's very nature: 'its soul, its inner experience'. The impressionists, he added, had failed to recognise the 'immaterial', 'transcendent' quality bestowed on nature by the 'inner musical ear'. See *Die Musik der Gegenwart* (Berlin and Leipzig: Schuster and Loeffler, 1921), p. 234.

[27] Thomas Mann, 'Richard Wagner und der *Ring des Nibelungen*' (1938), in *Thomas Mann: Gesammelte Werke*, vol. IX (Berlin: Aufbau-Verlag, 1955), p. 524.

[28] Bellaigue, 'L'opéra symphonique', 183.

the predominance of the sensual, a capitulation to feminine qualities. This was a theme that had emerged in Wagner's lifetime and continued to prove a convenient analogy during the early decades of the twentieth century. Reviewing the first Bayreuth festival, Eduard Hanslick expressed disapproval of the overwhelming effects of Wagner's music, likening them to 'the hashish dream of the ecstatic female'.[29] For Weissmann, writing in the twilight years of the post-Wagnerian era, music was waging a 'battle between the constructive power of rhythm and the refinements of an effeminate harmonic language'.[30] It is a battle that is often aligned in opera with the gender demarcations of the dramatic characters, and orchestral interludes, by pointing to those characters as their discursive 'source', prove to be a vivid means of defining music's identity. And if the orchestra can probe the 'inner' life of characters and even 'speak' on their behalf, there arises the question of its own imagined identity, of the implications of its assumed authority and chameleon-like character. Put another way, how does the orchestra exert power and construct 'truth' as it assumes the position(s) of narrator, of authorial figure, of a conglomeration of identities?

'Do I alone hear this melody?'

At the root of these questions is an understanding of music centred on its relationship to human subjectivity, a perspective that has been articulated by Lawrence Kramer.[31] For Kramer, music, as a historically specific, culturally determined practice, offers a trace of the particular sets of interests, desires, biases, and anxieties that shape subjectivity in a given historical, social, and cultural environment. Far from being some transcendent, timeless essence, music is a cultural activity (of composing, of performing, of listening) whose role and identity is never more nor less than what it is *prescribed* to be in a specific milieu. But it is also potentially an important determinant of subjectivity. By taking pleasure in music, the listener to a certain extent affirms and identifies with a subjectivity – a subject 'position' – assumed by the music. Pleasure, in other words, implies an element of legitimisation that aligns the listening subject with the set of attitudes and desires traced by the music, and this alignment becomes part of an ongoing cultural construction of subjectivity.

This is something that was well understood in the nineteenth and early twentieth century, but it was typically invested with a Romantic

---

[29] Eduard Hanslick, review in *Neue Freie Presse*, August 1876, in Robert Hartford (ed. and trans.), *Bayreuth: The Early Years* (London: Victor Gollancz, 1980), p. 84.

[30] Weissmann, *Musik in der Weltkrise*, p. 3.

[31] Lawrence Kramer, *Classical Music and Postmodern Knowledge* (Berkeley: University of California Press, 1995), pp. 21–4.

fervour in which music becomes capable of acting on the subject in a powerful, irrational, even dangerous way. In this sense it takes on a mystical, metaphysical quality illustrated in the so-called *Liebestod* of Isolde:

> Do I alone
> hear this melody
> which, so wondrous
> and tender
> in its blissful lament,
> all revealing,
> gently pardoning,
> sounding from him,
> pierces me through,
> rises above,
> sweetly echoing
> and ringing around me?

Here is music as transfiguring 'world-breath', a trace of the Will made audible to Isolde only by her desire for death. But underlying this metaphysics is the collapse of any distinction between what is external and what comes from Isolde herself. It is a music that has become both heard and produced at the same time. In this sense it exemplifies an understanding of music, adopted in post-Wagnerian opera, as persuasive precisely because its source is ambiguous: it is both mine and somebody else's. And here the orchestra, charged with realising Isolde's music, seems to re-create her experience so that a wondrous sound rings round and pierces us, the audience. The orchestra's invisibility comes to stand for the music's imaginary dimension, while the torrent of Wagnerian sound makes it seem all too real.

This is where orchestral interludes, by emphasising this very kind of ambiguity (indeed intensifying it in the absence of the singer), cease to be functional necessities and take on a value of their own. They become a means of anticipating their own reception, of incorporating the audience into musical drama. They seem consciously to encourage and mobilise a process of spectatorial engagement to which film theory, drawing on psychoanalysis, has addressed itself. Christian Metz, for example, has attempted to theorise spectatorial investment in cinema by likening the film experience to, among other things, the regressive condition outlined in Freudian dream theory.[32] By establishing an environment in which the spectator's usual demarcations of 'external' and 'internal' are subverted, Metz argues, cinema raises and problematises questions of

---

[32] Christian Metz, *The Imaginary Signifier: Psychoanalysis and the Cinema*, trans. Celia Britton, Annwyl Williams, Ben Brewster, and Alfred Guzzetti (Bloomington: Indiana University Press, 1977).

belief, fantasy, and identification. These are questions no less applicable to music drama and post-Wagnerian opera, which, like cinema, share cultural origins with psychoanalysis and which suggest an awareness of some of the same issues and concepts theorised by Freud. Yet the question of how a cultural practice such as music might interact with the subject plays no part in Freud's account of the mechanisms and topography of the psyche.

To do this we can turn, as Metz does, to the work of Jacques Lacan, a Freudian, but one who steers psychoanalytic theory towards a more acute awareness of the subject as a 'work in progress'. Central to Lacan's account of the subject is the ego, that illusory sense of 'self' formed through a series of identifications with people and objects. Lacan assigns a place of particular importance to the specular image and its capacity to captivate and propel us into identifications, but much of what he articulates here can be adapted to an understanding of the role of music in ego formation (and, as we shall see, 'music' becomes a central theme in the psychoanalytically based work of Julia Kristeva). Particularly relevant to the orchestral interludes is Lacan's insistence on the deceptive, ambiguous character of identification, which always involves a tension between the supposedly alien nature of that with which we identify and our need to treat it as part of ourselves, to make it our own. It is precisely this imaginary slippage between what is and what is not our own that the interludes, in the apparent absence of embodied performers, seem to stress.

Three principal themes, then, run through this study: the role of the interludes in promoting illusion and identification, their participation in the construction of music's identity, and the interaction of that construction with questions of gender and sexuality. Part of the value of the interludes for a critical investigation of music, moreover, lies in the implication that they represent only one, explicitly theatrical realisation of something also inherent in the so-called 'absolute' realm of instrumental music, and this suggestion underlies the study as a whole. Explored in association with the analysis of specific texts, these lines of enquiry offer a means of coming to terms with the ideological roots of this ambiguous, invisible theatre. Chapter 1 examines Frederick Delius's characterisation of music as transcendent and remote from worldly meaning, analysing a celebrated orchestral interlude from *A Village Romeo and Juliet* (1907) to ask how Delius's own compositional practice might suggest something much more tangible and physically grounded. In chapter 2 we encounter two very specific examples of music as cultural practice. In the orchestrally represented love scenes of Jules Massenet's *Esclarmonde* (1889) and Strauss's *Feuersnot* (1901), sexual ideology is vividly articulated in the form of musically constructed fantasies. An investigation of the interludes in *Pelléas et Mélisande* (1902) in chapter 3 expands on this notion to ask how Debussy might trace in music the form of a dream that encompasses the whole opera. Here the interludes are seen to illustrate and problematise the notion of musical difference and isolation, outlining the most repressed elements of the dream and opening spaces for momentary interjections of a music that seems utterly removed from its context.

The contradiction between music's perceived autonomy and its ability to articulate and reinforce ideology is explored in chapter 4, where orchestral 'eulogies' in *Götterdämmerung*, Hans Pfitzner's *Die Rose vom Liebesgarten* (1901), and Berg's *Wozzeck* (1925) are interpreted as models for the techniques of mass propaganda. In stark contrast to these thoroughly Wagnerian investments in audience sympathy and belief, the love scene in Franz Schreker's *Der Schatzgräber* (1920), the focus of chapter 5, seems to question its Wagnerian foundations and problematise belief. In this sense it would seem to offer reinforcement to Theodor Adorno's critique of Wagnerian music drama as a drive towards the stupefaction and domination of its audience. But Adorno disapproved of this love scene (and Schreker's music in general) on the basis of what he believed to be its pre-artistic appeal to the debased sensuality that he detects in mass culture. Caught between its celebration of pleasure and the body and its allegiance to an idealising art-tradition that frowns on such experiences, Schreker's music makes explicit a tension that had always been embedded in music drama and post-Wagnerian opera. In chapter 6 we return to the Wagnerian roots of the issue, focusing on the numerous orchestral interludes (and preludes) in *Der Ring des Nibelungen*, *Tristan und Isolde*, and *Parsifal* in an attempt to come to terms with this and other contradictions at the heart of music drama. Here the visceral impact of Wagner's music is confronted by an appeal to metaphysics, while the corporeality of the theatre is supposed to be transcended by a disembodied music.

1

A walk on the wild side

Music does not exist for the purpose of emphasising or exaggerating something which happens outside its own sphere. Musical expression only begins to be significant where words and actions reach their uttermost limits of expression.

The chief reason for the degeneration of present-day music lies in the fact that people want to get physical sensations from music more than anything else . . . In an age of neurasthenics, music, like everything else, must be a stimulant, must be alcoholic, aphrodisiac, or it is no good.

(Frederick Delius, 1920)

These excerpts from Delius's extravagantly entitled article 'The Present Cult – Charlatanism and Humbug in Music' raise two issues central to the debate over musical meaning at the turn of the century.[1] The first concerns music's perceived autonomy, its relationship to language, to society, to that 'which happens outside its own sphere'. What exactly is music's 'sphere' for Delius? The answer he provides in this article, as we shall see, appears to support the arguments of absolutist aesthetics, a position echoed by a number of the more prominent critics of his work. But, as an analysis of an orchestral interlude from *A Village Romeo and Juliet* will show, Delius's compositional practice is very much at variance with the arguments expressed in the article. The interlude, adopted for concert performance and separately entitled *The Walk to the Paradise Garden*, serves as a particularly instructive example, partly because it has been repeatedly hailed as the epitome of Delius's music, and partly because, as an orchestral interlude, it occupies territory claimed by both sides of the debate. As 'pure' instrumental music untouched by word or scene it can be read as an island of absolute music within the merely theatrical, and as a 'scene' central to the music drama it can be read as a vital moment of musical narrative.

---

[1] The article, one of Delius's few published writings on music, was commissioned by Philip Heseltine (a.k.a. Peter Warlock) for his journal *The Sackbut* (September 1920). It is reprinted in Christopher Redwood (ed.), *A Delius Companion* (London: John Calder, 1976), pp. 37–43.

The other issue raised by the excerpt is the question of music's relationship to the body, a relationship characterised by Delius in terms of sickness and artificial inducement. Expanding on these thoughts he reflects, with bitter irony, on what he sees as the physicality of contemporary music, its direct appeal to the body. It is this, above all, he concludes, that has brought about the 'degeneration' of music. From the perspective of postmodern theory, the argument forms part of a persistent denial of the body in Western culture. We might now ask how music could ever be disembodied. Richard Leppert has observed that audiences at a musical performance 'see it as an embodied activity':

> While they hear, they also witness: how the performers look and gesture, how they are costumed, how they interact with their instruments and with one another, how they regard the audience, how other listeners heed the performers.[2]

In Leppert's reading the body will always feature in musical performance and reception: the very physical activity of performing engages our attention, and the audience becomes a part of the performance. But what about the performance of an interlude such as 'The Walk to the Paradise Garden'? Here we have a passage in a music drama that calls for no stage bodies, that hides its performers in a pit, and that is usually performed in darkness before a closed curtain. The body seems excluded in this performance setting, but what happens in the musical text? Does Delius's music complement or resist the erasure of the body from the visual field?

'Strange wild music from the stream'

Delius drew his libretto freely from Gottfried Keller's *Romeo und Julia auf dem Dorfe*, one of a collection of stories published in 1856 under the title *Die Leute von Seldwyla*. Partly inspired by a newspaper report of the suicide pact of two young lovers, Keller's tale contrasts the pair's idealistic love with society's smug, complacent morality. Sali and Vreli, the Romeo and Juliet of the title, are separated not by a feud between patrician families but by a long-standing land dispute between their fathers, two neighbouring farmers. The struggle ultimately drives both farmers to ruin, and in an attempt to wrest Vreli from the control of her now deranged father Sali fatally wounds him. Left with nothing, the lovers find themselves shunned as beggars and outcasts everywhere they go. Finally they see death as the only way to be united and happy, and in a fantasised wedding they float out into the river on a hay barge.

[2] Richard Leppert, *The Sight of Sound: Music, Representation, and the History of the Body* (Berkeley: University of California Press, 1993), p. xxii.

There Sali pulls the plug from beneath the barge and the lovers sink with it beneath the waves.

Traditionally characterised as a 'poetic realist', Keller at first seems an unlikely source for a composer whose music so often turns away from brutal reality and seeks refuge in a highly idealised vision of Nature, what Ernest Newman called a 'poignant nostalgia'.[3] But Keller's tale, even as it seeks to confront a peculiarly nineteenth-century bourgeois hypocrisy, offered a framework that allowed Delius to shape a more timeless, ahistorical vision. In his libretto the impingement of reality on the world of the lovers loses much of its detail, while nature, already of some importance in terms of atmosphere in Keller's story, takes on a typically Delian role as the key to a fuller existence.

Central to this transformation is the role of the Dark Fiddler, for Keller a sinister outsider whose appearances are mysteriously tied up with the tragic fate of the lovers. He is heir to a strip of land that lies between the two fathers' fields, but as a bastard son his legal claim is forfeit, and it is the prospect of taking the land for themselves that propels the farmers into their disastrous struggle. In the opera the Dark Fiddler remains an outsider, but one who has shunned conventional morality for an unfettered existence outside the bounds of society, communing freely with nature. There remains a sense, as in Keller, that the Fiddler is somehow bound up with the lovers' destiny, but Delius portrays him as sympathetic towards Sali and Vreli, offering them an alternative vision of the world:

> And when you care to come
> into the world with me,
> the woods and dales we'll roam
> and your merry guide I'll be.

It is difficult not to draw parallels with Delius's own self-image as an outsider, a Nietzschean artist shunning conventional religion and morality in search of spiritual elevation in communion with nature, whether in the mountains of Norway or the garden of his home in Grez-sur-Loing.

The parallel is reinforced by the role of music: this strange figure, seemingly at one with nature, is also a musician whose music seems to mediate between humanity and nature. His distant voice is at first represented by a series of parallel ninth chords in the strings that Vreli and Marti identify as a strange-sounding breeze (Scene I, figure 21). Only gradually, after a baritone voice appears in the distance, do they identify it as the sound of singing. The Fiddler's words underline the connection ('but are we not comrades, o Vagabond wind'), presenting it

---

[3] Ernest Newman, 'Delius: The End of a Chapter in Music', *Sunday Times*, 17 June 1934, in Redwood, *A Delius Companion*, p. 99.

Example 1.1 Delius, *A Village Romeo and Juliet*, Scene 3

in terms of an idyllic communion: 'So long as you hear the wind singing through the branches, no sorrow will you know.' As he sings he accompanies himself on the fiddle (solo violin in the orchestra), following the melodic contour of the 'wind' music that had announced his arrival. Characteristic of that melody is a series of whole-tone phrases, harmonised in one particularly striking passage for solo violin as a Lydian inflection (figure 26). The phrase returns to play an important role in the Fiddler's second appearance six years later when the feuding farmers have brought ruin upon themselves. The Fiddler gloats over the consequences of their greed, but declares that he bears no ill will towards Sali and Vreli. He sings of his roaming life, and of the sound of the 'strange wild music from the stream' (Scene 3, example 1.1). The line draws a rich flood of music that recalls the Lydian violin passage, but now the vocal line suggests a Dorian setting, while solo violin gives way to full orchestra, swelling toward a *forte* climax followed by a cadential *ritardando* that seems to highlight the importance of the moment. In the final scene, as Sali and Vreli seek refuge and acceptance at an inn called the Paradise Garden, they encounter the Fiddler, surrounded by his 'vagabond' companions. Unable to accept an invitation to 'Come with us and live in freedom!', the lovers recognise their unsuitability to be 'outsiders' and their need to be accepted by the very society that shuns them. Knowing that acceptance will never come, they prefer 'to be happy one short moment', dying in each other's arms. As they enter their wedding fantasy, nature is indeed transformed into a 'garden of paradise', and the lovers hear that 'strange wild music from the stream':

> Listen!
> Far-off sounds of music
> waken trembling echoes,
> moving, throbbing, swelling,
> faintly dying in the sunset's fading glow.

The Fiddler is heard 'playing wildly', and the music that had signalled his first appearance returns to accompany him, its characteristic parallel ninth chords an apt musical symbol of that 'Vagabond wind', while its whole-tone meanderings seem to capture the 'freedom in nature' that the wind had always symbolised, a freedom that Sali and Vreli could never quite embrace.

'A writer of music pure and undefiled'

In *A Village Romeo and Juliet*, then, the relationship between music and nature surfaces on two levels. Music serves its traditional representative function of evoking nature as scenic background/mood/atmosphere, but in a reflexive move it is also thematicised within the diegesis. Drama and music combine to reflect on Music's role as the voice of nature. That 'strange, wild music from the stream' is the intoxicating, half-imagined sound that beckons us into a oneness with nature, a sound that is pointedly realised in the orchestra as something set apart from the music that surrounds it. Perhaps Delius is projecting himself, through the Fiddler, as the outsider-artist whose music can contribute to a renewed understanding of nature, pointing away from a decaying society.

Or perhaps, as Richard Capell has suggested, Delius is simply a musical 'landscape painter'.[4] One has only to look at the titles of Delius's works: *In a Summer Garden*, *On Hearing the First Cuckoo in Spring*, *North Country Sketches*, *A Song of the High Hills*. In *A Mass of Life*, his setting of passages from Nietzsche's *Also sprach Zarathustra*, Delius shuns Zarathustra's pagan sermons in favour of his poetic celebrations of Nature.[5] As for the operas, Capell writes of a 'static', 'timeless' quality, a 'oneness with Nature's immobility', and a 'lack of vivid accentuation' that 'brings about the effect of a dream rather than a drama'.[6] Walter Niemann, meanwhile, characterises Delius as a 'musical pastel painter', distinguishing his 'open air' vision of nature from the 'studio art' of French 'impressionist' composers such as Debussy.[7] Other critics, interpreting reactions of this sort as a belittling of Delius's artistry, have been eager to jump to his defence. For Constant Lambert, criticism of this kind distorts the meaning of Delius's music:

Many writers have laid stress on the great influence of Nature in his work and have almost classed him as a Nature poet in music. It would be safer to compare his works to landscapes with figures in which both elements are perfectly

---

[4] Richard Capell, 'Delius: Landscape Painter of Music', *Radio Times*, 4 December 1931, in Redwood, *A Delius Companion*, pp. 45–8.

[5] Delius thought of himself as a disciple of Nietzsche, cultivating what he felt were the traits of the Nietzschean artist. Zarathustra's invocation of nature's deep mysteries would have been very much in accord with Delius's views on the centrality of nature to human experience.

[6] Capell, 'Delius: Landscape Painter of Music', p. 48.

[7] Niemann, *Die Musik der Gegenwart*, p. 243.

balanced ... the human passion and its background of elemental Nature are inextricably woven.[8]

Delius, in other words, is not interested in scenic effect in and of itself, but in a subjective view of nature – in nature as idea. The landscapes in Delius's music, then, shun realism in favour of what Danish conductor and Delius specialist Paul Klenau termed the 'experience' of nature.[9]

Lambert's defence of Delius against charges of pictorialism are only part of a wider interpretative strategy that also addresses the relationship of his music to poetry and drama. The fact that 'one can relate his music to definite scenes and emotions' should not, Lambert argues, be taken as an indication that Delius is a 'literary composer'. On the contrary, 'he never allows himself to become shackled by either dramatic or pictorial considerations'.[10] Like many commentators, he emphasises what he calls the 'purely musical emotion of Delius's work'.[11] Neville Cardus takes a similar tack:

The truth is that Delius at his most typical is a writer of music pure and undefiled ... With Delius it is music or nothing. The words of Whitman, in *Sea Drift*, will not help you to enjoyment unless you also can follow the music's essence, its subtle and long-lengthed [*sic*] melodies, its instrumental and vocal combination, all of which are woven into a texture that can be sensed aesthetically only by the musical faculty, and by no other faculty whatsoever.[12]

The stress that Lambert and Cardus place on the 'purely musical' represents a challenge to charges of naïve tone painting and static pictorialism, and paves the way for a defence of Delius's operas. If the operas seem static and undramatic, it is only because the verbal and pictorial features on the surface of the music drama – musical landscapes, music–word interaction – have been mistaken for the inner layer of drama that resides in the music. This is the basis of Heseltine's defence of *A Village Romeo and Juliet*:

To praise the music of this drama and cavil at the drama, as so many critics have done, is simply to expose the fact that the meaning of the music itself has not been grasped; for the drama is literally but the overflowing of the music from the region of the audible into that of the visible.[13]

Here Heseltine echoes, and none too subtly, the Schopenhauer-inspired absolutism of Wagner's later theoretical writings with their appeal to

---

[8] Constant Lambert, 'The Art of Frederick Delius', *Apollo*, November 1929, in Redwood, *A Delius Companion*, p. 75.

[9] Paul Klenau, 'The Approach to Delius', *Music Teacher*, January 1927, in Redwood, *A Delius Companion*, p. 32.

[10] Lambert, 'The Art of Frederick Delius', p. 76.   [11] Ibid., p. 75.

[12] Neville Cardus, 'Delius: His Method and His Music', *Manchester Guardian*, 14 October 1929, in Redwood, *A Delius Companion*, p. 88.

[13] Peter Warlock, *Frederick Delius* (London: The Bodley Head, 1923), p. 88.

the metaphysics of instrumental music. Carl Dahlhaus sees this attitude exemplified in Wagner's theory of the continuous orchestral melody:

The idea of an 'endless' melody, always eloquent and meaningful, is . . . tendentially – applied to orchestral melody that is substance and not accompaniment within a music drama – an example of absolute music aesthetics: not of the phenomenon that Hanslick meant, but of the idea at which Schopenhauer aimed.[14]

Music, through the orchestra, eludes the mundane, the physical, the social, and speaks of a higher reality. As Heseltine put it in his analysis of Delius's *Requiem*:

It is almost unnecessary to add that the musical interest . . . centres in those sections where the living imagination is least impeded by the cere-cloths of materialism and least reminded of the stench of the charnel-house.[15]

Here we have, in the most vivid terms, the core of this absolutism: music as idea, as antidote to the material. Musical meaning is displaced into a realm removed from the signification of language or image.

Do these critics speak for Delius? 'The Present Cult' would suggest that they do. Much of the article represents little more than a diatribe against what he sees as the materialist, unemotional character of recent music. Delius can be seen to respond here to the sudden popularity of a music very distant from his own. In 1920, the year Delius's article was published, *A Village Romeo and Juliet* was restaged for the first time since its British premiere in 1910. But few works could compete with the sensation of the Stravinsky–Diaghilev ballets, and Beecham, conductor at both stagings of the opera, later recalled that it had come to seem old-fashioned, in terms of both music and staging.[16] Perhaps this explains the polemical and defensive tone of much of the article, and yet, for all its bitter posturing, there is much in it that proves illuminating.

Delius begins by decrying what he sees as a lack of respect for music as an art:

Music is a cry of the soul. It is a revelation, a thing to be reverenced. Performances of a great musical work are for us what the rites and festivals of religion were to the ancients – an initiation into the mysteries of the human soul.[17]

Echoing Wagner's 'art as religion' theory, Delius simultaneously places music on a pedestal while attempting to justify its social relevance as a means of communal self-understanding. By appealing to a mythical past, he succeeds in de-historicising musical experience in much the same way as his omission of detail and his idealisation of nature had

---

[14] Carl Dahlhaus, *The Idea of Absolute Music*, trans. Roger Lustig (Chicago: University of Chicago Press, 1991), p. 122.

[15] Warlock, *Frederick Delius*, p. 108.   [16] Beecham, *A Mingled Chime*, p. 144.

[17] Delius, 'The Present Cult', p. 38.

robbed Keller's tale of its immediate social critique. Delius goes on to offer some thoughts on musical meaning:

Music should be concerned with the emotions, not with external events. To make music imitate some other thing is as futile as to try and make it say 'Good morning' or 'It's a fine day'. It is only that which cannot be expressed otherwise that is worth expressing in music.[18]

Delius certainly echoes the language of absolutist aesthetics: music is distanced from 'external events' and confined to a realm of signification inaccessible to any other medium. But what are the implications for an orchestral interlude? Writing on 'The Walk to the Paradise Garden', Lambert observed:

[I]t is significant that the emotional climax and finest passage in his opera, *A Village Romeo and Juliet*, is the orchestral intermezzo in which no word is sung and (in its original form at least) no action takes place.[19]

Is this Delius's solution, to appoint the orchestra as medium of the climax of his opera? Do interludes allow his operas to live up to the absolutist arguments presented in Delius's article and by critics such as Lambert?

'Ever onwards towards the setting sun'

In 'The Walk' we are far from the melodramatic music of the fathers' quarrels, or the cacophony of the preceding scene, when the lovers had strolled through a village fair, only to attract stares and gossip. Unable even to join a dance, they set out for the Paradise Garden, 'and there we'll dance all night!'. As they leave the fair the curtain closes and the interlude begins. This is music that places the lovers in the midst of nature, music like that of their first meeting on the unclaimed land, or like the music that will well up around them in their *Liebestod*, drawing them 'where the echoes dare to wander'. But now, from the absolutist perspective, there are no voices to drown, no bodies or scenery to ground it in the mundane. Now music can capture the inner essence of nature, transcending the outward manifestation presented by the staged action. Beecham observed that in Delius's operas 'so long as the singers are off the stage the orchestra plays delicately and enchantingly, but the moment they reappear it strikes up fiercely and complainingly as if it resented not being allowed to relate the whole story by itself'.[20] Perhaps the resentment is also about being forced to stoop to grease-paint and spotlights. Only here, in the darkened theatre, can it enter its own domain, 'expressing,' as Delius writes, 'that which cannot be expressed

---

[18] Ibid., p. 39.   [19] Lambert, 'The Art of Frederick Delius', pp. 76–7.
[20] Beecham, *A Mingled Chime*, p. 144.

Example 1.2   Delius, *A Village Romeo and Juliet*, 'The Walk to the Paradise Garden'

otherwise'. Here music – supposedly pure and unfettered by stage action or word – enters its true element. But could Delius, who devoted so much of his compositional career to opera , really have resented the theatre in this way? Or were his sympathies always secretly with a music that was less than wholly 'pure'?

There can be no question that 'The Walk' refutes the simplistic notion of Delius as 'landscape painter', a term that conjures images of kitsch watercolours and consigns Delius, together with so much later English music, to the category of 'cow-pat' music. On one level the orchestra does represent the natural surroundings, creating a secluded idyll as the lovers journey hand in hand. Here Delius draws on familiar nineteenth-century (and specifically Wagnerian) musical signifiers of nature: a broad, sustained background of hushed strings, deliberately obscured rhythmic outlines, flowing melodic lines. But this is no descendant of the quasi-realistic effects of the Forest Murmurs in *Siegfried*. Everything seems filtered through subjective experience, a reflection of the lovers' own communion: it is that 'strange wild music from the stream' that the Fiddler had extolled. There is no landscape as such, but a surrounding as much *created* by Sali and Vreli as perceived by them. Relevant here is one particularly prominent motif, presented in its most characteristic form as an ascending triplet pattern (example 1.2). It has appeared, always in the orchestra, in the context of the lovers' search for happiness together (for example, Sali's line in Scene 3, 'If we two hold together, all may yet come right again,' and later, in Scene 4, 'Come, we will wander together into strange lands'). The motif seems to encapsulate their search for acceptance, its melodic pattern of incrementally increasing intervals a spatial metaphor for a journey into the unknown. Heseltine sums up this quest when he writes of *A Village Romeo and Juliet*:

The whole work is charged with an atmosphere of mystery: through it all there blows a wind as from a far country . . . What lies beyond is shrouded in mystery, but there is no staying the journey onwards, ever onwards towards the setting sun.[21]

---

[21] Warlock, *Frederick Delius*, p. 88.

It is music that seems to come *from* Sali and Vreli, and its conspicuous presence in the interlude implies that the lovers are behind this music, that we are experiencing this walk through their ears.

The impression of a music that emanates from Sali and Vreli is vividly set up in Scene 4 when Sali and Vreli dream of that one tradition of conventional society for which they most long and from which they are excluded: a wedding. In a pantomime scene replete with bells and chorus, they are married in the old village church. Strangely sombre (more like a funeral at times) and infused with a disjointed, surreal quality appropriate to a dream, it seems to articulate the lovers' separation from the reality they crave and the inevitability that death will represent their real wedding. 'The Walk', then, can be seen to pick up on this idea of 'orchestra as unconscious'. In some ways as dream-like as the wedding scene, it seems to trace a journey through the psyche, through memories and desires not quite accessible to the (conscious) voice. Perhaps this was the role Delius was trying to reinforce when, around 1906, he revised the opera and expanded the interlude from its originally published version: in the original edition the always orchestral ascending-triplet motif was absent from the interlude and from the opera as a whole.[22]

Not that the triplet motif is the only leitmotivic feature of 'The Walk'. So extensive are the interlude's thematic/motivic quotations, in fact, that it functions as a retrospective of the whole drama. All the opera's most prominent leitmotifs and recurring themes are represented, some originally vocal lines, others orchestrally based, and all directly related to Sali and Vreli. Such dependence on dramatic associations certainly contradicts Delius's assertion that music should not concern itself with 'external events', but it hardly challenges the absolutist premise that music is remote from the kind of meaning (visual and linguistic) on which theatre depends. It could suggest, in fact, that music is only able to fulfil a dramatic and reflective role such as this one by associating itself artificially with the stage by means of the leitmotif. But leitmotivic meaning arguably represents only one semantic layer here.

For all the suggestions that this music comes from Sali and Vreli, there are two important suggestions of another imagined source. From figure 42+6 woodwinds present a lyrical, descending theme that eventually becomes the basis at figure 43+3 for the interlude's first real surge of orchestral sound, a *mezzo forte* descending sequence for strings accompanied by undulating horns and ascending-scale figurations in

---

[22] According to Jelka Delius, 'The Walk' was expanded before the opera's premiere (Berlin, 1907). In a letter to Philip Heseltine dated 28 September 1929, she writes: 'The Entr'acte of the *Village Romeo* was composed or changed in 1906 for the Berlin performance.' Cited in Robert Threlfall, *Frederick Delius: A Supplementary Catalogue* (London: Delius Trust, 1986), p. 25.

Example 1.3   Delius, *A Village Romeo and Juliet*, Scene 6

Example 1.4   Delius, *A Village Romeo and Juliet*, 'The Walk to the Paradise Garden'

winds. This lyrical 'eruption' marks the climax of the first half of the interlude, but its source is ambiguous. Although clearly related to some of the opera's prominent leitmotifs, it also represents a new departure with an identity of its own. In fact the theme represents less a recollection of past material than an anticipation of the final scene, as Sali and Vreli see and hear nature transformed into a 'garden of paradise' (example 1.3). There the theme is sung by Sali, joined by Vreli's lyrical counter-melody. The move is a proleptic one, an anticipation of events that have yet to transpire, and it resembles the effect in literary narrative when as yet undefined themes or symbols are introduced, to be clarified only later. In this sense the theme in 'The Walk' begins to construct a narrating subject that 'knows' what Sali and Vreli do not, but it is a construction that only solidifies as the narrative progresses, when we become more aware of what was being anticipated.

A more far-reaching effect is initiated at figure 50, the dynamic climax of the interlude (example 1.4). It begins with a *forte* statement of the ascending-triplet motif in its familiar melodic form, but at figure 50+5

28

the motif becomes a *fortissimo* seventh chord in the minor mode, a form completely unlike any of its previous incarnations. It introduces a melodic descent that recalls the opening theme of the opera (one that has acquired too many associations to be adequately named) and also anticipates the 'See the moonbeams' theme, while its Dorian character evokes the Fiddler's 'strange, wild music'. This leads to a quotation at figure 50+7 of a three-note motif from Scene 4, Vreli's lament over the ruin that has befallen Sali and herself. Such a sudden concentration of leitmotivic and modal suggestion arguably renders any individual connotations unimportant in the face of what is a flood of reflectiveness, of perspective. It is as if the music's relationship to the lovers has become infused with a distance that speaks *about* rather than *from* them. And yet the impact of the passage rests on characteristics much more immediate than leitmotivic content and reflectiveness. What comes across most forcefully is its dramatic contrast with the tone of the interlude thus far. Where 'The Walk' had previously evoked images of pleasure, of idyllic solitude and immersion in nature, it is now charged, if only briefly, with a sense of intensity and tragedy that is distant from the lovers' reverie. The climax subsides to give way once again to a Delian idyll, but it seems to leave its mark on the remainder of the interlude. At figure 52+6, for example, a meandering chord stream rooted in B major is brought to a halt with a very Wagnerian cadence (a plagal progression in which the subdominant is followed by its minor-mode counterpart embellished with an added sixth). Familiar from the closing bars of *Götterdämmerung* and *Tristan*, it has almost a trope value that carries a strong sense of epic closure and transcendent finality.[23]

Yet the interlude continues for another twenty bars, resuming the musical discourse that the cadence had interrupted. It is as if the cadence represented a temporary intrusion of that narrative position that had emerged at the climax, a position that seems to place a diegetic frame around the interlude, perhaps around the whole opera. And at figure 53+7 two chordal progressions produce a similar effect (example 1.5). The first, a *pianissimo* tonic major seventh to subdominant, seems to echo the quiet pleasure and longing of the interlude, but the second, beginning with an augmented-sixth chord, has the effect of casting a shadow over the serenity, of introducing a brief glimpse of lurking tension before relenting to the tranquil B major that will bring the interlude to a close. Again that other perspective seems to break through, disturbing and competing with the overall sense that this

---

[23] The altered subdominant is actually very familiar as the harmonic setting for one of the motifs quoted frequently in the interlude (see figure 51+6), but its symbolic value seems transformed in this cadential setting, with full scoring and dynamic shading that seem to announce, in truly Wagnerian fashion, the importance of the moment.

Example 1.5   Delius, *A Village Romeo and Juliet*, 'The Walk to the Paradise Garden'

music comes from Sali and Vreli. It is a rift that is confirmed when the curtain opens to reveal the Fiddler and the Vagabonds at the Paradise Garden: we have 'arrived' there before Sali and Vreli. The Fiddler tells the story of the feuding farmers and their children who fell in love. Might he be the narrator implied in the interlude?

'The Walk' seems immersed in the pleasure of the lovers' secluded journey and their oneness with nature. But it constructs a more knowledgeable narrator who seems to articulate just how temporary that pleasure is, and offers a hint of the tragedy in store. Trapped by their conventional values and unable to heed the Fiddler's call to roam in search of that 'strange, wild music from the stream', Sali and Vreli are condemned. They are neither accepted in their own surroundings, nor able to break out of them. They fail to see that the experience of their journey is not something temporary and transitional, but precisely the goal. Delius seems to make the same point about his interlude when he assigns it such a meaningful role within the opera. Cited by Lambert to demonstrate Delius's independence from 'dramatic or pictorial considerations', it turns out to be a turning point in the narrative and a site of vivid imagery. Far from limiting itself to a realm of 'purely' musical signification, it relies on its associations both with the specific dramatic plot in which it is embedded and with the broader plots of shared understanding that made such music meaningful for *fin-de-siècle* audiences. Subtle and richly ambiguous, narrativity in 'The Walk' depends on a cluster of effects, rather than being limited to the leitmotif. And if music here seems to 'transcend' its dramatic associations, as Heseltine would have it, this surely reflects on Delius's discomfort with the stage. That is, the kind of heightened experience that 'The Walk' has represented for so many in relation to the staged scenes is an *effect* of an undeniably successful musical crystalisation of the drama, and not some quality intrinsic to music.

Beyond the body?

Perhaps one of the reasons for the success of the interlude is that in its attempt to capture the sheer pleasure and desire that Sali and Vreli experience it highlights a quality of Delius's music that neither he nor his supporters seem prepared to acknowledge, a quality that might help to account for its consignment to the fringes of the musical canon. Confronting contemporary musical experience, Delius's tone becomes increasingly bitter and pessimistic. Music has lost its meaning in modern society, he insists, not because it has grown irrelevant, but because society has betrayed it:

> Appreciation of art which has been born of profound thought and intensity of experience necessitates an intellectual effort too exhausting for most people of the present day. They want to be amused: they would rather feel music with their bodies than understand it with their emotions.[24]

Delius here establishes a polarity between, on the one hand, emotion and intellect, associated with profundity and intensity, and, on the other, the physical experience of music, equated with amusement. *A Village Romeo and Juliet*, and particularly its attitude to the characters as embodied subjects, might be seen to reflect Delius's disdain for physicality in music. Just as nature is musically represented 'as if in the distance', offstage voices position human figures as out of sight, disembodied. In his first appearance, the Fiddler seems to emerge out of the sonorous landscape, becoming visible only after two verses of his song 'O wandering minstrel'. The wedding dream in Scene 4 features an invisible church choir 'sounding from the distance', and towards the end of the scene, long before the village fair of the next scene becomes visible, we hear the stereotypical triadic phrases of yodelling 'Peasants in the distance': musical traces of a pleasure that beckons all the more because of its distance. In the final scene, distant bargemen are heard but never seen, their voices mistaken by Vreli for angels. Not only are we denied the site/sight of production, but the voices, positioned backstage, are robbed of their immediacy. The effect is one of displacement, of locating bodiless voices within a musical landscape that resists physical presence. The 'distant sound' evoked by Delius is, for Adorno, a recurring theme in post-Wagnerian opera:

> [I]n it music pauses and is made spatial, the near and the far are deceptively merged, like the comforting Fata Morgana that brings the mirage of cities and caravans within reach and makes social models appear magically rooted in nature.[25]

For Delius that ideal social model is not the bourgeois society which has entrapped Sali and Vreli but the promised life that lies 'beyond the setting sun'.

[24] Delius, 'The Present Cult', p. 40.
[25] Theodor W. Adorno, *In Search of Wagner* (1952), trans. Rodney Livingstone (London: Verso, 1981), p. 86.

We can also detect a more subtle distancing of human figures based on the relationship of their voices to the orchestral discourse. In contrast to the scenes centring on human action – the death of Vreli's father, Vreli's lament – the nature scenes tend to position the voices as mere interruptions of the orchestral fabric, as though they were enveloped by the sound of nature. Embodied and granted the power of words, these voices nevertheless fail to wrest the focus of attention away from the orchestra. (One is reminded here of Delius's dictum that singers should act not from the stage, but from the music.)[26] It is as though the orchestra were compensating for the embarrassing physical presence of the characters by sweeping their voices along in a flood of music that threatens to carry them into the distance. This is true of the idyllic rendezvous in Scene 3, in which Sali and Vreli claim less musical attention than the 'wild land' itself. Running through the prelude and the scene itself is music filled with Delian signifiers of a benign nature: backstage horns (again marked 'as if in the distance'), long-breathed melodic lines shaped from bird calls, modal phrases. All seem designed to present a vivid landscape that – *pace* Lambert – belittles the human figure. What happens in 'The Walk to the Paradise Garden', then, might represent a different realisation of this relationship. We have seen that the representation of nature here seems filtered through Sali and Vreli as subjects, but we might equally reverse this perspective and suggest that representations of nature redefine the subjectivity of Sali and Vreli. Here the lovers' embodied form and voices are dispensed with altogether, leaving their subject positions to be conveyed by the same medium as nature: the orchestra. Sali and Vreli are present, but disembodied, wordless, and in a sense dispersed into nature, so that a sense of spatial (dis)placement again comes to the fore.

For the 1920 staging at Covent Garden Beecham introduced a short pantomime in the course of the interlude. It was, he maintained, 'the only way in an English theatre to secure comparative silence'.[27] The curtain opens to reveal Sali and Vreli walking hand in hand. They sit down on the moss, and as the cuckoo motif emerges they kiss 'long and tenderly'. They continue on their way and the curtain closes for the remainder of the interlude. The scenario found its way into later published versions of the score, and has been included in more recent productions of the opera. By presenting the interlude as a teasing game of 'now you see them, now you don't', Beecham's pantomime further draws attention to the gap between embodiment and disembodiment that runs through the opera. For a few moments Sali and Vreli are embodied in the form of singers, but they emerge from and return to a

---

[26] Cited in Warlock, *Frederick Delius*, p. 68.   [27] Beecham, *A Mingled Chime*, p. 144.

sonorous form that seems remote from the body. It is as if their desire were being dispersed once more into their surroundings, channelled into nature.

'Moving, throbbing, swelling'

The model of desire traced by the *Tristan* orchestra, with its ceaseless motion, its constant ebbing and flowing, is arguably one that played a vital role in shaping *fin-de-siècle* musical constructions of sexuality. Desire is, to use Wagner's own words, 'unquenchable', 'a longing forever renewing itself – a fevered craving', extinguishable only in the 'bliss of dying'.[28] Lawrence Kramer has drawn parallels between the construction of sexuality in *Tristan* and Freud's concept of libidinal desire.[29] Central to this model, he argues, is the characterisation of desire as 'free-flowing subjectivity', 'detachable from the human body'. Desire as libido resists attaching itself to any particular object, and so opens up 'the unprecedented possibility of idealising sexuality as the means by which the body transcends itself'.[30] For Kramer, *Tristan* traces this model musically in a number of ways: postponed resolutions, harmonic motion by semitones, avoidance of firm cadential points, and rhythmic fluidity. He sees a parallel, for example, between the constant, unchannelled flow of desire and the avoidance of clearly defined cadences that might signal clear direction or closure. The climactic effects of cadential resolution are always accompanied by a resistance to resolution, just as climax in the libidinal model of desire merely represents a diversion and never a total satisfaction of desire.

Many of these musical characteristics are to be found in *A Village Romeo and Juliet*. There are in fact some moments of rather obvious appropriation – *Tristan* chords and Wagnerian cadential patterns – and Robert Anderson's characterisation of the opera as a '*Tristan* for the young and innocent' is appropriate in more ways than one.[31] Harmonic ambiguity, one of the hallmarks of the *Tristan* style, is possibly the most characteristic feature of Delius's music, and cadential postponement is a Delian trait that has often led to charges of directionlessness and monotony. But this raises an aspect of Delius's music that seems foreign

---

[28] Richard Wagner, programme note to *Tristan und Isolde*: Prelude (1860), *SSD* XII, pp. 346–7.

[29] Lawrence Kramer, *Music as Cultural Practice, 1800–1900* (Berkeley: University of California Press, 1990), pp. 135–75.

[30] Ibid., p. 175.

[31] Robert Anderson, '*A Village Romeo and Juliet*', in *The New Grove Dictionary of Opera*, vol. IV (London: Macmillan, 1992), p. 1008.

to the whole Wagnerian ethos: harmonic stasis. For all its postpone-
ments and diversions, both large- and small-scale, Wagner's harmonic
language remains firmly goal-oriented. While much of the music of
A Village Romeo and Juliet could be described in similar terms (particularly the opening scenes centring on the fathers' feud), the gradual plot
shift towards the interior world of Sali and Vreli is accompanied by a
subversion of this teleological view of harmonic syntax.

In many ways it reaches its apex in 'The Walk', where the harmonic
language seems oriented more towards colour and sensual effect than
towards immediate or long-range goals. The modulation at figure 50, for
example, marks the beginning of forty-four concluding bars in which
B major and its subdominant function as static harmonic fields that
are repeatedly embellished but, with the exception of the narrative
'intrusion' at figure 50+5, never challenged. Characteristic here are the
almost constant tonic pedals that bring all but decorative harmonic motion to a standstill. Upper voices generate chord streams, chromatic
slippage, and modal embellishments (such as the Dorian sixths beginning at figure 51+6), but in so doing they only seem to reinforce the
sense of stasis. It is this same static B major that returns to conclude
the opera as the hay barge sinks into the river and the voices of the
distant bargemen fade. Sustained B major chords briefly shift modally
in a last echo of a cuckoo motif that has accompanied Sali and Vreli
throughout the opera, before rising to a *fortissimo* climax centred on
a more dissonant and jarring version of the augmented-sixth chord
at figure 53+9 of 'The Walk'.[32] But just as its earlier counterpart had
quickly relented, so this chord (actually an embellished *Tristan* chord)
gives way to a quiet sustained B major chord that fades gently into
silence.

Stasis, immersion, a blanket of sound: these are qualities that suggest
not an elusive desire but a *sustained* pleasure that surrounds and courses
through the subject. And, as both 'The Walk' and the opera's closing
moments make clear, the source of that pleasure is to be found in the
sensual embrace of nature, in the caresses of what the Fiddler calls the
'wind singing through the branches'.[33] As Delius constructs it, nature is a
metaphor for a desire that always seems to beckon from the distance and
urge us towards what we seem to lack, but it equally and paradoxically

---

[32] Its vehemence here perhaps symbolises the last intrusion from that narrative position
that articulates the tragedy of the lovers' inability to experience the pleasure offered to
them, except in death.

[33] After conducting a concert that included 'The Walk to the Paradise Garden' and excerpts
from *Tristan*, Malcolm Sargent is reported to have remarked: 'With Wagner I felt I was
in the bedroom, with Delius in the open air.' Cited by Christopher Palmer in liner notes
to audio recording of *A Village Romeo and Juliet*, Argo 430 275-2, 1989.

stands for a palpable, material, corporeal pleasure. This is an ambiguity that emerges in the final scene of the opera in the words of Sali and Vreli:

> See the moonbeams kiss the woods,
> the fields and all the flowers,
> and the river softly singing
> glides along and seems to beckon.
> Listen!
> Far-off sounds of music
> waken trembling echoes,
> moving, throbbing, swelling,
> faintly dying in the sunset's fading glow.

Tinged with the metaphysical but profoundly erotic, this is an understanding of nature as beyond the horizon and simultaneously in contact with the body. Walt Whitman, whose verse Delius set on several occasions, conveys a sense of this double construction in 'Song of Myself' (1882) when he glorifies nature in terms of Romantic vision ('Earth of departed sunset – earth of the mountains misty-topt!') and characterises in erotic terms the experience of swimming in the sea: 'Cushion me soft, rock me in billowy drowse,/ Dash me with amorous wet'.[34] Something of the pleasurable experience connoted here and in Delius seems to re-emerge even in Heseltine's lofty prose:

Whoever has known true ecstasy has already encompassed past and future, and having once attained is initiate, immune from delusion. He is at one with Nature and strides fearlessly into the darkness.[35]

Timelessness and ecstasy: this is the Delian experience *par excellence*, and it is the experience that 'The Walk' celebrates, mapping the idyllic union of Sali and Vreli onto a sensual immersion in nature.

If nature is the source of pleasure, then music is its voice. It is that 'strange, wild music from the stream' that throbs and swells. Again Whitman captures this eroticised fusion of music and nature:

> The orchestra whirls me wider than Uranus flies,
> It wrenches such ardors from me I did not know I possess'd them,
> It sails me, I dab with bare feet, they are lick'd by the indolent waves,
> I am cut by bitter and angry hail, I lose my breath,
> Steep'd amid honey'd morphine, my windpipe throttled in fakes of
> death.[36]

---

[34] Walt Whitman, 'Song of Myself', in Bradley Sculley and Harold Blodgett (eds.), *Leaves of Grass* (New York: W. W. Norton and Co., 1973), p. 49.
[35] Warlock, *Frederick Delius*, p. 135.   [36] Whitman, 'Song of Myself', p. 56.

Music as love and death: this is the sense that emerges in Delius's *Liebestod*. As the lovers' voices intertwine, running triplets in winds and cello syncopations provide a quivering, undulating accompaniment. The barge sinks and we are left with that B major blanket of orchestral sound: a tonic pedal in the basses, a pulsing ostinato rhythm in the low brass and strings, and a sustained 'sheen' in the violins. Here is music of extraordinary physical impact, a music that traces those 'throbbing, swelling' echoes with its own throbbing pulse, that courses through the body with the vibrations of its deep pedal, that 'swells' to a palpable flood of sound. For all the elusive distance of the 'strange, wild music', for all its metaphysical connotations, it returns here decisively to the body. If the opera seems at times to construct a desire in which the body can 'transcend' itself in libidinal fashion, at others to celebrate a sustained pleasure, then it is ultimately the very materiality of Delius's music that proves decisive (as it arguably does in *Tristan*, too).

Kramer is right to characterise libidinal desire as an idealisation of sexuality, and like any idealisation it is vulnerable to a material grounding. This is something that 'The Walk' demonstrates as vividly as anything in Delius's opera. Its very opening is characterised by that musical 'throbbing' of the libretto (syncopated ostinato in the strings), while the sequential descent by cellos and basses seems to hollow out a sonorous foundation that suggests a metaphysical reading (as though Nature were resounding in a Mahlerian sense), but also something that is *felt* through the body as much as heard. In the midst of long harmonically static episodes, the spotlight is repeatedly thrown on timbre, on the sensual pleasure of Delius's often kaleidoscopic orchestration (the cuckoo motifs at figure 47 create a vivid *Klangfarbenmelodie*), and on the sonority of non-functional harmonies such as the Dorian-sixth embellishments beginning at figure 51. Also characteristic is a rhythmic fluidity and layering: while pedal basses threaten to stifle rhythmic energy altogether, high strings and winds counterpoint with running figurations (figure 49). The effect is one of 'stillness in motion', a seductively aimless drift disturbed only by those brief narrative intrusions. Far from the establishment, postponement, and release of tension that characterise musical constructions of desire, 'The Walk' depends on an abatement of tension, an image of pleasure that celebrates being over becoming.

On first observation, the whole thrust of the interlude seems to be towards escapism, isolation, and autonomy. Communion with nature is presented in *A Village Romeo and Juliet* as an antidote to a stained and corrupt social existence. If society has alienated us from nature, music promises to heal the wounds and draw us into a blissful union. The wordless, mostly invisible medium of Delius's interlude is perfectly suited to an aesthetic that credits music with the capacity to leave the mundane world behind. Freed from the distraction of the stage and mercifully devoid of visible, performing bodies, music is free to operate in what Delius calls 'its own sphere'. But Nature, as constructed by Delius, is more than a pastoral metaphysics, and his music here asserts its relation to the body and its capacity to assume a narrative burden alongside word and image.

2

What the conductor saw

If Delius defines one possible construction of sexuality in music, quite another emerges in the orchestrally represented love scenes of Massenet's *Esclarmonde* and Strauss's *Feuersnot*. Here the articulation of pleasure gives way to an erotics of desire that depends precisely on the postponement and manipulation of pleasure, on its elusiveness and the satisfaction of overcoming that elusiveness. Out of this model emerges a narrative structure in which the kind of intrusions we detected in 'The Walk' take on the character of frustrations integral to the impact of closure. Like Delius's interlude, too, these love scenes offer a reflection on the materiality of music, but in doing so they touch on questions of representation and 'realism' in ways that seem inimical to Delius's music. And if musical sensuality in 'The Walk' seemed to contradict Delius's declared aesthetic, in Strauss it becomes part of a self-proclaiming manifesto.

Fantasy scenes

A familiar technique in cinematic sex scenes is the slow pan or fade that effects a discreet and timely withdrawal from the scene of passion. Displaced by cuts or surrogate images and evoked by appropriately ardent music, the scene is restored only when lust has turned to post-coital repose. Although in one sense dictated by the demands of censorship and the cultural taboos that surround sexual representation, the technique can also be interpreted as a compelling means of signifying sex, one that succeeds all the more for what it resists revealing. *Esclarmonde* and *Feuersnot* offer an operatic prototype, one in which the orchestra is called upon to represent sexual encounters between characters now silenced and hidden from view. What is denied to the eyes is granted to the ears, a manoeuvre that, according to the critics, provoked a sensational reaction. Music, it seems, was deemed capable of testing the very limits of theatrical representability, of revealing what the stage dare not reveal. As direct substitutions for the staging of a sexual encounter, these orchestral interludes offer a vivid illustration of the hermeneutic codes embodied in the musical signification of sex and sexuality in the context of *fin-de-siècle* culture.

Equally, however, they can be seen to participate in the cultural definitions of sexuality and gender. No matter how vivid their musical effects, the interludes are nevertheless presented in a context of absence. Actors, scenery, and words are withdrawn to leave only the orchestra, a lack that positions the interlude as a kind of fantasy in relation to the 'reality' of the staged action. Psychoanalysts Jean Laplanche and Jean-Bertrand Pontalis define fantasy as a setting out of desire 'in which what is prohibited is always present in the actual formation of the wish'.[1] It is, in other words, a response to what is denied in reality, a substitution in which the subject reshapes reality according to its own wishes. In the interludes music becomes a signifier of the illicit; it reveals a scene that is simultaneously happening – it is as real as any of the staged scenes – and yet hidden and unreal. It is within this gap between the explicit and the imaginary, between tolerated and censored, that the interlude engages with fantasy. Here the prohibited partly surfaces, and the shape of the subject's desire is covertly documented. Both scenes can be seen to address and ultimately reinforce the male subject, remodelling the perceived threat of female sexuality as desire for him. If music is capable, as Carolyn Abbate claims, of resisting the objectification of women in libretto plots and 'subvert[ing] the borders we fix between the sexes', then these orchestral scenes reveal that, by appropriating 'feminine' voices as sources of masculine pleasure and empowerment, it can also magnify that objectification and reinforce those borders.[2]

Commissioned for the 1889 Exposition Universelle in Paris, *Esclarmonde* opened at the Opéra-Comique on 15 May for the first of 101 performances. Massenet and his librettists, Alfred Blau and Louis de Gramont, dubbed it an *opéra romanesque*, a reference to the libretto's origins in the medieval romance *Partenopeus de Blois*.[3] In a move characteristic of so many of Massenet's operas, the male title figure of the literary source finds himself replaced by the leading female character. Esclarmonde, daughter of the Byzantine emperor Phorcas, succeeds to her father's throne, but must keep her face veiled in order to retain the magical powers he has taught her. When she reaches the age of twenty a tournament will decide her hand, and the victor will remove the veil.

---

[1] Jean Laplanche and Jean-Bertrand Pontalis, *The Language of Psycho-Analysis*, trans. Donald Nicholson-Smith (New York: Norton, 1973), p. 318. While it owes a great deal to Freud's analyses of fantasy, the model developed by Laplanche and Pontalis also attempts to address what the authors feel are a number of discrepancies in Freud's definitions.

[2] Carolyn Abbate, 'Opera; or, the Envoicing of Women', in Ruth A. Solie (ed.), *Musicology and Difference: Gender and Sexuality in Musical Scholarship* (Berkeley: University of California Press, 1993), p. 258.

[3] Demar Irvine, *Massenet: A Chronicle of His Life and Times* (Portland: Amadeus Press, 1994), pp. 163–4.

Her resolve is tested, however, when she falls in love – or at least lust – with Roland, count of Blois. How could she ever hope to entice him without breaking her vow? The answer proposed by her sister is to use her magical powers to bring Roland to her. Transporting him to an enchanted island, Esclarmonde overwhelms Roland with marvellous sights and sounds, declares herself to be 'beautiful and desirable', and seduces the bedazzled knight. Esclarmonde's plan backfires, however, when the bishop of Blois later learns of the tryst and tears the veil from her face. Disgraced, Esclarmonde is forced to renounce Roland in order to save his life at the hands of Phorcas. But the beneficent Phorcas does not revoke Esclarmonde's claim to the throne, and when the tournament is held to decide her hand, it is none other than Roland who triumphs.

Critical reaction was very mixed, much of it coloured by the politics of the Wagner debate.[4] Victor Wilder, music critic for *Gil Blas*, welcomed a new 'strength and robustness which one would not have expected in [Massenet]',[5] but lamented 'certain brutalities' in the orchestration which he equates with 'symphonic drama':

We have to face it this time ... the new work embarks under full sail on the impetuous flood of the music of the future.[6]

One of the features identified as Wagnerian was, not surprisingly, the presence of leitmotifs in the score. But critics also noticed the prominent role given to the orchestra. Bellaigue observed that it is above all the orchestra 'which sings, which recounts, which describes'.[7] Like many of the critics, he drew attention to one orchestral interlude in particular.

It takes place in Act II during the love scene on the enchanted island and serves as a transition to the second tableau of the act, in which Roland awakens in a magic palace. Accompanied by a chorus of spirits, the love duet of Roland and Esclarmonde reaches its climax at the words 'Voici le divin moment, c'est l'heure de l'hyménée!' The chorus fades into the distance with a repeated 'Hymen!' on the *Tristan* chord, and a curtain descends on the scene. René Brancour provides a particularly shrewd commentary:

At a given moment the tree, sensing that the shadow of its leaves will not adequately veil the transports of the sorceress and her tenor, makes a discreet sign to the stage-hand. A prudish curtain then lowers to shield the eyes of

---

[4] For a discussion of Wagnerisms in *Esclarmonde* see Steven Huebner, 'Massenet and Wagner: Bridling the Influence', *Cambridge Opera Journal* 5 (1993), 223–38.

[5] Victor Wilder, *Gil Blas*, 17 May 1889, cited in Eugène de Solenière, *Massenet: Etude critique et documentaire* (Paris: Bibliothèque d'Art de la Critique, 1897), p. 47.

[6] Ibid., p. 46.

[7] Camille Bellaigue, 'Revue musicale', *Revue des Deux Mondes* 83 (1 June 1889), 701–2.

the equally prudish audience. But what use these chaste precautions! The ears substitute for the eyes, and the orchestra, overcome with voluptuous pleasure, spares them no detail.[8]

Bellaigue enthused that

we witness with our ears what we could not with our eyes. Never before, I believe, has such an accurate and detailed musical description of the physical manifestation of human affection been made (you see that I try to express myself becomingly).[9]

Brancour's reference to the 'prudish curtain' points to one practical motivation for representing a love scene through an orchestral interlude. Liberal as the French censors may have been at this time – and they certainly represent a marked contrast to enforcement in other parts of Europe[10] – the sexual act was hardly likely to be tolerated on the stage of the Opéra-Comique.

At the same time, interpreting the interlude as a compromise to the censor obviously fails to do it justice; as Brancour observes, 'what use these chaste precautions!'. Eugène de Solenière remarked that 'it is impossible for music to be more carnal – I would even say more aphrodisiac – than this symphonic interlude'.[11] Richard O'Monroy described how, during the *scène d'amour*,

all the spectators became aroused to paroxysm. The men's eyes narrow in rapture, the ladies hide behind their fans. They shout bis, yes, an erotic frenzy.[12]

For Bellaigue this 'detailed musical description' is simply a substitution of ears for eyes. He continues:

[I]t is all noted down and gradated: the violins begin softly, then the violas answer the call for help, then the rest of the strings; the sonorities swell, the tempo rushes head-long, and it all leads to a general climax that is terribly significant.[13]

By building towards and dying away from a central climax based on tempo and orchestral sonority, the interlude, in Bellaigue's reading,

---

[8] René Brancour, *Massenet* (Paris: Libraire Félix Alcan, 1922), p. 98.

[9] Bellaigue, 'Revue musicale', 704.

[10] Frederic Hemmings traces the gradual weakening of state censorship of the theatre in France at the end of the nineteenth century. He notes that by the final decade of the century bans and enforced modifications had become increasingly rare and rulings were often ignored. In 1905 the Chambre des Députés withdrew the salaries of the theatrical censors, effectively putting an end to state censorship of the theatre. See Hemmings, *Theatre and State in France, 1760–1905* (Cambridge: Cambridge University Press, 1994), pp. 221–5.

[11] Solenière, *Massenet*, xxvii.

[12] Richard O'Monroy, *Gil Blas*, 17 May 1889, cited in Solenière, *Massenet*, p. 47.

[13] Bellaigue, 'Revue musicale', 704.

shadows the dynamics of the sexual act. So vivid is the representation, indeed, that Bellaigue accuses Massenet of a lack of 'aesthetic delicacy'. The effect, he argues, is the 'union of two bodies' rather than 'two souls' and the 'debasement of the musician's ideal'.[14]

'Those females who haunt us in our dreams'

In the *scène d'amour* Esclarmonde is the seducer, luring both Roland and the audience into her realm of pleasure. Like her sisters Thaïs and Manon she is a woman of abundant sexual energy and limited self-restraint. Her desire for Roland knows no bounds. It arouses intense jealousy within her when she hears of a potential rival for his affections; it compels her to resort to sorcery and risk a betrayal of her royal destiny. Roland appears as little more than a powerless object of that desire, overwhelmed and libidinally overmatched. For Bellaigue, Esclarmonde

seems as desirable, to use her own word, as she is desiring, but only for the senses. Women who make all the advances and take all the initiative in love can hardly be loved; or rather, they can be loved initially out of politeness and then with a great deal of pleasure (providing they are beautiful), but it is an incomplete and inferior love.[15]

Like the music of the interlude, Esclarmonde represents a physical debasement of something more noble. Bellaigue manages to combine a view of Esclarmonde as fantasy figure – a veiled temptress rife with desire – with an attitude of moral superiority. She is a concubine, an object to provide 'a great deal of pleasure' but not worthy of true 'love'. The 'voice' of her desire is music, a feminine music that entices and enfolds the hapless male. From the beginning of their encounter on the enchanted isle, it is Esclarmonde who wields power. It is she who has transported him there and intoxicated his senses with an array of images and sounds worthy of *The Tempest*. She appears, veiled and mysterious, and lures him into submission with her siren song. Roland is swept into the embrace of her seductive, feminine music with what Jules Lemaître described as 'supple melodies, long and caressing like waves or like women'.[16] The curtain descends and the orchestra echoes her arching phrases sung to the words 'Oui, je suis belle et désirable!' Released from the confinement of the body, her music takes on an uncanny sense of emanating from her inner being. It is as if the loss of a physical locus invites us to trace the source of the music in the heart of the psyche. And if the music is anything to go by, that psyche is a fluid, polymorphous place, its music characterised by flowing melodic lines and a pulsing

---

[14] Ibid.   [15] Ibid., 699–700.
[16] Jules Lemaître, *Billets du Matin*, 14 May 1889, cited in Brancour, *Massenet*, p. 99.

Example 2.1   Massenet, *Esclarmonde*, *Scène d'amour* (p. 103)

rhythm (example 2.1). Her music has subtly changed, however. Gone is the stable harmonic context of its original appearance, replaced by the ambiguous support of a half-diminished chord. Given free rein, her feminine musical discourse seems empowered and, for the first time, genuinely threatening to male control. It appears capable of breaking down tonally the barriers that still applied in the embodied world of the stage. Male authority seems destined to defeat in this irrational feminine realm of the sensual.

As the widely quoted epithet 'Mademoiselle Wagner' suggests, an image of Massenet as feminised artist circulated in the critical discourse of the *fin de siècle*.[17] Santillane described him as the 'musician of woman and of women', adding that he followed Gounod by driving music beyond 'Marguerite's bedroom' and into 'Manon's boudoir'.[18] Solenière compared his appeal to that of a *'femme fatale* whose embrace is diseased and whose power is lethal'.[19] From this perspective Massenet's music empowers woman, lending a voice to what Bellaigue called 'women who take all the initiative'. But if they suggest an envoicing, these observations also project those voices onto fantasy figures – the *femme fatale*, the prostitute – that typically embody *fin-de-siècle* conceptions of female sexual excess. Debussy wrote of

Massenet's insatiable desire to find in music the necessary documents for a complete history of the feminine soul. For they are all there – those females who haunt us in our dreams! . . . The harmonies are like arms, the melodies like the napes of necks. We gaze into the ladies' eyes dying to know their thoughts.[20]

[17] Henry Finck, *Massenet and His Operas* (New York: John Lane Company, 1910), p. 70.
[18] Santillane, *Gil Blas*, 5 October 1895, cited in Solenière, *Massenet*, p. 133. Santillane is obviously a *nom de plume* that takes its cue, like the name of the journal, from the novel *Gil Blas de Santillane*.
[19] Solenière, *Massenet*, xxxi.
[20] Claude Debussy, 'Massenet: D'*Eve* à *Grisélidis*', *La Revue Blanche*, 1 December 1901, in Richard Langham Smith (ed. and trans.), *Debussy on Music* (New York: Alfred A. Knopf, 1977), pp. 56–7.

In this view Massenet's music reveals what is otherwise only dreamed. It offers a window on the feminine, on those women who 'haunt us in our dreams'. What Debussy seeks might be better described as a 'complete *male* history of the feminine soul'. Like Solenière and Santillane, his image of the feminine in Massenet's music is bound up with fantasy. Far from offering a voice to woman, Debussy's reading presents her as the object of the male gaze, a figure revealed in dreams and documented in music.

As she lures Roland towards erotic fulfilment, Esclarmonde announces her destiny: 'Celle qui s'est donnée/Va s'unir à son amant' ('She who gives herself/Will be united with her lover'). Although Esclarmonde may stray into uncharted waters, her ultimate goal is merely the safe and welcome return of a C major that has come to stand for duty and phallic power, the same emphatic C major that heralded Phorcas's announcement of abdication and his imposition of strict conditions of succession on his daughter. Pleasure in this scenario will derive from the journey itself, from the tantalising postponement of the climax. Appropriating thematic material from the love duet, Esclarmonde flirts agonisingly with C major while avoiding cadential closure. Harmonically, the interlude seems to close in on C stepwise, first from below as A flat gives way to A major/minor and then B flat. But any further stepwise motion is suspended when B flat major is interrupted by a prolonged but unresolved dominant preparation on G. This harmonic motion manifests itself melodically as a prominent chromatic shift from B flat to B natural. Then C major seems to be approached stepwise from above as D minor is established, only to be similarly interrupted by a sustained G7. As the crescendo builds, a harmonic struggle ensues between the G7 chord and D minor, the latter now undermined by a persistent G pedal. Melodically, the result is a tense alternation between B flat and B natural that seems to demand an upward resolution onto C. Finally, D minor gives way as the B flat shifts decisively to B natural, and after four bars of *tutta forza* preparation the much anticipated C major bursts emphatically forth (example 2.2). This agonising postponement of C is actually a recapitulation, transposed down a semitone, of the climax of the love duet, with the difference that, while the first climax settled firmly on D flat for no more than two bars before modulating, the *scène d'amour* affirms and reaffirms its goal with repeated and unambiguous cadences. Only a brief *pianissimo* passage for strings provides a fleeting reminiscence of the chromatic striving of the crescendo, and a reminder that desire is only quelled for the moment.

Esclarmonde's arching lines return, now firmly rooted in C and robbed of their dangerous allure. The rhythmic fluency of the interlude now lost, a series of tentative repeated chords dissolves into the portentous C major invocation of the Prologue, now intoned *pianissimo*. Susan

Example 2.2   Massenet, *Esclarmonde, Scène d'amour* (p. 104)

McClary has interpreted diatonic closure in *Carmen* and *Salome* as a need to purge female chromatic excess for the sake of the 'social and tonal order' of the dominant male discourse.[21] But there is no need to *impose* closure upon Esclarmonde; true to her promise, she willingly submits. Having seduced us with her feminine musical discourse, Esclarmonde has returned us unscathed to a state, albeit temporary, of reason and authority.

'She who gives herself'

When the curtain rises again, Roland finds himself transported away from the magic island and laments the end of the 'sweet night of love' with its 'burning ecstasy'. Now the passion is only a memory, a faded dream. Reminiscing, the befuddled tenor draws brief glimpses of the love music from the orchestra, but they remain mere fragments of their former selves. In his longing to return to the previous night, Roland throws a light on the desire that has circulated in this fantasy scene. With its seductress who desires and yet submits, a climax teasingly postponed, and a bewildering realm of feminine music, the *scène d'amour* presents a passive male fantasy of seduction. Esclarmonde is empowered only so as to place the male subject in a (pleasurable) passive position; she remains merely an object within the fantasy scenario. Her dominant position, in other words, is calculated and framed by the limits of the fantasy.

If Massenet's powerful females and passive fantasies appear to subvert traditional gender roles, it is surely only part of a broader male

[21] Susan McClary, *Feminine Endings: Music, Gender, and Sexuality* (Minnesota and London: University of Minnesota Press, 1991), p. 100.

45

strategy of reinforcement. Exploring the cultural reinforcement of male subjectivity, Stephen Heath has referred to

that fringe of ignorance which 'the woman' poses even as 'she' is set up to establish identity – the woman confirms the man, giving a clarity of position, but then also projects an absolute otherness, different, in contradiction, potentially threatening – and which has thus, continually, to be made up, securely fictioned.[22]

By characterising this fictioning process as 'continual', Heath implies that it responds to specific historical circumstances. Laplanche and Pontalis make a similar point when they suggest that fantasy scenarios – what they call the 'fantasmatic' – are 'constantly drawing in new material'.[23] Kaja Silverman takes the suggestion a step further, arguing that the fantasmatic scene 'is being continually drawn into new social and political alignments, which may even lead to important "scenic" changes'.[24] In other words, the fantasy scenario is located in a specific historical and cultural environment, one that impacts profoundly upon its constitution and its effect.

The fantasmatic scene at the root of the *scène d'amour* relies on scenic 'props', tropes that identify it and make it meaningful. Esclarmonde's 'feminine' music, with its pulsing rhythms and flowing melodic lines, is an effect that relies, like Wagner's Rhinemaidens, on nineteenth-century constructions of female sexuality in terms of water, fluidity, and polymorphism. As Jules Lemaître put it, 'melodies ... like waves or like women'. In this construction it is the instability and uncontainability of female sexuality, its elusive Otherness, that is emphasised. The climax-oriented form of the interlude, meanwhile, can be interpreted as a phallic vision of sexual experience, one that, unlike *A Village Romeo and Juliet*, celebrates desire over pleasure. McClary has identified the gradual climax as an image of male sexual pleasure, one so universalised that it comes to represent *the* pattern of sexual fulfilment.[25] This is an effect clearly understood by the critics of *Esclarmonde*, particularly Bellaigue with his description of a 'general climax that is terribly significant'. Taken together, these textual effects present a sex scene motivated and initiated by the Other of 'feminine desire', but ultimately shaped and controlled by the phallus.

The musical erotics of *Tristan* loom large here, too. Like the Act II love duet and Isolde's Transfiguration, the melodic pattern is one of persistent upward chromatic movement based on repeated motivic cells,

---

[22] Stephen Heath, *The Sexual Fix* (London: Macmillan, 1982), p. 92.

[23] Laplanche and Pontalis, *The Language of Psycho-Analysis*, p. 317.

[24] Kaja Silverman, *The Acoustic Mirror: The Female Voice in Psychoanalysis and Cinema* (Bloomington and Indianapolis: Indiana University Press, 1988), p. 218.

[25] McClary, *Feminine Endings*, 126–7.

while harmonically the final resolution grants reward after a tension un-
bearably heightened. The seemingly endless postponement of cadential
closure, the breathless quality of the strings' staggered climb towards
melodic climax, and the harmonic ambiguity are effects very much in accord with the libidinal model of desire that Kramer detects in *Tristan*. But
Tristan and Isolde can only reach satisfaction in that 'miraculous world
of Night' where, as Kramer observes, the 'boundary between subject and
object collapses'.[26] Esclarmonde, by contrast, seeks no transfiguration.

Nor does she represent, like the *femme fatale*, an embodiment of male
anxiety. Far from threatening or altering, Massenet's female figures offer
the possibility of hedonistic indulgence. Their goal is a pursuit of their
own sexual desire that harmonises with that of the male. Massenet's
Salomé, unlike her counterpart in Wilde/Strauss, ultimately dreams
only of a mutually loving union, a dream that John the Baptist comes to
share. Though plagued with sexual excess in themselves, Massenet's
lustful heroines ultimately submit themselves to the fulfilment of
male pleasure. Placed in a position of power within the fantasy, the
female reveals that all she really desires is the male, and in doing so
characterises female sexuality in terms of pleasuring him. Here is the
femme fatale without the mortal threat, a figure who disperses anxiety in
the name of pleasure.

Such base pleasures, of course, have no place in the lofty realm of
masculine art, and so, while embraced, they are also dismissed hypo-
critically as the product of a feminised artist. Perceiving a threat to the
integrity of the canon from this sensual, hedonistic music, the critics
construct an authorial subject that is absolved of responsibility. Constructions of authorial identity also figure prominently in the music of
Strauss. Here, however, the source lies not in critical reception, but in a
conscious authorial strategy. In *Feuersnot* that construction centres on an
orchestral *Liebesszene* in which the sexual triumph of the 'hero' comes
to stand for Strauss as man, while this mini symphonic poem mirrors
Strauss as artist.

'All warmth springs from woman'

In 1898, still smarting from the critical drubbing of *Guntram* at its Munich
premiere four years earlier, Strauss met Ernst von Wolzogen, a satirical
novelist, theatrical director, and later founder of the *Überbrettl* cabaret.
Unlike his half-brother Hans von Wolzogen, one of the most prominent
members of the Bayreuth 'inner circle', Ernst had found little demand
for his services in theatrical circles. Of particular disappointment was his
failure to secure a directorship at any of the court theatres in Munich, an

[26] Kramer, *Music as Cultural Practice*, p. 147.

experience that left him, like Strauss, with a lingering bitterness towards the city. Together, Strauss and Wolzogen hatched a plan for an operatic revenge that would mock the 'Philistine' citizens of Munich, and the search began for suitable material. Strauss was intrigued by a Flemish legend, translated into German as *Das erloschene Feuer von Audenaerde* (*The Extinguished Fire of Audenaarde*) and published in an 1843 collection entitled *Niederländische Sagen*.[27] It concerns a young man who is spurned and humiliated by the object of his affections. He tells his story to an old magician, who resolves to exact revenge on the youth's behalf. Casting a spell that extinguishes every fire in the town, he declares that fire will only return from the young woman who had denied love. She is forced to strip in the town square and bend over so that each citizen can ignite a candle from a flame springing from her anus.

Needless to say, such a crudely violent plot was deemed unsuitable, at least in its original state. (Erich Urban later expressed the wish that Wolzogen and Strauss had resisted altering the tale, which he described as 'coarse, and yet at the same time, subtle'!)[28] Wolzogen set about devising a modified version and in March 1899 reported to Strauss:

I now have the following idea: *Feuersnot* – one act – scene of action, Munich in legendary Renaissance times. The young hero lover is himself a magician; the Great Old Man, his master, who was once thrown out by the good people of Munich, never appears in person at all. The malicious young girl, pressured by the council and the citizens, must in the end sacrifice her maidenhood to the young magician in order to redeem the town from their 'Feuersnot' [fire famine]. When love unites with the magic of genius, even the greatest Philistine must see the light![29]

Wolzogen enticed Strauss by introducing a number of autobiographical parallels. The old magician was to become Reichart der Meister, an obvious reference to the wizard of Bayreuth, whose shadow is still all too evident in much of *Guntram*. His apprentice, Kunrad, would then represent Strauss himself. This gave Wolzogen the opportunity to allude to Wagner and Strauss in the text, make ironic use of Wagnerian language, and even incorporate punning references to their names and to his own. Strauss proved a match for the irony and symbolic allusion in Wolzogen's text. He paralleled the Wagnerian language with Wagnerian references of his own and – not unexpectedly from the composer of *Ein Heldenleben* – quotations from his own music, particularly *Guntram*.

[27] William Mann, *Richard Strauss: A Critical Study of the Operas* (London: Cassell, 1964), p. 23.

[28] Erich Urban, review of *Feuersnot* in *Die Musik* 1 (1901), 418, cited in Franzpeter Messmer, *Kritiken zu den Uraufführungen der Bühnenwerke von Richard Strauss* (Pfaffenhofen: W. Ludwig Verlag, 1989), p. 23.

[29] Letter to Strauss, cited in Franz Trenner, 'Richard Strauss und Ernst von Wolzogen', *Richard Strauss Jahrbuch* 1953, 111–12.

The 'fire famine' was to be made all the more dramatic by setting the action on midsummer's night, when the town would be illuminated with solstice fires. If magic was to be symbolic of artistic creativity, then fire would be its medium:

All creative power springs from sensuality [*Sinnlichkeit*]. Creative spirit possesses the magic power to fashion a living entity out of nothing. Now, if this magic can only become effective through the fire of the senses, then I claim full right to clutch this fire to myself wherever I may find it. Each true artist is a Prometheus who creates mankind in the likeness of God. But he has no need to steal the distant light of heaven for his creation; he can take fire from the earth, since:

> 'All warmth springs from woman,
> All light stems from love...'

That is the moral of this little poem.[30]

Wolzogen's quotation is taken from Kunrad's lengthy address to the people of Munich in which he chastises their neglect of sensuality, adding that 'only from hot, young, maidenly bodies does the fire spring forth anew!' Fire is equated not only with the artist's medium, but with libidinal energy, an energy nourished only by woman.

Contrary to the tone of mockery in much of the libretto, Kunrad's address strikes a note of deadly seriousness, despite its series of punning references. *Sinnlichkeit* was to be respected, neither avoided nor degraded. A similar attitude is evident in Wolzogen's prescription for the ideal cabaret:

No prudishness in the erotic, but at the same time no deliberately provocative sultriness and no clumsy obscenity.[31]

It is difficult to accept, however, that Wolzogen was not aware of the provocative nature of his dénouement, particularly in the conservative context of opera. If, as Leopold Schmidt observed, Wolzogen makes the 'prudent' move of hiding the encounter behind the stage,[32] little room is left for misinterpretation.

Diemut, Wolzogen's 'malicious young girl', has spurned and embarrassed Kunrad. Enraged, he has plunged the town into darkness, demanding Diemut's 'maidenhood' in exchange for the fire. Responding to the desperate (and threatening) pleas from the populace, Diemut admits Kunrad to her bedroom located above the darkened stage. Through

---

[30] Ernst von Wolzogen, *Wie ich mich ums Leben brachte: Erinnerungen und Erfahrungen* (Brunswick and Hamburg: Westermann, 1922), pp. 146ff. Cited in Trenner, 'Richard Strauss und Ernst von Wolzogen', 112–13.

[31] Trans. in Miriam Stevens, *Turn-of-the-Century Cabaret* (London: Routledge, 1989), p. 125.

[32] Leopold Schmidt, *Aus dem Musikleben der Gegenwart* (Berlin: A. Hofmann and Co., 1909), p. 113.

her window a faint glimmer of light appears, growing stronger until, at the moment of truth, all the fires in the town burst forth once more.

Here was an opportunity for the master of programme music, the Strauss who was soon to shock the musical public with a graphic bedroom scene in *Symphonia domestica*. The combination of a musical sex scene with Wolzogen's occasionally lewd language did not escape the scrutiny of the authorities. Mahler encountered resistance from both the Viennese censor and the Hofoper administration when he proposed a production there in 1901,[33] and performances at the Berlin Hofoper in 1902 were abruptly suspended when the work met with the disapproval of the Kaiser's wife. Strauss wrote bitterly to his parents: 'the priests and sanctimonious wives have denounced *Feuersnot* to the Kaiser [Wilhelm II], and the Kaiser has strictly forbidden further performances'.[34] Even in a concert arrangement the *Liebesszene* was to prove more than adequate to the task, as Colette testifies:

That a love scene? My God, if I went into such tumultuous ecstasies I'd be afraid of what my neighbors downstairs might say. The programme was right: a 'scene' it was, not a duet. One would have thought there were fifteen of them, not just two.[35]

If Wolzogen's scenario provided fuel for the fire, then Strauss's music clearly fanned the flames into an inferno.

---

[33] Mahler wrote to Strauss in August 1901: 'So far I only know that our highly moral Intendant, who manages to be on equally good terms with the Graces, the nine muses and with our holy patron saints, wishes to inhibit the performance. All my representations and appeals to "common sense" seem to have been in vain.' In Herta Blaukopf (ed.), *Gustav Mahler–Richard Strauss: Correspondence 1888–1911*, trans. Edmund Jephcott (London: Faber and Faber, 1984), p. 60.

[34] In Willi Schuh (ed.), *Richard Strauss: Briefe an die Eltern* (Berlin: Atlantis Verlag, 1954), p. 264. In contrast to the relaxation of censorship in France, Germany was in the midst of controversy over the issue. A proposed bill providing sweeping anti-obscenity provisions under the Criminal Code was introduced in the Reichstag in 1900. Partly an attempt to avoid ambiguous judicial definitions of the word 'obscene' (*unzüchtig*), the bill stipulated that offending material would no longer have to be judged obscene, but rather, 'capable of giving offence through gross injury of feelings of shame and morality'. The bill had the full support of the conservative majority, but through a combination of parliamentary manoeuvring by the socialists and left liberals and government embarrassment over widespread protest the portions of the bill dealing with obscenity on the stage were dropped. It was in the tense aftermath of this narrow defeat that the *Feuersnot* scandal in Berlin arose. See Peter Jelavich, *Munich and Theatrical Modernism* (Cambridge, Mass.: Harvard University Press, 1985), pp. 141–2.

[35] Colette, review in *Gil Blas*, 23 March 1903, in Langham Smith (ed. and trans.), *Debussy on Music*, p. 163.

The master's apprentice

The *Liebesszene* begins very quietly with a developed version of Kunrad's main character-motif (example 2.3, figure 216). The opening key, A major, represents a resolution of the extended diminished seventh with which the townsfolk had cried out to Diemut to restore the fire. This moment, it seems, holds out the hope of a solution to their *Feuersnot*. Here, in this foreboding series of sustained chords with their shimmering triplet accompaniment, is the glow of the magic fire and the heritage of the master (Reichart and Richard). A musical dialogue then develops, in which Diemut is represented by a purely orchestral rendition of the simple folksong that she sang at her first appearance in the opera (example 2.4, figure 217). The song's text draws on the summer

Example 2.3   Strauss, *Feuersnot*, Liebesszene

Example 2.4   Strauss, *Feuersnot*, Liebesszene

solstice tradition of handing out sweets, and Wolzogen typically incorporates some rather obvious *doubles entendres*: 'alle Mädeln mögen Meth' ('all girls like mead'). With its simple chorale style, this folksong stands in stark contrast to the sophisticated music of Kunrad's 'response' (figure 218). Diemut is very much the *bürgerlich* ideal partner, while Kunrad knows of another, metaphysical world, a world over which he is beginning to assume mastery. In terms of sonority, Kunrad's music is characterised by full, thickly orchestrated textures, Diemut's by transparent, chamber-like scoring. Accompanied by a delicately orchestrated ensemble of solo cello and horns, Diemut's melody is scored for flute doubled by solo violin. The result is an ethereal sound-world dominated by 'feminine' colours (in *Ein Heldenleben* it is the solo violin that represents the female figure of the 'hero's companion'). The distinctness of Diemut's music is reinforced by an offstage harp positioned behind her house, as if to locate her in a space that is, for now, Other to Kunrad. In a second appearance of the folksong (figure 219) the harp is joined by offstage harmonium ('sweet register') and glockenspiel ('very soft and full'). Kunrad, meanwhile, has command of the orchestra in the pit – no offstage ensembles for him.

Soon the Diemut 'voice' adopts a motif that has been associated with her resistance to Kunrad (example 2.5, figure 222, the motif marked 'flehend'). It originally emerged immediately after their first encounter (figure 67), when Kunrad, unable to contain his longing any further, suddenly leapt towards the surprised Diemut and planted a kiss 'fest auf den Mund'. This sudden familiarity provoked outrage among the bystanders and brought humiliation for Diemut, who now found herself the object of ridicule and ribald humour. The motif returned repeatedly in the aftermath of the kiss, most memorably as Diemut cried out in shame at Kunrad's 'disgraceful' behaviour (figure 71). Characteristic

Example 2.5   Strauss, *Feuersnot*, *Liebesszene*

Example 2.6   Strauss, *Feuersnot, Liebesszene*

of the motif is a tritonal harmonic relationship, most often between D minor – which is implied only melodically in the *Liebesszene* version – and A flat 7. It is an apt musical image of Diemut's embarrassment and indignation, an abrupt harmonic dislocation that symbolises her desire to escape Kunrad's attentions and all the public scrutiny that has accompanied them.[36] Indeed in the *Liebesszene* Strauss emphasises the motif's association with Diemut's resistance, indicating in the score that it should sound 'imploring' ('flehend'). But it seems to have little effect on Kunrad, whose music continues its relentless surge. Suddenly, Diemut's final *molto agitato* utterance (figure 224+5) is swept away by an explosive F sharp major motif (= V of B) (example 2.6). The motif finds its melodic origins in the 'Kunrad' motif of example 2.3, but in its current rhythmic guise it recalls the moments before the infamous kiss. There

---

[36] In a dramatic reversal, Kunrad appropriates this tonal pairing when he casts his spell, extinguishing all the fires in Munich (figure 159).

53

Example 2.7   Strauss, *Feuersnot*, 'libido' motif

Example 2.8   Strauss, *Feuersnot*, *Liebesszene*

it had conveyed the growing tension of Kunrad's desire, bursting forth as he leapt towards Diemut (example 2.7, figure 66). Its return in the *Liebesszene* suggests a parallel outburst of aggression on Kunrad's part. Again Kunrad seems to have invited himself where no other invitation was forthcoming. Together with the new, much more emphatic episode that it triggers, the motif suggests that Kunrad, aroused by the surging flames of libidinal energy, has put an end to foreplay and initiated intercourse. Gentle persuasion has given way to physical force.

The tempo is now marked 'sehr leidenschaftlich bewegt' (very passionately agitated), and thematic material overlaps in a dense, frenzied contrapuntal texture. What emerges most forcefully, however, is a graphic realism of extraordinary intensity. One theme in particular, previously unheard, seems to represent what we might call an erotic topos (example 2.8). Characterised by a halting, fitful rhythm and a rising chromatic melodic line, the theme is repeated sequentially over a chromatically ascending harmonic sequence that recalls the Act II love duet of *Tristan und Isolde*. As in *Tristan*, the harmonic-melodic sequence creates the impression of gradual climax, an effect reinforced through dynamics and acceleration of the tempo. Yet nothing in *Tristan* could prepare us for the graphic quality of Strauss's mimesis and the earthy eroticism it conveys. Wagner's lovers never quite lose sight of their metaphysical perch, but Kunrad seems to have put aside the mantle of the master and substituted some very down-to-earth pleasure for mystical sermonising. The final few bars of the interlude resort to a crude musical frenzy highlighted by a chromatically ascending sequence for horns that anticipates the whooping effect in the prelude to *Der Rosenkavalier*. And just as the musical erotics in the *Rosenkavalier* prelude are marked 'parodistisch', so this climax – including a tongue-in-cheek allusion to the destruction of Valhalla (figure 227+8) – represents something of a

54

parody of the kind of musical hyperrealism that offended so many of Strauss's critics.

'A new subjective style'

The parody element, however, seems to have escaped most critics. Many, including Erich Urban, detected a tension between Wolzogen's satirical, cabaret tone and the many passionate, seemingly straight-faced moments of Strauss's music.[37] Carl Söhle praised the *Liebesszene* as the highlight of the score, but regretted that Strauss's music would always seem external to the dramatic situation, 'for as a whole [the scene] can only pass for a farce, and so this sudden *Tristan*esque fervour of the two lovers ... gives the impression of something forced'.[38] Oscar Merz, meanwhile, bemoaned Strauss's 'stiff' response to Wolzogen's satire, suggesting that it was only in passages such as the 'invisible love scene' that he 'composed with his heart', writing 'grand and expressive' music, 'rich in serious, substantial ideas'.[39]

For Strauss the critical reaction to *Feuersnot* exemplified a general misunderstanding of what was modern in his works. In his last diary entry (19 July 1949) he offered some parting thoughts on the issue:

In nearly all of the biographical articles which I now find myself reading in profusion, I miss the correct attitude, particularly towards the libretto of *Feuersnot*. One forgets that this by no means perfect work ... still introduces into the nature of the old opera a new subjective style at the very beginning of the century – a sort of upbeat. Why do people not see what is new in my works, how in them man plays a visible role, as only in Beethoven – this begins already in the third act of Guntram (the renunciation of collectivism), *Heldenleben*, *Don Quixote*, *Domestica* and in *Feuersnot*. There is a conscious tone of mockery, of irony, of protest against the conventional opera text, the individual newness. Hence the cheerful satire of Wagnerian language.[40]

What the critics failed to recognise in *Feuersnot*, Strauss suggests, was its satirical critique of the 'old opera' (read Wagnerian music drama). *Feuersnot* represented for Strauss a new 'subjectivism' that would reject the collective in favour of a Nietzschean celebration of the individual. Guntram's 'renunciation of collectivism' – his rejection of the metaphysical redemption represented by submission to a brotherhood

---

[37] Urban, review of *Feuersnot*, 418, cited in Messmer, *Kritiken zu den Uraufführungen*, p. 23.

[38] Carl Söhle, *Musikalisches Wochenblatt* 32 (1901), 665–6, in Messmer, *Kritiken zu den Uraufführungen*, p. 25.

[39] Oscar Merz, *Münchner Neueste Nachrichten*, 22 November 1901, in Messmer, *Kritiken zu den Uraufführungen*, p. 28.

[40] Richard Strauss, 'Letzte Aufzeichnung' (June 1949), in Willi Schuh (ed.), *Betrachtungen und Erinnerungen*, 2nd edn (Zurich: Atlantis, 1957), p. 182.

of minstrels – marked the first step in this new direction. The suppression of the individual in the metaphysics of Schopenhauer and Wagner would give way to the triumph of the individual subject in the art of the new century. Kunrad embodies that new subject, and it is the establishment of his dual role as both apprentice to the master and master in his own right that is critical in *Feuersnot*. This, as Strauss suggests, is the reason for the satire on Wagnerian language, a satire that extends to both libretto and music. It is within the context of this Wagnerian parody that the new subjectivity emerges. In Wolzogen's text it centres on *Sinnlichkeit*, on taking the 'fire from the earth' in place of the 'distant [metaphysical] light of heaven'. In Strauss's music it emerges most clearly in the *Liebesszene*, with the contrast between the Wagnerian opening and the subsequent exaggerated realism. It is a recognition of this deliberate exaggeration, this satirical contrast, that Strauss misses in the *Feuersnot* criticism.

Seeing with ears

Colette's charge of exaggeration can be seen to echo a much wider critical perspective on Strauss, one that tended to view his realism with suspicion. Robert Hirschfeld summed up some of these doubts in a review of the first Viennese performance of *Salome* (1907):

> In the age of illustration even the terrible event at the well, the falling and rolling of the dear head, must be demonstrated by the orchestra. O this famous exactitude! ... And what is now the upshot of the heartbreaking moment? ... The public cranes its neck toward the orchestra and wants to know how Richard Strauss did that.[41]

In this view technique overwhelms content, a theme taken up by Adorno when he characterises Strauss's music as embodying the 'concept of compositional technique as self-sufficient virtuosity'.[42] This is also the basis of Niemann's assessment of Strauss's merely 'external' appeal to the senses, a 'musical illustrator of the stage', a 'colouristic commentator on the dramatic action'.[43] Rudolf Louis singled out Strauss's virtuosic visual suggestiveness as the defining characteristic of his music:

> No musician before now has ever advanced nearly so far in the art of letting the listener *see*, as it were, with his ears. This is the source of Strauss's unique

---

[41] Robert Hirschfeld, review in *Wiener Abendpost*, 26 May 1907, trans. Susan Gillespie in Bryan Gilliam, *Richard Strauss and His World* (Princeton: Princeton University Press, 1992), p. 335.

[42] Theodor W. Adorno, 'Richard Strauss: Zum 60. Geburtstag: 11. Juni 1924', in *Zeitschrift für Musik* 91 (1924), 289–95, trans. Susan Gillespie in Gilliam, *Richard Strauss and His World*, p. 410.

[43] Niemann, *Die Musik der Gegenwart*, p. 122.

and personal strength, that he has developed the ideal, elevated gestures of the tonal language of Liszt into a gestural language of great specificity that undertakes quite seriously not only to interpret the events of an external plot in tone (by revealing the music that is latent in them) but to draw them until they are recognizable to the inner eye.[44]

What was once 'elevated' has become in the hands of Strauss 'specific', a development, Louis adds, that has 'enriched music's expressive means but which finally turned out to be a dead end'.[45] Leon Botstein presents Strauss's music in terms of the challenge of musical narrative:

Strauss was not embarrassed by the musical illustration. His point was that by telling a story in music, the emotional and psychic impact of that story would transcend any parallel effort to represent reality in visual or literary terms.[46]

In this view, realism, far from a liability, becomes one of the strengths of Strauss's music.

James Hepokoski, following Fredric Jameson's theories, interprets this realism as a form of critique. Focusing on *Don Juan*, he characterises realism as a powerful force in the deconstruction of the metaphysics of music embodied in Strauss's Wagnerian heritage:

In its embracing of some sort of non-transcendent, everyday concreteness and secularized representation, much of Strauss's *Don Juan* (and the later tone poems even more) subjects the prevailing concept of a mystical, autonomous music to a rigorous critique.[47]

In the *Liebesszene* the sudden, powerful entrance of the horn theme (example 2.6) and the subsequent graphic imagery can be interpreted very much in these terms. Where the interlude has until now centred itself on the magical flow of the libidinal fire, its focus shifts to the bodily and the mechanical. What had been a *Tristan*esque metaphysics of sexuality becomes an earthy, vulgar eroticism calculated for sensational effect. Just when an audience is being led to expect a mystical union, it is confronted with graphically depicted intercourse; the mystical and the metaphysical are utterly grounded and given embodiment.

Here, in the clearest possible terms, is the Straussian manifesto, an unabashed artistic credo. Here, Strauss seems to say, is where the apprentice parts company with the master, where the ghost that haunted

---

[44] Louis, *Die Deutsche Musik der Gegenwart*, p. 177, trans. Susan Gillespie in Gilliam, *Richard Strauss and His World*, p. 309.

[45] Ibid.

[46] Leon Botstein, 'The Enigmas of Richard Strauss: A Revisionist View', in Gilliam, *Richard Strauss and His World*, p. 24.

[47] James Hepokoski, 'Fiery-Pulsed Libertine or Domestic Hero? Strauss's *Don Juan* Reinvestigated', in Bryan Gilliam (ed.), *Richard Strauss: New Perspectives on the Composer and His Work* (Durham, N.C.: Duke University Press, 1992), p. 155.

Guntram is exorcised. And yet, in keeping with the mocking spirit of the work, the whole process is comically exaggerated. If the mysticism and magic of the first half of the interlude come to seem inflated and illusory in the down-to-earth world of the later realism, then equally that realism emerges as grotesque and vulgar in relation to the restraint of Kunrad's fire music. Out of this critique emerges Strauss the artist, a figure whose self-projection ushers in the twentieth century with what he calls a 'new subjective style'. On one level the suspension of staged action for a brief symphonic poem creates an obvious *mise-en-abyme* of Strauss the tone poet. In this sense the *Liebesszene* can be seen to construct an imaginary composer who heroically evades the censorship of the theatre and represents in music what is prohibited from visual and verbal representation. But, as we have seen, this composer-subject is aligned in no uncertain terms with the hero of the plot. If Kunrad's sexual 'triumph' confirms his identity and reinforces his ego, then it also, through an explicit process of identification, constructs the composer-subject. This subject is 'Strauss', here placed in inverted commas to distinguish what is a textually constructed figure from Strauss the actual, historical composer. Like the hero of *Ein Heldenleben* or the family man in *Symphonia domestica*, this figure represents a fictional projection of a Straussian identity. He is the Strauss whose story is told and retold in symphonic poem and opera. In *Feuersnot* his identity as artist is based on Wolzogen's *Sinnlichkeit*, on the interrelationship of sexuality and creativity. With a heady brew of magic and fire, revenge and seduction, the *Liebesszene* constructs an artist-subject from musical representations of libidinal desire.

Mastering the fire

But how is this libidinal exchange conveyed in music? Embedded within Diemut's folksong is a phrase associated with the sacred power of solstice, and the *Subendfeuer* (solstice fire) that symbolises its libidinal magic. The motif is characterised by harmonic motion in thirds, initiated by an abrupt shift down a major third to the flattened submediant. In both appearances of the folksong in the *Liebesszene*, the flattened submediant then serves as a dominant preparation for music associated with Kunrad. In the first example the G major of Diemut's song shifts dramatically to an E flat 7, preparing the arrival of the A flat music associated with Kunrad's wooing of Diemut earlier in the opera (example 2.4, figure 218).[48]

---

[48] Given the Wagnerian references in *Feuersnot*, it is probably no accident that the two principal keys of the love duet in *Tristan* (A flat and B) return here in the love duet (figure 122+25) and the *Liebesszene* climax (figure 225).

Example 2.9   Strauss, *Feuersnot*, *Liebesszene*

When the folksong is next heard, the comparable shift, F–C sharp (example 2.9, two bars before figure 220), sets up an almost note-for-note repetition (figure 220) of the F sharp minor music originally heard when Kunrad anticipates mastery of the magical fire of his craft: 'Soll ich die Flammen meistern' (figure 99+9). Here harmonic preparation is complemented by a motivic exchange. In both versions of the 'mastery of fire' music, flickering semiquavers and tremolos, representative of the magical flames, weave around the ominous sustained chords. It is only in the *Liebesszene*, however, that the origins of that fire seem to be traced. Beginning with the second (F major) appearance of the Diemut folksong, Strauss adds tremolo violins and a flowing semiquaver counter-melody in solo viola. And in what might be called a timbral intensification, the cello harmonics of the first folksong are taken up first by violas and later by violins. When the 'mastery of fire' music takes over (figure 220) it adopts the tremolo, echoes the 'sheen' of the string harmonics, and incorporates the counter-melody as the flickering patterns of the fire music; the implication is that the magic of the flames has spilled over from Diemut's folksong. The fact that musical traces of the libidinal flames become more perceptible in the second of the two Diemut passages suggests that Diemut's desire is being awakened only gradually, that the fire within her is growing only in response to Kunrad's passion.

Together with the harmonic preparation of Kunrad's music in Diemut's folksongs (example 2.4, two bars before figure 218, and example 2.9, two bars before figure 220), the musical flames suggest that Kunrad's creative fire finds its source in the sacred fire of Diemut's desire – what Wolzogen calls the unification of 'love with the magic of genius'. It is a fire that empowers Kunrad and fuels his seduction further.

The 'shame' motif (example 2.5) also seems to attest to the awakening of Diemut's desire, or, rather, to the weakening of her resistance. If we compare its interruption of Kunrad's 'mastery of fire' music in the *Liebesszene* (example 2.5, figure 222) with the original uninterrupted version (example 2.10), we find that the interruption of the 'shame' motif does not actually take Kunrad's music off course. For all the dislocating effect of its D minor to A flat 7 leap, the motif immediately yields to the originally expected F major of Kunrad's music (figure 101+3), displacing only the harmonically static passage enclosed in brackets in example 2.10. In its subsequent appearance (example 2.6, figure 224+5) the 'shame' motif proves equally ineffective harmonically. Here the brief D minor oboe arpeggio gives way to a fully harmonised D7, an arrangement that lends greater emphasis to the tritonal relationship with the A flat 7 that follows. Yet the rising chromatic line that closes the motif twice leads the accompanying voices back to the harmonic point of departure, in this case F sharp major (example 2.6, figure 224+6 and figure 225). The increasing urgency of Diemut's protests is belied by a circularity that suggests the futility of her denial in the face of Kunrad's lure. Her attempt to resist Kunrad is configured as utterly ineffective,

Example 2.10   Strauss, *Feuersnot*, 'mastery of fire' music

perhaps half-hearted. Indeed, setting aside the oboe's D minor – which is, after all, only melodically implied, and fleetingly at that – we find that both the Diemut 'interruptions' open with the flattened submediant relationship (C–A flat 7, F sharp–D7) characteristic of the *Subendfeuer* motif. Now even this voice of resistance seems to participate in the libidinal exchange.

Light from self-love?

The problem is that Kunrad seems merely to be replaying his (failed) attempt at seduction earlier in the opera. There, too, he had deployed the 'mastery of fire' music (figure 99+9) and the winding thirds of the A flat passage in example 2.4 (originally heard at figure 140). In that encounter, Diemut, seeking revenge for the humiliation caused by Kunrad's uninvited display of affection, had pretended to respond to his exaggerated poeticisms and promises of a wedding under the flaming sky of midsummer's night. She had offered to smuggle him up to her bedroom in a suspended basket, an invitation that the eager Kunrad had gladly accepted. Dangling in midair, Kunrad had continued his seduction rhetoric, suggesting that only with Diemut's guidance would he truly understand magic. His false modesty seemed to find an apt musical image in the cloying thirds (figure 140) that return, verbatim, in the *Liebesszene* (example 2.4, figure 218). Only when the basket was far above the ground had Diemut revealed her true feelings, taunting him with the suggestion that he use his magical powers to fly up to her. The whole 'love duet' had come about only because Kunrad had believed Diemut's encouraging words, because, in his desire for Diemut, he had projected that desire onto her. The situation in the *Liebesszene*, meanwhile, seems to repeat the state of affairs; Diemut's invitation to Kunrad is based on coercion, not desire. Her discourse may appear to trigger and fuel Kunrad's music, but since Diemut finds herself in this position only under duress, how can she be considered the source of this empowerment? It would seem that the source of fire/libido lies not in Diemut, but in Kunrad's desire *for* Diemut. Her music is surely Other because it is presented from Kunrad's subject position, hence her eviction from the orchestra pit to a backstage ensemble. From this perspective the harmonic preparation embedded in Diemut's folksong appears to be Kunrad's appropriation of her discourse. The only active libido here is Kunrad's, flowing in a narcissistic circle.

Hepokoski explores the question of appropriation in his analysis of the seduction episodes in *Don Juan*. Responding to interpretations that equate a musical figure with the second of Don Juan's conquests, he counters that it may in fact 'be' her, but only in the limited sense that, in actuality, it is nothing more than Don Juan's perception – or Strauss's construction – of her as something beautiful to be possessed.[49]

The question of who this conquest is, then, would really never enter the picture because we remain at the level of a fantasy construction. Possession would appear to characterise Wolzogen's attitude towards the feminine. He speaks of claiming 'full right to clutch this fire to myself wherever I may find it' and taking 'fire from the earth' in the form of woman – the image is one of masculine power and privilege. Wolzogen's pronouncements are presented in too serious a vein to be dismissed as ironic; these ideas, as he claims, represent the 'moral' of the drama. Yet, to this point in Strauss's interlude, Wolzogen's 'inspiration' appears to have been configured as little more than narcissism. Kunrad appears to be either blissfully ignorant of the artificiality of the situation or determined to evade the truth and continue to behave as if his desire were reciprocated. Is Strauss offering a critique of Wolzogen's philosophy, deconstructing the 'light from love' as light from self-love?

The answer emerges only in the latter half of the interlude. If the Diemut 'voice' of the *Liebesszene* has been presented until now as little more than an appropriation by Kunrad, it has at least proved capable of interrupting Kunrad's discourse, as though symbolic of some lingering doubt in his mind. But with the graphic musical narrative that begins at figure 225 (example 2.6), those doubts appear to have been put to rest. For the first time Diemut's behind-the-scene ensemble is heard simultaneously with Kunrad's music, enthusiastically reinforcing its B major tonality with glissando and sustained dominant seventh. The final climax returns to this F sharp 7, suspending it abruptly for a dramatic pause as all the fire and light returns to Munich (example 2.11, figure 228+7). And what should return but Diemut's folksong, now ringing out *fortissimo* for full orchestra to signal that it is no longer Other for Kunrad. Most meaningful of all, though, is the reversal of the flattened submediant relationship of the fire motif. Now inverted to become an ascending major third, that progression takes us from the F sharp 7 to the emphatic B flat that will conclude the opera. The magic of the libidinal fire has served its function and reverses itself, turning outward to restore the external fire to Munich.

How did this sexual fulfilment come about? Is Kunrad still fantasising? Is Diemut again feigning attraction to Kunrad, the deed that enraged him and bruised his ego in the first place? The implication is, rather, that Diemut has responded to Kunrad's seduction and has become aroused herself. The graphic music of the latter half of the

[49] Hepokoski, 'Fiery-Pulsed Libertine', p. 165.

Example 2.11   Strauss, *Feuersnot*, *Liebesszene*

Liebesszene represents a tide of phallic power that sweeps Diemut along. No sign of resistance is left – the two voices have become synchronised, the desire revealed as mutual. The point is affirmed moments after the interlude when we hear the lovers' voices in a duet sung 'sweetly' behind the scene. Their lines harmonise in thirds, then imitate each other as Kunrad and Diemut address each other adoringly; Diemut confirms Kunrad's triumph, hailing him as 'Meister'. It is not simply that, from the perspective of Kunrad's fantasy, Diemut's resistance has vanished. The magician did not employ all the powers of his craft only to be deceived again. Rather, Diemut is positioned as actually responding to Kunrad. The *Liebesszene* presents a picture of mutual sexual fulfilment, paving the way for a post-coital declaration of love.

In retrospect, then, the first half of the interlude no longer appears as a scene of narcissism, but rather as a gradual arousal of Diemut's as yet unconscious desire for Kunrad. Diemut may not have been aware of it at the time, but she wanted Kunrad and returned the flow of libido that became Kunrad's inspiration. Outwardly she has progressed from total resistance at the beginning of the interlude to complete sexual abandon at the end. But Strauss's music relates – in hindsight – an inner story of repressed desire released by Kunrad's seduction. Perhaps, indeed, she had always desired him, even when she went to such pains to humiliate him. Only in the *Liebesszene*, however, does she finally admit it to herself.

In this sense the *Liebesszene* represents an important corrective to the false love duet, displacing repression with released desire and rejection with affirmation. Kunrad's failure in the earlier scene to persuade Diemut seems to call into question the power of his discourse. For all the sugary allure of the thirds in example 2.4 or the foreboding intensity of the 'mastery of fire' music, Kunrad failed to win Diemut over. His powerlessness – his impotence – is symbolised by the basket, in which

63

Example 2.12   Strauss, *Feuersnot*, Diemut's revenge

Example 2.13   Strauss, *Feuersnot*, mocking chorus

he must place his trust, but which cedes control to Diemut. Suspended in midair, his power gives way to vulnerability and his aggression to fear. The situation is illustrated musically when Kunrad's music is actually appropriated by Diemut and subjected to distortion and fragmentation. At figure 145+9, for example, as Diemut mocks the dangling Kunrad, she repeatedly quotes the opening phrase of the cello's melodic line from the 'mastery of fire' music (see lower cello line in example 2.9). The orchestra echoes with quotations of its own, finally reducing the phrase to a parody of itself (example 2.12, figure 146+7). And as a final insult, figure 225 (example 2.6), that symbol of Kunrad's virility, is actually taken up as accompaniment to a chorus of mocking bystanders (example 2.13, figure 150+3). What happens in the *Liebesszene*, then, represents a restoration, a reappropriation, of Kunrad's music. In place of the mocking quotations of the earlier duet, we now have a musical exchange in which Diemut's music serves, tonally and thematically, as the source and preparation for Kunrad's. Now the first appearance of the folksong tonally prepares the seductive thirds from the basket scene (example 2.4, figure 218), while the second both prepares the tonality of the 'mastery of fire' music (example 2.9, two bars before figure 220) and lends to it the string sound-effects of libidinal magic. And as if to avenge its appropriation, the triplet motif of example 2.13 (figure 150+3) enters in four-horn glory to bring an end to the seduction and initiate the sexual gratification that had earlier been denied Kunrad. Now, as the genuine power of his voice is brought to bear, there is no mockery of Kunrad. Instead of the long-winded, diffuse discourse of his first attempt, Kunrad has concentrated all the resources of his craft, compressing his musical material into a powerful and persuasive out-pouring. Here, surrounded by darkness, Kunrad's music seems to find renewed potency. Temporarily called into question, his magic is ulti-mately revealed as authentic and irresistible. Diemut may have denied Kunrad once, but this time she will be caught up in his spell and swept along, 'sehr leidenschaftlich bewegt'.

'Pleasure in spite of herself'

Far from subjecting Wolzogen's narcissistic 'light from love' to a cri-tique, Strauss's *Liebesszene* ultimately embraces the lie, giving it new embodiment in the form of music. In its refusal to expose Kunrad's self-deception for what it is, the *Liebesszene* touches on a much broader male fantasy, one that views a woman's refusal as a denial of her own desire. It is a fantasy in which, to quote Elizabeth Cowie,

the man really knows the woman wants what he has, despite her protestations, and will find pleasure in spite of herself in his sexual activities on her. He shows her what she always wanted all along, which is also himself; hence the fantasy is also an affirmation that he is the desired object.[50]

What Cowie outlines is a process of affirmation that redefines the fan-tasy object as a desiring subject. It is this affirmation through fantasy that underpins Wolzogen's doctrine and emerges so clearly in Strauss's music. And in Strauss's case, it is a fantasy that affirms two distinct identities within the subject. What we might call the Strauss thematic – man versus artist – is played out again and again in his music. In *Ein Heldenleben*, *Symphonia domestica*, and *Intermezzo*, a tension is outlined between sophisticated artist on the one hand and Bavarian *Bürger* on the other. Music, for Strauss, is a means of articulating this tension as part

[50] Elizabeth Cowie, 'Pornography and Fantasy', in Lynne Segal and Mary McIntosh (eds.), *Sex Exposed: Sexuality and the Pornography Debate* (London: Virago Press, 1992), p. 147.

of the projection of an identity. In the *Liebesszene* 'Strauss the artist' is mirrored in the vivid contrast between the metaphysical heritage of the Meister and the graphic illustration that follows. But this artistic persona must be reconciled with the bourgeois subject who lives on Sendlinger-gasse, the ordinary man who desires and needs to be desired. Critical to the definition of both figures is Diemut (read Pauline). She is the feminine Other who fires his creative spirit, the 'hero's companion' of *Ein Heldenleben*, and the sensual muse à la Wolzogen. But she is also the domestic partner of *Symphonia domestica* and *Intermezzo*, who shares a bourgeois existence with Strauss/Kunrad. Neither image excludes the other, each serving as a means of reinforcing one of the Straussian identities. True to Wolzogen's doctrine, this Strauss-subject is defined by the feminine: 'All warmth springs from woman . . .'.

Neither of them averse to a little sensationalism, Massenet and Strauss exploit the orchestra to make known the unknowable, to speak the unspeakable. The critical reception of these interludes leaves little doubt as to music's capacity to signify sexuality for *fin-de-siècle* audiences. By drawing upon musical and broader cultural tropes, musico-dramatic associations, and the perceived relationship between music's patterns of climax and those of sexual behaviour, these orchestral scenes prove able to respond to contemporary constructions of sexuality. Indeed, many of the critical comments would seem to indicate that the traditional elevation of sexuality associated with artistic representation – what Peter Gay terms the 'doctrine of distance'[51] – is endangered. Massenet and, to a greater extent, Strauss seem to test the limits of representability, no doubt with one eye on the box office.

At the same time, they successfully avoid the traditional taboos associated with sexual representation, taboos that centre around the visual and verbal. How does one censor musical sex? For all its pictorial and literary possibilities, can music be credited with the kind of specificity, the capacity for explicit detail, that so often provokes censorship? Perhaps in Strauss's case it can, and yet initial resistance to the *Liebesszene* of *Feuersnot* soon petered out in a way that would be unimaginable if Strauss and Wolzogen had chosen to stage the encounter. Strauss succeeded in smuggling a sex scene into a temple of 'art' where any staged representation would have been unthinkable. Explicit his music may be, but it is received with a tolerance that would be unlikely in the case of an explicit image or verbal description. Music can 'say sex and sexuality', to use Heath's words,[52] but it operates covertly. It bypasses the discourses associated with the illicit portrayal of sex, circumventing the traditional

---

[51] Peter Gay, *The Bourgeois Experience*, vol. I: *Education of the Senses* (Oxford: Oxford University Press, 1984), pp. 391–9.

[52] Heath, *The Sexual Fix*, p. 109.

preoccupation with word and image as potentially transgressive signifiers of the sexual realm.

What emerges clearly in these sex 'scenes' is the repositioning of female sexuality in terms of something enticing and ultimately empowering to the male. By giving the impression of surrendering the musical discourse to woman, *Esclarmonde* engages with a passive fantasy of seduction that seeks to define feminine sexual excess in terms of the pleasurable. *Feuersnot* tackles another male fear – the female power of refusal – suggesting that resistance can be overcome through seduction so that woman is revealed to want it after all. Just as Diemut's 'no' riddles the male ego with doubt, her exposed desire represents a reaffirmation of his identity. Dispersed through the orchestra, her voice, once a symbol of resistance, emerges as one of reassurance and affirmation. In the context of *fin-de-siècle* culture, textual fantasies like these can be seen to have offered an opportunity to reconstruct the feminine in terms that confronted or quelled male fears over the sexual emancipation of women.[53] At a time when feminine desire seemed awakened and dangerously independent, fantasies that located the male as the object of that desire took on a special relevance. They offered to reshape an increasingly incomprehensible and threatening reality into a secure and pleasurable alternative. The threat of the 'new woman', reconfigured as the pleasure-seeking enchantress or the unconsciously desiring 'woman next door', finds itself powerfully dispersed by these fantasmatic musical narratives. Here music becomes an effective tool in the advancement of an imaginary knowledge of the feminine and the subsequent reinforcement of male subjectivity.

[53] Some of these fantasies are explored in Elaine Showalter, *Sexual Anarchy: Gender and Culture at the Fin de Siècle* (New York: Viking, 1990), and Bram Dijkstra, *Idols of Perversity: Fantasies of Feminine Evil in Fin-de-Siècle Culture* (Oxford: Oxford University Press, 1986).

3

Lost in the forest

That orchestral interludes might represent brief fantasy scenarios or dream-like idylls opens up the question of larger-scale projections of interiority in which the impression of the discourse emanating from one of the dramatic subjects expands to embrace large portions of an opera, even the entire work. Relevant here is Strauss's *Salome*, analysed by Lawrence Kramer and Carolyn Abbate in terms of the implied authorship of the title figure.[1] Singling out the execution scene, Abbate interprets Strauss's orchestral music as a projection of Salome's inability to hear what is happening in the cistern below. Rather than correct Salome's mishearings, Abbate argues, Strauss multiplies them, adopting Salome's subject position and 'envoicing' her.[2] Kramer interprets the music of the entire final scene as Salome's, concluding that even the opera's final violent gesture fails to frame and silence her, that she 'appropriates too much of the composer's own voice to be fully negated'.[3]

Taking this kind of reading to one of its possible conclusions, producer Pierre Strosser staged another turn-of-the-century opera, *Pelléas et Mélisande*, as a product in its entirety of Golaud's mind,[4] and Katherine Bergeron has explored the theoretical and critical implications of such a reading, presenting the scenes and images of the opera as exterior projections of Golaud's desire.[5] Given the period's preoccupation with the idea of the unconscious and interiority, a *fin-de-siècle* opera such as *Pelléas* would seem to lend itself strongly to interpretations rooted in

---

[1] Abbate, 'Opera; or, the Envoicing of Women', and Lawrence Kramer, 'Culture and Musical Hermeneutics: The Salome Complex', *Cambridge Opera Journal* 2 (1990), 269–94.

[2] Abbate, 'Opera; or, the Envoicing of Women', pp. 247–8.

[3] Kramer 'Culture and Musical Hermeneutics', 29. Both Abbate and Kramer seem to overlook the possibility that the very completeness of the gesture of 'envoicing' is what gives it its fantasmatic power, that the illusion of empowerment is only a prop that masks appropriation and ultimately heightens the masculine sense of withstanding and controlling feminine authority.

[4] Opéra de Lyon, 1995.

[5] Katherine Bergeron, 'Mélisande's Hair, or the Trouble in Allemonde: A Postmodern Allegory at the Opéra-Comique', in Mary Ann Smart (ed.), *Siren Songs: Representations of Gender and Sexuality in Opera* (Princeton and Oxford: Princeton University Press, 2000), pp. 160–85.

psychological theory. But Maurice Maeterlinck, whose play Debussy set to music almost intact, resisted what he saw as an all too individualistic and worldly account of human subjectivity. In *Le trésor des humbles* (1896) he writes:

Neither those who believe in a God, nor those who disbelieve, are found to act in themselves as though they were sure of being alone. We are watched, we are under strictest supervision, and it comes from elsewhere than the indulgent darkness of each man's conscience![6]

'Psychology', he believed, had 'usurped the beautiful name of Psyche', and should be replaced by a new 'transcendental' psychology that would pay heed to the 'mysterious spiritual phenomena' acting silently on every soul.[7] Susan Youens takes Maeterlinck's position as a basic premise when she explores the representation of destiny in *Pelléas* as an all-powerful and unknowable agency.[8] But before we take Maeterlinck's language as a cue to read *Pelléas* in more metaphysical, non-psychological terms, we need to understand something of the extraordinarily wide-ranging exchange of ideas on psychology at the time, much of it centred in France. It was there that the late nineteenth-century climate of positivism encouraged the development of a 'nouvelle psychologie' based on supposedly strict 'scientific' approaches to observation and diagnosis. Figures such as Jean-Martin Charcot, Hippolyte Bernheim, and Pierre Janet laid the framework for the medical institutionalisation of psychologically based disciplines. Charcot's lectures and demonstrations at the Salpêtrière hospital on hypnosis and its relationship to hysteria attracted students to Paris from all over Europe, while Bernheim's competing theories on hypnosis established an international reputation for the so-called Nancy School of psychiatry. For Janet, a researcher at the Salpêtrière and later Professor of Experimental Psychology at the Collège de France,[9] the possibilities for diagnosis and treatment seemed endless: 'all patients, from the simple rheumatic to the general paretic, will have their psychology minutely investigated in all its details'.[10]

But Janet's work also offers a glimpse of the range of the debate in the name of psychology. Educated as a philosopher, he sought theoretical

---

[6] Maurice Maeterlinck, *The Treasure of the Humble* (1896), trans. Alfred Sutro (London: George Allen, 1905), p. 63.

[7] Ibid.

[8] Susan Youens, 'An Unseen Player: Destiny in *Pelléas et Mélisande*', in Arthur Groos and Roger Parker (eds.), *Reading Opera* (Princeton: Princeton University Press, 1988), pp. 60–91.

[9] Pierre Janet, 'L'anesthésie hystérique', *Archives de Neurologie* 23 (1892), 323–52, trans. in Henri F. Ellenberger, *The Discovery of the Unconscious: The History and Evolution of Dynamic Psychiatry* (London: Allen Lane, 1970), p. 321.

[10] Janet was appointed to the post in 1902.

engagements between philosophy and psychology, and his interests brought him into contact with ideas that seem to occupy the opposite end of the ideological spectrum from the *nouvelle psychologie*. The medical and scientific appropriation of psychology was countered by the assertion of metaphysical and occult readings that shared with science the desire to investigate human subjectivity and to map out the limits of consciousness, while seeking to go beyond what Maeterlinck calls the 'indulgent darkness of each man's conscience'. In 1885 Janet conducted experiments on a patient named Léonie in which he demonstrated that he could hypnotise and plant mental suggestions not only in direct contact but at a distance of one kilometre. Made public at the Société de Psychologie Physiologique, his experiments provoked a telling reaction, for not only was the work taken seriously by his scientifically oriented colleagues, but it generated interest among researchers in the field of parapsychology, some of whom travelled to see Léonie for themselves. They included a delegation from the Society for Psychical Research, an organisation founded in Cambridge in 1882 for the promotion of investigation into paranormal psychical activity. Janet later recalled that the reports on his work by parapsychologists took on a sensationalistic tone:

These experiments, which the representatives of paranormal psychology have published and popularised in my opinion too soon, have since that time been cited and used in all works on the unknown faculties of the human mind. In viewing these citations and this abuse of my former observations, I have always had a feeling of astonishment and regret.[11]

The incident demonstrates the contested territory between the different approaches and methodologies, and the extent to which the nature and scope of psychology was open to debate. What Maeterlinck objects to in psychology as it has come to be understood are its connotations of individualism, of worldly humanism. Rather, he argues, psychology needs to transcend the individual and embrace the remote and unknowable forces that act upon us. Philosopher Henri Bergson, a colleague of Janet at the Collège de France, encapsulated this opposition when he declared in *Matter and Memory* (1896) that his goal would be to establish a reconciliation between psychology and metaphysics, between materialist and scientifically rooted observation and an acknowledgement of psychical phenomena beyond immediate verification or sensory perception.[12]

Dreams represented an important focus on all sides of the debate over psychology. Central to the scientific investigation of dreams was their

---

[11] Pierre Janet, *Autobiography*, in Carl Murchison (ed.), *History of Psychology in Autobiography*, vol. I (Worcester, Mass.: Clark University Press, 1930), p. 125.

[12] Henri Bergson, *Matter and Memory* (1896), trans. Nancy Margaret Paul and W. Scott Palmer (London: Swan Sonnenschein, 1911), p. 234.

perceived relationship with mental illness. Alfred Maury's 'Nouvelles observations sur les analogies des phénomènes du rêve et de l'aliénation mentale' (1853) and *Le sommeil et les rêves* (1861) are cited frequently in the literature of the late nineteenth century, not least in the work of Freud, for whom the investigation of dreams represented in part an extension of his work on hysteria and hypnosis in the late 1880s and 1890s (Freud visited the Salpêtrière and the Nancy School in the 1880s and translated essays by Charcot and Bernheim into German). *The Interpretation of Dreams* (1900) opens with an introductory survey of research on dreams. Its title, 'The Scientific Literature on Dreams', seems pointedly to exclude the traditions of metaphysical and occult dream analysis, and Freud repeatedly deconstructs the association of dreams with, for example, premonition and prophecy.

But in fact *The Interpretation of Dreams* proves itself quite open to less scientifically oriented investigations of dreams; Freud repeatedly cites the work of the Marquis d'Hervey de Saint-Denis on hypermnesic (enhanced memory) dreams and lucid dreaming, and he regrets his inability to acquire the research on hypermnesic dreams published in the *Proceedings of the Society for Psychical Research*. He also refers three times to Schopenhauer's 'Essay on Spirit Seeing and Everything Connected Therewith', an essay largely devoted to the analysis of dreams. There Schopenhauer investigates the relationship of dreams to premonition and clairvoyance (*Wahrträumen*), phenomena that seem remote from the clinical, scientific tone of *The Interpretation of Dreams*.[13] But what Freud seems to value in accounts such as these is the insight they offer into the topography and mechanisms of the psyche, particularly the nature of the unconscious and the means by which dreams organise and represent unconscious thoughts. A number of ideas in Schopenhauer's reading of dreams, both in the 'Essay on Spirit Seeing' and elsewhere in his writings, strongly anticipate some of the theories outlined in *The Interpretation of Dreams*, and Freud was later to acknowledge Schopenhauer as a pioneer in the discovery of the unconscious:

Probably very few people can have realised the momentous significance for science and life of the recognition of unconscious mental processes. It was not psycho-analysis, however, let us hasten to add, which took this first step. There are famous philosophers who may be cited as forerunners – above all the great

---

[13] Arthur Schopenhauer, 'Essay on Spirit Seeing and Everything Connected Therewith', in *Parerga and Paralipomena* (1851), trans E. F. J. Payne (Oxford: Clarendon Press, 1974), vol. I, pp. 247–58. In support of his argument for the relationship between dreams and mental disorder, Freud quotes Schopenhauer's observation that 'the dream may be characterised as a brief madness, madness being looked upon as a long dream' (Schopenhauer, 'Essay on Spirit Seeing', p. 252; Freud, *The Interpretation of Dreams*, p. 122).

thinker Schopenhauer, whose unconscious 'will' is equivalent to the mental instincts of psycho-analysis.[14]

Freud's reference to 'science and life' suggests, like much of his work, a desire to reconcile the scientific with the more broadly cultural implications of his work, and his reference to the will demonstrates a willingness to embrace aspects of Schopenhauer's thinking, even if its metaphysical implications are ultimately questioned.[15]

Maeterlinck once claimed to have read all of Schopenhauer, and he expressed a particular preference for *Parerga and Paralipomena*, the collection of writings in which his 'Essay on Spirit Seeing' was published. In a sense Maeterlinck's work could be seen to represent a more strictly metaphysical inheritance of Schopenhauer's thought. Premonitory dreams, Schopenhauer argues, 'put in the strongest light the strict necessity of all that happens'.[16] They are, in other words, the signposts of our fate, but signposts so difficult to interpret 'that in most cases we understand them only after their prediction has come true'.[17] Premonitions are common in Maeterlinck's plays from the period of *Pelléas*, but, like Schopenhauer's signposts, they offer their characters no power or knowledge. Rather, characters such as Mélisande have little more than a vague sense of their own destiny, and, as Susan Youens points out, it is destiny itself, rather than the human characters, that assumes agency in *Pelléas*. This fits with Maeterlinck's rejection of traditional psychology and his call for a more 'transcendent', metaphysical understanding of the psyche, and Youens suggests that Maeterlinck takes his metaphysics a stage further than Schopenhauer, dislocating its determining powers further from human subjectivity and investing them with an Otherness that is truly unknowable.[18]

But this drives a wedge between Maeterlinck and psychology when in fact the situation is much more fluid. In a sort of mirror image to Freud's sympathetic handling of metaphysical theories, Maeterlinck's essays from the period suggest a desire to redeem rather than abandon psychology. His demand in *Le trésor des humbles* is for a new psychology, and the language in his essays is often indebted to psychology, even when his ideas are at their most metaphysical or even occult. In *Le temple enseveli* (1902) he recounts his experiences with mediums, and suggests that the best of them 'know how to substitute for their own consciousness the

[14] Sigmund Freud, *Introductory Lectures on Psycho-Analysis* (1916–17), in James Strachey (ed. and trans.), *The Standard Edition of the Complete Psychological Works of Sigmund Freud* (London: Hogarth Press, 1953–74), vol. XV, p. 143.
[15] Addressing a session on Freud's ideas at the International Congress of Medicine in London in 1913, Janet expressed reservations about the 'metaphysical' nature of psychoanalysis. See Ellenberger, *The Discovery of the Unconscious*, p. 344.
[16] Schopenhauer, 'Essay on Spirit Seeing', p. 254.   [17] Ibid., p. 255.
[18] Youens, 'An Unseen Player', p. 63.

consciousness and even a part of the unconscious of those who consult them'.[19] He defines the poetic symbol as something that 'will be quite unconscious, will take place without the poet's knowledge, often despite him, and will be almost always well beyond his thought'.[20] Perhaps like Thomas Mann, who called Schopenhauer the 'psychologist of the will',[21] Maeterlinck understood the relationship between metaphysics and psychology in more than purely black and white terms.

It could be argued, in fact, that by the last decade of the nineteenth century psychological language and concepts (in their many schools and guises) were so pervasive that any engagement with questions of subjectivity would betray their influence, intentionally or not. Bergson, who, as we have seen, sought a *rapprochement* between psychology and metaphysics, shows how elastic psychological discourse could be. In March 1901 (just over a year before the premiere of Debussy's opera) he delivered a lecture entitled 'Les rêves' at the Institut Psychologique in Paris. In it he expanded on some of the theories on mental association outlined in *Matter and Memory* and addressed the question of the access of dreams to the unconscious. His approach, cautious and widely informed, is not out of keeping with the more scientific literature on dreams, and he refers approvingly to Freud's discussion in the recently published *The Interpretation of Dreams* of the role of repression. In his conclusion he turns to the question of dreams during deep sleep:

This deep slumber is that on which psychology ought to direct its effort, not only to study the structure and functioning of unconscious memory, but also to investigate the more mysterious phenomena which are the subject of psychical research.[22]

He goes on to admit that he has not devoted enough study to this field to comment further but commends the work of the Society for Psychical Research. (In fact in 1913 he assumed the presidency of the society, which counted among its 'corresponding members' Freud, from 1911, and Maeterlinck, from 1914.) In taking this metaphysical turn towards the end of the lecture, Bergson seems to abandon traditional psychology for parapsychology, but he presents this as a natural continuum rather than a radical disjunction.[23]

[19] Maurice Maeterlinck, *Le temple enseveli* (Paris: Fasquelle, 1902), p. 293.

[20] Cited in Jules Huret, *Enquête sur l'évolution littéraire* (Paris: Bibliothèque-Charpentier, 1901), p. 120.

[21] Thomas Mann, 'Schopenhauer' (1938), in Hermann Kurzke and Stephan Stachorski (eds.), *Essays*, vol. IV (Frankfurt: S. Fischer Verlag, 1995), p. 301.

[22] Bergson, 'Dreams' (1901), in his *Mind-Energy*, trans. H. Wildon Carr (London: Macmillan, 1920), p. 109.

[23] In *The Unknown Guest* Maeterlinck characterises the scientific, rational bias of Western culture as a preference for the conscious over the unconscious, and he quotes from

Youens argues that in *Pelléas* Maeterlinck avoids any 'psychologising', treating his characters as will-less puppets controlled by the metaphysical strings of destiny.[24] Yet, as she concedes, Golaud fails to fit the puppet mould; he defies the passivity of his fellow characters, acts wilfully and ultimately experiences guilt.[25] His behaviour in the final act reveals him to be at the mercy, *pace* Maeterlinck, of his conscience, engaged in an agonised process of self-examination and denial that speaks of nothing if not the split between conscious and unconscious theorised by psychology and psychoanalysis. Golaud is a flesh-and-bones character in a world that Debussy aptly compared to a tapestry.[26] It is the contrast between Golaud and his unreal surroundings that compellingly argues for a reading in which Allemonde is understood as a projection of Golaud's tortured psyche, and Debussy's remark that the play is characterised by an 'atmosphere of dreams' suggests the possibility of reading its other-worldly quality as Golaud's dream.[27] Relating the opera to *fin-de-siècle* theories of dream and dream interpretation offers to further illuminate and historicise its representation of interiority and the unconscious.

The interludes of *Pelléas* seem to reinforce this kind of reading. As Robin Holloway has shown, the Wagnerian presence in the interludes is surprisingly strong, and, like Wagner's orchestra, Debussy's music seems to offer windows onto the psyche of the opera's characters.[28] If *Pelléas* is Golaud's dream, the interludes, following the traditional Wagnerian alignment, become a projection of Golaud's unconscious. When the discursive patterns of the interludes seem to follow the kinds of mechanisms and processes that Schopenhauer, Bergson, and

---

Bergson: 'in his very fine presidential address to the Society for Psychical Research on the 28th of May, 1913, [Bergson] said that he had sometimes wondered what would have happened if modern science, instead of setting out from mathematics, instead of bringing all its forces to converge on the study of matter, had begun by the consideration of mind; if Kepler, Galileo and Newton, for instance, had been psychologists: "We should certainly," said he, "have had a psychology of which to-day we can form no idea, any more than before Galileo we could have imagined what our physics would be; a psychology that probably would have been to our present psychology what our physics is to Aristotle's. Foreign to every mechanistic idea, not even conceiving the possibility of an explanation, science would have enquired into, instead of dismissing a priori facts, such as those which you study; perhaps 'psychical research' would have stood out as its principal preoccupation."' Maeterlinck, *The Unknown Guest*, trans. Alexander Teixeira de Mattos (New York: Dodd Mead, 1916), chapter 5, section 15.

[24] Youens, 'An Unseen Player', p. 70.   [25] Ibid., pp. 85–6.

[26] Debussy, letter to Henri Lerolle, 28 August 1894, in François Lesure (ed.), *Claude Debussy: Correspondance 1884–1918* (Paris: Hermann, 1993), p. 104.

[27] Claude Debussy, 'Why I Wrote *Pelléas*' (programme note, Opéra-Comique, April 1902), in Langham Smith (ed. and trans.), *Debussy on Music*, p. 75.

[28] Robin Holloway, *Debussy and Wagner* (London: Eulenburg, 1979), pp. 76–95.

Freud detected in dreams, the suggestion is not simply that Debussy was acquainted with literature on dreams or psychology. Rather, in a more indirect and rich sense, Debussy's music can be understood to respond to Symbolist ideas and imagery, themselves indebted to Romantic and idealist conceptions of dreams and the unconscious. Nor did the more positivistic psychological understanding of dreams emerge *ex nihilo* as some form of neutral, objective description: it was itself a product of ideas circulating much more widely. Gotthilf von Schubert's influential *Die Symbolik des Traumes* (*The Symbolism of Dreams*, 1814), with its scholarly but highly poetic account of the visual language of dreams (*Traumbildsprache*), had already demonstrated the overlap and exchange possible in discourses on dreams.[29] What we encounter, then, are cultural tropes with the potential to surface in philosophy, literature, drama – or music. Aligned in the nineteenth century with inwardness and indecipherability, music already had a long tradition of association with dreams, an association made most explicit through opera with its scenes of reverie, hallucination, and sleep walking. The interludes in *Pelléas* take their place in this tradition, responding to it and contributing further to the construction of ideas about dreams and the relationship between the conscious and the unconscious.

There are, however, cardinal moments in the interludes that seem to disrupt and exceed this reading of the opera as Golaud's dream, as if something has challenged the capacity of the dream to represent it. Youens characterises the interludes as spaces in which 'Destiny conducts her wordless operations', and her alignment of music with the unknowable tallies convincingly both with Debussy's repeated descriptions of music as a mysterious force and with our (admittedly limited) knowledge of Debussy's involvement with esotericism and the occult.[30] Her reading is never more apt than in these disruptive moments, when the discourse seems to be suspended and Maeterlinckian destiny seems to intrude in the guise of a music utterly removed from its context. But these moments can also be read as a grounding of the metaphysical. Far from some transcendence that eludes the body, they can be understood to be marked by a material immediacy that asserts the body's presence. Here we will turn to the psychoanalytically based work of Julia Kristeva, who uses the idea of music to theorise intrusions of materiality into representation. But this will also raise problems, among them the suspicion that the traditional alignment of music with an inaccessible metaphysics remote from ordinary signification is replaced here by an equally idealised construction based on a materiality that *precedes* signification.

[29] Gotthilf von Schubert, *Die Symbolik des Traumes* (Bamberg: Kunz, 1814).
[30] Youens, 'An Unseen Player', p. 62.

'Do you know where I have brought you?'

As the first scene of Act I closes, Golaud confesses himself as lost as Mélisande. It is his first acknowledgement of vulnerability in an encounter that has so far placed him in a position of knowledge, and it triggers a curtain that veils an uncertain journey through the forest. If Mélisande, the *princesse lointaine* of male fantasy, embodies Golaud's sexual desire, then the unknown of the forest would seem to represent the unknown of his own psyche, perhaps that impenetrable region that is the unconscious. By setting off into that entangled darkness, Golaud signals the beginning of an interior voyage that will be projected in the scenes that follow. In the meantime, however, Debussy's interlude captures the first steps of that journey and its sense of bewilderment. The interlude at first draws all its musical material from the preceding scene. An appropriately meandering triplet pattern, first heard at Golaud's initial entry, predominates, at first restricting itself to the D Aeolian that lends the first scene such a timeless, vaguely archaic quality. Gradually it wanders into the whole-tone scale, another feature of the opening scene and an appropriate image of disorientation with its rejection of any centre or gravitational pull. Gradually the 'forest' material is displaced by a motif that will soon be explicitly associated with Golaud (example 3.1, presented here in one of its fullest forms). One element of this motif, the dotted quaver with semiquaver, then forms the basis of a new, rather pompous and stately episode marked 'le rythme très accentué'. Here the harmonic ambiguity of the forest gives way to clearly defined cadences, and the meandering rhythm to carefully paced, heavy accents. Juxtaposed with this material and stated only once is a motif first heard when Golaud identified himself as son of Arkel. It is at this point that the curtain opens on Scene 2 to reveal Geneviève and Arkel in the castle of Allemonde. The meaning of the transition to the stately style now becomes clear. We might also interpret the presence within the scene of the opening fragment of the Golaud motif as symbolic of his connection with the castle. What is certain, however, is the function of transition, of gradual displacement undertaken by the interlude. Where in Maeterlinck's play the shift is abrupt and unmediated, Debussy's music effects a gradual transformation that leads from the forest via an image of Golaud to the castle of Allemonde.

Example 3.1   Debussy, *Pelléas et Mélisande*, 'Golaud' motif

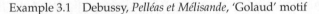

The process is above all one of filling in a gap, creating a smooth coherence out of raw material that had appeared fragmentary. In Freud's theory of dreams, the latent content of a dream is subjected to unconscious mental processes that differ from conscious thought in their tendency to manipulate, distort, and fragment material in seemingly irrational, chaotic ways. One of the outcomes of this process is a form of censorship that effectively protects the conscious ego from any direct access to the unconscious. This transformation of material, what Freud calls the 'dream work', relies on a number of formal techniques. Condensation, for example, is a compression or fusion of material into combinations that become unrecognisable to consciousness, and displacement transposes one object onto another, seemingly unrelated, object, thereby disguising its identity. Here Freud drew on several influential accounts of the mechanisms of dreams, and again France was to prove an important source of ideas. He cites Maury's *Le sommeil et les rêves*, with its discussion of the associative mechanisms of dream images, Joseph Delboeuf's identically titled work of 1885, with its concept of 'rapprochement forcé' (enforced convergence), and Yves Delage's 'Essai sur la théorie du rêve' (1891), which articulates the concepts of condensation and displacement.[31] All share the idea that distortion is fundamental to the grammar of dreams. The result of this distortion, Freud argues, is a lack of coherence that is unacceptable to consciousness:

It is the nature of our waking thought to establish order in material of that kind, to set up relations in it and make it conform to our expectations of an intelligible whole.[32]

Bergson echoes this notion in his lecture on dreams when he argues that the remembered content of the dream is a reinterpretation:

The conversations that the dreamer supposes he has heard are for the most part reconstituted, completed, amplified at waking.[33]

For Freud this reinterpretation of the raw material of the dream work – what he calls 'secondary revision'– is associated with the preconscious, a state in which material is not yet directly accessed by consciousness, but one which lacks the repressed character of the unconscious.

---

[31] Sigmund Freud, *The Interpretation of Dreams* (1900), trans. James Strachey (New York: Avon Books, 1965), pp. 91–2, 212. These ideas owe something in turn to more general theories of mental association in which thoughts are understood to recall other thoughts based on metaphorical likeness or on proximity (their temporal proximity in memory or the physical proximity of their referents). Schopenhauer, for example, uses the terms 'similarity' (*Ähnlichkeit*) and 'proximity' (*Verhältnis*), while Bergson refers to 'similarity' (*ressemblance*) and 'contiguity'(*contiguïté*).

[32] Freud, *The Interpretation of Dreams*, p. 537.   [33] Bergson, 'Dreams', p. 105.

Example 3.2   Debussy, *Pelléas et Mélisande*, Act III (p. 141)

Not that secondary revision operates only after the completion of the dream work. Rather, 'from the very first the demands of this second factor constitute one of the conditions which the dream must satisfy'.[34] If the characteristic effects of condensation and displacement are to fragment and withdraw, secondary revision creates 'interpolations and additions'.[35] In so doing, it fills in the gaps and attempts to make out of the dream a relatively comprehensible narrative. The qualification 'relatively' is important here because even a dream that has undergone a maximum of secondary revision clearly retains an element of disconnectedness and incoherence that is capable of baffling conscious attempts to decipher it. Christian Metz is quick to make this point when he analyses film in terms of dream theory, adding that film narrative seldom conveys the sense of 'true absurdity' so characteristic of dreams.[36] Film, he suggests, might be compared to a dream in which secondary revision has been vastly extended, leaving only a trace of the primary (i.e. unconscious) processes of condensation and displacement.

With this qualification in mind, we can see how the first interlude of Act I represents a form of secondary revision. As Freud suggests of secondary revision, the interlude functions to create 'interpolations and additions' where there had previously been only a gap. Withdrawing gently from the first scene, it offers a genuine transition to the following scene by gradually introducing material appropriate to that scene, but still recognisably related to the familiar material of the first scene. In the first interlude of Act III the transition is as smooth and gradual, and here it relies not only on the relationship of its musical material to the scenes, but on a carefully presented tonal pivot (example 3.2). The emphatic, heavily orchestrated episode in D sharp Aeolian that

---

[34] Freud, *The Interpretation of Dreams*, p. 537.   [35] Ibid., p. 527.
[36] Metz, *The Imaginary Signifier*, p. 120.

78

dominates the first part of the interlude fades very gradually to a pair of brief, almost half–hearted phrases. In its place, *pianissimo* horns and low woodwind intone a sustained minor third (A–C) over a D sharp in basses and timpani. Horns and woodwind fade away, leaving a solo trumpet to fill in a diminished seventh with an F sharp, finally adding a B natural. Only timpani and basses remain to await the entrance of a new C minor episode for low strings evocative of the dungeons in the following scene. The diminished-seventh chord contains the first and third degrees of the tonalities of both the previous episode and the subsequent dungeon music. Meanwhile the B natural serves as a leading tone to the dungeon scene, and the A natural anticipates the Dorian sixth that will be produced in the C minor episode by parallel motion. As a pivot, it works not only because of these common tones, but because it appears in a sort of silent no-man's-land between them, functioning as a kind of independent mediator.

'Visiting cards' from the ego

That both interludes derive their musical building blocks from adjacent scenes suggests another aspect of Freud's theory of the dream work. Freud's analysis of dreams led him to believe that it was rare for secondary revision to create original interpolations. Rather, he argues, 'it employs anything appropriate that it can find in the material of the dream-thoughts'.[37] Here music could be understood as an important model in that the reliance of nineteenth-century musical languages on the reworking, transformation, and development of existing material gives it a metaphorical value for other discourses. So, for example, the structure of literary narratives could be (and was) likened to 'symphonic development' or 'theme and variations'. Debussy's interludes could not be described as symphonic in the sense in which the term has been applied to the motivic webs of many late nineteenth-century operas, but they do manipulate a number of basic recurring musical ideas. This is a feature not only of the two interludes cited thus far, but of all the interludes in the opera. Rather than introducing original ideas, they tend to centre themselves on the re-presentation and reworking of existing material. This can take the form of the postludes and preludes central to the transitional function of the interludes, and often involves the quotation of motifs – such as the meandering forest idea – that are more or less isolated to a particular scene, unifying and, in a sense, defining it musically. But the interludes also represent a concentration of more wide-ranging motifs in the Wagnerian leitmotif tradition. If the question of the leitmotivic role within the scenes recalls a long and tortuous

---

[37] Freud, *The Interpretation of Dreams*, p. 328.

debate – from Debussy's own defensive anti-Wagnerian rhetoric to the leitmotif-hunting of Maurice Emmanuel to more recent investigations of Wagnerian influence[38] – the interludes place us on rather firmer ground. In fact, there are few bars in the interludes that do not quote or develop clearly recognisable leitmotivic material. While even the most zealous 'leitmotifers' are unlikely to unearth the kind of sprawling web we encounter in the *Ring*, the motifs in *Pelléas* on whose identity and importance there tends to be critical consensus – essentially those associated with the principal characters – prove to be fundamental to the musical material in the interludes.

One motif in particular, that associated with Golaud (example 3.1), functions almost like a mantra throughout the interludes. In fact there are only two out of the opera's eight interludes in which it does not appear in some form, and in most of the other six it forms the basis of extended and prominent musical episodes. The climactic interlude following Golaud's violent confrontation with Mélisande in Act IV, for example, represents almost a musical fantasy based on the Golaud motif. A clue to the motif's dramatic meaning emerges in Act I, Scene 1, when it appears as Golaud is trying to explain how he became lost in the forest, first to himself (!) and later to Mélisande. It is as if the motif looked back at Golaud from outside; in later scenes it becomes a means of evoking him when absent or of announcing his arrival – this despite Debussy's criticism of Wagner's 'visiting cards'.[39] The emphasis, then, is on Golaud's external image, whether the self-explanation/presentation of the first scene, or references to him from other vantage points.

There is one type of dream to which Freudian theory assigns a particularly prominent role for the ego. In what Freud calls 'punishment dreams', a residue of pleasurable but forbidden thoughts is transformed by the ego into an unpleasurable dream as a means of punishment. The dream thus derives not from the repressed (pleasurable) material in itself, but from an unconscious wish to be punished for that pleasure. Set in motion by the ego, the wish for punishment remains itself

---

[38] 'Certainly', Debussy wrote, 'my technique (which consists of doing away with all "techniques") owes nothing to Wagner. In his music each character has, so to speak, his own "prospectus", his photograph, his "leitmotif" which must always precede him. I confess to finding this method a trifle blatant.' 'Critique des critiques: *Pelléas et Mélisande*', *Le Figaro*, 16 May 1902, trans. in Roger Nichols and Richard Langham Smith, *Claude Debussy: 'Pelléas et Mélisande'* (Cambridge: Cambridge University Press, 1989), p. 80. The publication of Emmanuel's study of *Pelléas* in 1926 challenged Debussy's self-assessment, uncovering a leitmotivic web worthy of *Tristan*. Maurice Emmanuel, *Pelléas et Mélisande: Etude historique et critique* (Paris: Mellottée, 1926). More recently, Carolyn Abbate has analysed the early drafts of the opera with a view to revealing Debussy's attempts to cover the traces of Wagnerism in his compositional method. 'Tristan in the Composition of *Pelléas*', *Nineteenth-Century Music* 5 (1981), 117–41.

[39] Nichols and Langham Smith, *Claude Debussy: 'Pelléas et Mélisande'*, pp. 80–1.

Example 3.3   Debussy, *Pelléas et Mélisande*, 'Mélisande' motif

unconscious, but unlike the unconscious wishes of most dreams it is not repressed. Rather, it is the ego's *reaction* to what is repressed. Perhaps, then, the insistent presence of the Golaud motif throughout the opera can be interpreted as the judging voice of Golaud's ego. It is that critical voice that haunts Golaud's every action, setting in motion the tragic, punishing images of the dream that ultimately leave Golaud in a state of pathetic remorse.[40] The repetitions of the motif, then, represent its attempt to assert its control over the primary processes of the dream work. While the dream work manipulates and seeks to maximise the repressed pleasure, the ego seeks to monitor and punish that pleasure. It is hardly any wonder that it should emerge with such fury in the Act IV interlude after Golaud's sadistic encounter with Mélisande in Scene 2.

Its first appearance, in the prelude to Act I, seems to set out the whole conflict at the root of the dream. The primeval Aeolian of the forest alternates in two-bar phrases with the Golaud motif: the unconscious is answered by the ego. Emerging from the midst of the conflict is a figure, 'doux et expressif', that will be associated with Mélisande, or better, the object of desire that Mélisande embodies (example 3.3). She is, like Diemut, the 'x' that fills out the void of Golaud's desire, a position that is confirmed by her utterly enigmatic, mysterious nature. Adding support to this reading, the Golaud ego motif now gravitates towards it, as if asserting its own presence and holding Mélisande's in check. In the interlude that precedes Mélisande's arrival in Allemonde (Act I, Scene 3), the two motifs are juxtaposed in such a way that the Golaud motif almost completely disguises that of Mélisande, suggesting the ego's control. And in the first interlude of Act II it twice interrupts the joyous, carefree music that has spilled over from the well scene, deadening its rhythmic vitality with a menacing sustained pedal in the basses.

The picture that emerges is one of self-reflection and recrimination consistent with the mechanism of punishment dreams. In some ways the activity of the ego intersects neatly with the process of secondary revision; both represent a reaction to the repressed material of the unconscious, a means of dealing with the threat of that material. But the ego's control is far from unwavering, as the interlude following the tower scene in Act III demonstrates. Here, in a richly scored climax marked

---

[40] This function of self-observation and self-punishment would be associated in Freud's later theory with the superego.

'profondément expressif', the characteristic rhythms of the Golaud motif become an undulating, throbbing accompaniment figure to sustained statements of the Mélisande motif in the strings. It is as if the Golaud motif has been appropriated by Mélisande's, forced to serve as its support. Here the repressed desire seems to gain the upper hand, if only temporarily. Perhaps it is this weakening of the ego's resolve, this caving in under the pressure of desire, that provokes it into retaliation and brings on the relentless punishment that will characterise the dream from now on. What seems clear, however, is that the interludes represent a site of considerable volatility and conflict.

'Can you hear the sea behind us?'

A similar tension can be seen emerging in the various scenic representations in the interludes. By introducing or rounding out the *mises en scène* of the staged action, the interludes create a dovetail effect that smooths out the more jarring contrasts of the play. In this sense the scenic representations are transitional, contributing to the process of secondary revision. But the very prominence of the scenic element in play and opera has powerful resonances within Freud's theory of the primary process. In his discussion of the dream work, Freud makes the important point that the admission of the latent dream thoughts into the content of the dream is partly governed by their representability. Material, he suggests, is often displaced into other forms in order to facilitate representation, a process that may involve a transfer from verbal to visual form:

A thing that is pictorial is, from the point of view of a dream, a thing that is *capable of being represented*: it can be introduced into a situation in which abstract expressions offer the same kind of difficulties to representation in dreams as a political leading article in a newspaper would offer to an illustrator. [41]

The dream work, then, will resort to visual images as the most satisfactory means of representing the abstract. Certainly the forest, if understood as a symbol of the unconscious, traces a site of unrepresentability: the unconscious can only be traced in its transformed manifestations. The same can be said of the chasm in the dungeon scene. With its impenetrable depth and its 'stench of death', it serves as an apt symbol of the repressed desires consigned to the unfathomable reaches of Golaud's unconscious. This raises the problem of representability and the Symbolist dissatisfaction with language, with its semantic inadequacy and its inability to touch on ideas without distorting them. As Bergson put it in 1889, 'the word with well-defined outlines, the rough and ready

---

[41] Freud, *The Interpretation of Dreams*, p. 375.

word . . . overwhelms or at least covers over the delicate and fugitive impressions of our individual consciousness'.[42] Substituting symbols becomes a means of rewiring the linguistic, representational short circuit. It addresses a fundamental suspicion of representation and its perceived tendency to disfigure, substituting a process of deferral that, in a sense, approaches ideas from the side and catches representation unawares. This has implications both for the creative process and for reception. As we have seen, Maeterlinck valued the poetic symbol as a product of the unconscious with the potential to evade the limitations of the poet's always limited and limiting conscious mind, and we can detect behind this the Romantic association of artistic creativity with the unconscious. The dream state provided Romantic aesthetic theory with an ideal model for unconscious creativity, an attitude summed up in Joseph Ennemoser's observation that 'the essence of dream is a potential life of genius'.[43] If artistic creativity is likened to a dream, then the process of deciphering meaning in art takes on the characteristics of dream interpretation, and here the potential arises for avoiding an all too direct meaning. Schopenhauer highlights the challenges of interpreting dream 'allegories' when he warns against

the assumption that the events in the dream ha[ve] a fixed meaning valid once for all about which a lexicon could therefore be made . . . On the contrary, the allegory is expressly and individually suited to each and every object and subject.[44]

The sense of indecipherability, substitution, and slippage evident here seems to anticipate Symbolist scepticism toward representation and meaning in language.

Freud, too, warns of the 'peculiar plasticity' of dream material and the challenges it presents to interpretation.[45] He suggests that the process of visual displacement can become a nodal point for condensation, as, for example, when one image embodies a number of thoughts or concepts. In doing so, it can also serve the aim of censorship, disguising and compressing the repressed material of the unconscious.[46] In this sense visual displacements can mark a site of extreme psychic intensity, a site in which the censoring aspects of the dream work are most called for. Maeterlinck's forests, wells, and caves could thus be read as visual displacements of highly repressed material, and this might also be true of the representational displacements in the interludes. The

[42] Bergson, *Time and Free Will: An Essay on the Immediate Data of Consciousness* (1889), trans. F. L. Pogson (London: George Allen and Unwin, 1910), p. 132.

[43] Joseph Ennemoser, *Der Magnetismus in Verhältnisse zur Natur und Religion* (Stuttgart and Tübingen: Cotta, 1842), pp. 335–6.

[44] Schopenhauer, 'Essay on Spirit Seeing', p. 255.

[45] Freud, *The Interpretation of Dreams*, p. 387.   [46] Ibid., p. 375.

musical *mise en scène* outlined in the interludes would represent a trace of the dream's primary processes, a site of some of the most repressed material drawn on by the dream work. Might we then ask whether the interludes in some respects represent not a concentration but a lack of secondary revision? On the level of the act the interludes certainly provide a narrative coherence and smoothness missing from the play, but if we turn to the level of the scene we encounter a rather different picture. As much as Maeterlinck's dramatic style is characterised by abrupt non sequiturs and sudden shifts in focus, the scenes in *Pelléas* present relatively uncomplicated narrative outlines: scenes of encounter, of mutual discovery, of revelation, and of death. The play is, for all its Symbolist pretension, a 'superior variation on the admirable old melodrama', as Mallarmé put it.[47] Debussy's music for the scenes, meanwhile, eschews any recognisable, independent form in favour of an orchestral continuum divided into period-like structures, each shaped by the division of Maeterlinck's text into narrative 'blocks' or subsections. It gives the impression, in other words, of tracing the form of the text intimately. (This is not to suggest that either dramatic or musical discourse is uncomplicatedly linear, but rather that both are anchored by a reasonably conventional narrative thrust.)

By contrast, the interludes often suggest a highly fragmented narrative structure. Possibly the simplest example occurs when the interlude seems to abandon its transitional function and interpolates material associated with an earlier scene in the opera. In the interlude following the letter scene in Act I (Scene 2), a brief postlude gives way to a passionate twelve-bar passage (alluded to above) that juxtaposes the Golaud and Mélisande motifs. It seems to represent one of the battles with desire that will return in a number of later interludes. But as quickly as it emerges, it yields to introductory music for the final scene of the act, the first encounter of Pelléas and Mélisande. Perhaps the intensity of Debussy's interpolation foreshadows the trauma (for Golaud) of that first encounter, but it is nevertheless an interpolation that, like Delius's 'Walk', seems to disrupt the diegesis as defined by the play's narrative order.

In their original form, the interludes in *Pelléas* avoided even this simple form of interpolation in favour of a postlude–prelude format. But, as is well known, Debussy was forced to lengthen several of them when it became apparent that the existing versions would not allow sufficient time for the numerous set changes required by Albert Carré's elaborate staging. Conductor André Messager recalled collecting the music for the expanded interludes page by page from an 'ill-tempered

---

[47] Stéphane Mallarmé, 'Théâtre', *National Observer*, 1 July 1893, in Henri Mondor and G. Jean-Aubry (eds.), *Oeuvres complètes* (Paris: Gallimard, 1945), p. 330.

and raving' Debussy.[48] What the audiences heard at the premiere on 30 April 1902 is a matter for conjecture, for although first-hand testimony confirms the existence of expanded interludes, it is also clear that the interludes were further modified during subsequent revivals. As David Grayson has shown, the most compelling evidence of these alterations is to be found in the manuscript full score and a recently discovered manuscript viola part used for the first forty-two performances of *Pelléas* until printed parts became available in the 1906–7 season.[49] Although the manuscripts cannot clear up the question of which versions were performed during each of those first four seasons, the numerous patches, deletions, and recopied pages do bear witness to a continual process of modification and, for most of the interludes, expansion.

What the manuscript scores also reveal is that, in expanding the interludes, Debussy altered them substantively, modifying their role in the opera and ultimately their meaning. Grayson shows, for example, that the first interlude of Act II, originally a very brief orchestral link of ten bars, was transformed in three stages to become a fairly extensive interlude of forty-seven bars averaging almost three and a half minutes in performance.[50] In that first version the interlude functioned much as curtain music to provide a brief postlude to the music of the well scene and a two-bar introduction (with Golaud motif) to Scene 2, where we find Golaud nursing an injury sustained just as Mélisande dropped her ring in the well. In its expanded form the interlude introduces what Grayson terms 'composite' motifs, material in which elements of two motifs are equally recognisable.[51] One composite fuses the characteristic dotted rhythm of the Golaud motif with the initial melodic outline of the Mélisande motif, while another achieves the same effect with the motifs of Golaud and Pelléas. And as if to sum up the process, one last composite combines that same initial Golaud rhythm with a melodic cell that will accompany Pelléas's advances to Mélisande in the tower scene and in the final love scene. Compressed into these composite forms, the motifs seem to exemplify that convergence of 'overdetermined' material that Freud associates with condensation. And like the effects of the primary process in general, this expansion of the interlude seems to generate fractures in the discourse that admit a multiplicity of meaning. Grayson hints at such a reading when he suggests that the expanded versions represent a 'liberation' from a 'purely narrative function'

---

[48] André Messager, 'Les premières représentations de *Pelléas*', *Revue Musicale* 7/7 (1 May 1926), 207, trans. in David A. Grayson, 'The Opera: Genesis and Sources', in Nichols and Langham Smith, *Claude Debussy: 'Pelléas et Mélisande'*, p. 191, n. 32.

[49] David A. Grayson, 'The Interludes of *Pelléas et Mélisande*', *Cahiers Debussy* 1988–9, 100–22.

[50] Ibid., pp. 113–20.   [51] Ibid., p. 117.

that 'enrich[es] the subconscious and psychological aspects of the interludes'.[52]

This kind of substantive as well as quantitive difference can be seen in a number of the interlude expansions. In the interlude of Act IV a simple transition was expanded to become a climactic moment of self-examination, a great release of pent-up pressure centred on that ever-watchful image of the ego, relieved only by single quotations of the Mélisande and Pelléas motifs. The interlude following Golaud's confrontation with Mélisande over the missing ring (Act II, Scene 2) was expanded to embrace recollections of the first scene of the act. As Mélisande leaves weeping, sombre echoes of the Mélisande motif – reminiscent of the Kareol music in *Tristan* – surface in the strings. But in the midst of this bleakness, the fleeting semiquavers of the well music emerge furtively, only to disappear into the gloom, while a childlike arrangement of the Pelléas motif makes a brief appearance. Again the focus is on the love triangle, its players, and their interrelationship.

Perhaps it is to the development and intensification of this triangle that we can trace the strengthening of the ego's punishment. By focusing more and more on the most intense psychical material – on the conflict between desire (Mélisande) and the frustration of desire (Pelléas) – the ego retraces the origins of its own aggression. The interludes, particularly in their expanded form, resemble fissures that have opened up onto sites of intense conflict. They betray the pressure of the latent, unconscious material, subjecting it to transformations like those of the dream work. The more linear narrative of the original interludes is sacrificed in favour of a multidirectionality characterised by gaps and interruptions, simultaneity and juxtaposition. They are sites, surely, which suggest the failure of secondary revision, where the traces of the primary process are most evident.

The extent of the interludes' participation in dramatic representation places Debussy's music in an awkward position. When Symbolist aesthetics privileged music above all, it had in mind not actual music but the 'condition' of music, its supposedly non-representational character. Music served as a metaphor for the avoidance of crude signification. So, for example, in his review of Maeterlinck's play, Mallarmé wrote that 'in this art, where everything becomes music in the real sense, even the addition of a single, pensive violin part would be unnecessary'.[53] From this perspective Debussy's music becomes redundant, an excessive doubling of Maeterlinck's 'music'. This would seem to apply in particular to those points in Debussy's score when representation comes to the fore, when, for example, Maeterlinck's visual symbols are evoked through musical description or when Debussy's music is saturated with

[52] Ibid., p. 119.   [53] Mallarmé, 'Théâtre', p. 330.

leitmotifs. This is theatre music in the crudest sense. Is Debussy's music not merely supplementary here? The problem with this perspective – and the whole Symbolist reading of music – is its assumption that music is antithetical to representation, that to draw music into a representational role is to betray its essence. But what if music is granted the capacity to construct its own symbolism, to offer its own representational displacements analogous to those visual displacements at the core of Maeterlinck's symbolism? The sea is evoked in Debussy's music by a particular musical vocabulary: muted brass, rocking rhythmic patterns, ripple effects from trills. Our understanding of this representation is partly made possible through association with the stage, but it is also a musical vocabulary based on a shared, established meaning and it will surface again in *La mer*. Cultural familiarity allows us to associate certain musical techniques with the sea, and in this sense music has a representational language that can be as meaningful as (sometimes more so than) words or images. Dream interpretation offers an interesting parallel here, because although, as we have seen, Freud warns of the 'peculiar plasticity' of dream material, in later editions of *The Interpretation of Dreams* he speculates on the historical and cultural foundations of symbols and on the possibility that dream symbolism is linked with these wider shared networks of association: 'this symbolism is not peculiar to dreams, but is characteristic of unconscious ideation . . . and is to be found in folklore, and in popular myths, legends, linguistic idioms, proverbial wisdom and current jokes, to a more complete extent than in dreams'.[54] Similarly, musical language and gestures can be said to acquire meaning by circulating in culture and becoming embedded within various media and forms of discourse (opera, song, theatre, popular genres, ceremonial use, etc.).

As for leitmotifs, any interpretation that focuses on fixed associations between musical and dramatic ideas is bound to view their formation as a derivative process. But leitmotifs do not necessarily depend on their associations to establish meaning. The fanfare connotations of the 'royal' Golaud motif say as much about its meaning as any accompanying words, and the instrumentation and arabesque form of the Mélisande motif conjure well-established associations with femininity, particularly via opera. (That these associations are culturally established and not intrinsic does not separate music from language: words also acquire meaning and have no inherent relationship with what they signify.) More than this, the leitmotifs in *Pelléas* prove capable of constructing meaning in ways that go beyond subservience to the stage or mere introductions or continuations. The interludes grant them a semantic

---

[54] Freud, *The Interpretation of Dreams*, p. 386. This observation was added in the 1909 edition.

power that is neither 'purely musical' nor dramatic and representational in a merely imitative sense (these are issues to which we shall return in the context of Wagner's practice).

Beyond the symbolic

What we have not addressed, however, are those moments in the interludes that seem to go beyond scenic representation and leitmotif. These are intrusive, arresting moments that seem out of context with their surroundings and seem to grant the interludes an occasionally uncanny Otherness. In his review of the premiere, André Hallays, music critic of the *Revue de Paris*, emphasised the contrast between scene and interlude:

When the curtain is raised, [the orchestra] magnifies the beauty of the decor on the stage, animating it and, with an irresistible spell, filling it with intimations of fragrance and light. When the curtain is lowered, the symphony continues between the various tableaux; sweet, fluid, almost groping like a dream, it gives the impression of a curtain of fine, shifting mist lit by a pale, distant star.[55]

By characterising the music as 'groping' (*tâtonnante*) and 'mysteriously veiled', Hallays captures the multidirectional, disorienting quality of the interludes that has been our focus. But he also locates this difference in the context of performance. And by emphasising the orchestra's interaction with the stage during the scenes, Hallays draws attention to the absence of the visual in the interludes, an absence that is central to their effect. This, he seems to imply, is what gives the interludes a shrouded, distant, pale quality. Released from the 'irresistible spell' that flows from orchestra and image, the spectator enters a twilight world of dreams.

The question then arises as to whether this absence might find a parallel in the musical text, whether there is any sign of a breakdown in the musical links with the scenes. This brings us back to the interlude following the well scene, for it is within the final expansions of this interlude that we can detect a trace of that very absence. Immediately preceding a two-bar statement of the Golaud motif that will usher in Scene 2 is a five-bar passage for unison strings that seems to hover, directionless, awaiting an injection of momentum that will propel the interlude towards the new scene (example 3.4). Situated between a thickly textured *Tristan*esque section and the Golaud motif, the passage appears to function as a transition (Grayson refers to it simply as a 'linking passage').[56] But to interpret it in terms of what precedes and what follows is to assign

---

[55] André Hallays, '*Pelléas et Mélisande*', *Revue de Paris*, 15 May 1902, 411–20, cited in Johannes Trillig, *Untersuchungen zur Rezeption Claude Debussys in der Zeitgenössischen Musikkritik* (Tutzing: Hans Schneider, 1983), p. 203.

[56] Grayson, 'The Interludes of *Pelléas et Mélisande*', p. 118.

Example 3.4 Debussy, *Pelléas et Mélisande*, Act II (p. 75)

it a functional, teleological character that seems out of place. Rather, the passage seems to renounce its relationship to the discourse which surrounds it. In contrast to the well-defined, even foursquare rhythmic character of the music before and after it, the passage blurs its rhythmic values and metrical outline with a combination of ties and duplet–triplet alternation, and an indication to hold back the tempo ('retenu'). It seems almost not to exist within any organised temporal framework, a moment when time and momentum seem unimportant.

As a single melodic line, too, it represents an extraordinary economy and sparseness in relation to the surrounding music, whether the almost contrapuntal texture of the sombre passage that precedes it or the rich block chords of the Golaud motif. Harmonically, it can be read as an extension of the anticipatory function of the block chords from which it emerges. If the third and fourth bars of example 3.4 represent a dominant preparation of B (=C flat), the string passage implies a diminished seventh on A sharp (=B flat) with its own introductory leading tones (A natural and C). The diminished seventh then 'resolves' onto the B dominant seventh in the final bar of the excerpt. But again we rob the passage of its essentially goalless character. As it drifts gradually upwards through the diminished chord, it begins to sound as if it might just continue circling through the chord indefinitely, and in this sense the actual resolution appears arbitrary. That sense of circularity is enhanced by the arrangement of the passage into a statement and answer, pitting low violins against violas and cellos in the high register. The two statements are timbrally distinct and separate, and yet so similar. The effect is one of echo, suggesting that the voices will continue to answer one another as they circle through the chord.

This leaves one obvious question: is the passage based on leitmotivic material? Grayson points to the origins of melodic cell x in one of the versions of the Mélisande motif, and melodic cell y in a derivative of the Mélisande motif that he describes as 'one of the opera's most complex'

89

motifs.[57] Drawing on the commentary by Michel-Dimitri Calvocoressi, he labels it the 'threat motif', since it is associated with the shadow that Golaud casts on the other characters. But the dramatic associations are so diffuse and its musical allusions so understated that leitmotivic connections are arguably undermined: it appears in connection with, for example, Arkel's advice to Pelléas in Act I, Scene 2, to delay his departure until Golaud's return; Mélisande's declaration in Act IV, Scene 2, that Golaud no longer loves her; and Pelléas's indecision in Act IV, Scene 4, as to whether he should see Mélisande again. If anything defines this music, it is surely its isolation – an isolation fostered by rhythmic, textural, and harmonic difference – and its foregrounding of timbre, the sheer physical, sensual quality of its sound. In other words, the passage seems to value immediate, material musical presence over literary representation. This is not to suggest that it somehow removes itself from the leitmotivic chain, but rather that it situates that particular form of signification as one element – and not necessarily the most important one – among several others. Perhaps in the context of opera, with its powerful intertextuality, any music will always be representational of the drama, but here there is a sense of plurality of meaning that defies the limiting effect of the leitmotif. For as much as we may drastically misrepresent the leitmotif when we attach simple labels to it, there remains something rather obvious, exaggerated, and ultimately confining about its deployment in many of the interludes.

The uncanny effect of this moment finds a parallel in Julia Kristeva's theory of the semiotic. In *Revolution in Poetic Language*, Kristeva analyses the poetry of Mallarmé, among others, in an attempt to come to terms with what she characterises as a 'space underlying the written', a space that is 'rhythmic, unfettered, irreducible to its intelligible verbal translation'.[58] It is a site of *jouissance*, of surplus, of discharge. Drawing on the Freudian theory of the drives, Kristeva presents this space as a transgression from the dynamic, pluralised force of the unconscious into the regulated sphere of signification. If language seeks to contain and repress the drives, it can also discharge them, with the result that 'meaning is constituted but is then immediately exceeded by what seems outside of meaning: materiality'.[59] The origins of this materiality, Kristeva argues, are to be found in a pre-Oedipal, 'pre-verbal functional state that governs the connections between the body (in the process of constituting itself as a body proper), objects and the protagonists of family structure'.[60] This 'semiotic' state is dominated by the flow and stasis,

[57] Ibid., p. 106.

[58] Julia Kristeva, *Revolution in Poetic Language*, trans. Margaret Waller (New York: Columbia University Press, 1984), p. 29.

[59] Ibid., p. 100   [60] Ibid., p. 27.

collision and separation of the drives, activity that is 'checked' both by
biological constraints (the operations of the primary process) and social
relationships. But neither external 'objects' and 'subjects' nor the child's
relationship to its own body are as yet perceived in terms of object and
subject. Rather, the child's experience is one of ceaseless heterogeneity
that precedes the perception of difference essential to signification, and
Kristeva uses the term 'chora' (in Plato a receptacle that resists identification or naming) to denote its presymbolic character. It is a state
exemplified by the sense of complete continuity that the child still enjoys with the mother's body.

Only with the formation of the ego, illustrated in Lacan's 'mirror
stage', does the child take up a position in relation to objects and constitute itself as subject. By identifying with its image in the mirror the child
becomes aware of a 'self' and the separation of that self from the rest of
its environment. That separation is sealed with the Oedipal phase, and
the child's enforced detachment from dependence on the mother. The
entry of the phallus becomes a symbol of the substitution of imaginary
plenitude with difference and lack.[61] Now the child leaves behind the
semiotic and enters the symbolic order, where difference and lack are
the order of the day. If the semiotic is defined by 'drives and their articu-
lations', the symbolic is the 'realm of signification, which is always that
of a proposition or judgement, in other words, a realm of *positions*'.[62]
The boundary that separates the two modalities – what Kristeva terms
the 'thetic phase' – is the symbolic's positing of signification, its separation of subject and object.[63] Not that the semiotic and symbolic are
mutually exclusive. Rather, Kristeva sees the two working in dialectical
oscillation within language. Without the semiotic, the symbolic would
be empty of meaning, while the constraints imposed by the symbolic
produce a signifying practice out of what would otherwise be delirium.
Indeed Kristeva is careful to point out that the semiotic, as something
beyond representation, can actually be conceived only from the position
of the symbolic and is traced only by infractions within the symbolic.
The idea of a semiotic prior to the symbolic is merely a 'theoretical
supposition', since any awareness of its existence represents an already
symbolic representation.[64]

Mallarmé's poetic language, Kristeva argues, is a practice marked by
the infractions of the semiotic. By emphasising poetic rhythm and the
timbre of words, Mallarmé 'musicalises' language, calling attention to
its materiality and creating a space for the drives. Together with this
musicality, Mallarmé's poetry represents a liberation from traditional
grammatical constructs. By freeing language from some of its signifying
constraints it provides an opening for the repressed semiotic. It also

[61] Ibid., pp. 47–8.　　[62] Ibid., p. 30.　　[63] Ibid.　　[64] Ibid., p. 68.

'pre-alters' representation by calling attention to its very foundation.[65] In place of stable relationships between signifier and signified, Mallarmé's poetry foregrounds the overdetermined quality of the signifier, exposing representation as an unstable and often arbitrary chain of signification. It thus calls into question the unity of signifier and signified posited by the symbolic.

The value of the Kristevan semiotic in relation to *Pelléas* lies in its ability to articulate a sense of release from the leitmotivic web and the foregrounding of an immediate, sensual quality, and it is surely an appropriate image for the string passage in example 3.4. Though always symbolic in the sense that it retains a relationship to the leitmotivic chain – not to mention the symbolic associations that any music will always embody – the passage is very much 'about' its sheer timbral presence. Nor is it an isolated example. A brief diminished-seventh passage in the interlude preceding the dungeon scene has been characterised as a kind of mediator between the surrounding episodes (example 3.2), but again this represents a very teleological view. Roger Nichols possibly captures more of what the passage is about when he describes it as 'spine-chilling'.[66] Like example 3.4 it seems removed from its context, an effect suggested by Debussy's marking, 'très lointain'. Time comes to a standstill, and out of the silence emerges a distant trumpet, intoning, in a reversal of example 3.4, a diminished triad followed by a single semitone. It is the briefest utterance, giving way once more to a silence punctuated by the barely audible roll of timpani and three D sharp pizzicato pulses from the basses, a faint, dying echo of what had once been a passionate outburst in D sharp Aeolian. The moment is striking, an intrusion from another place whose effect is indeed, as Nichols points out, physical. Again we can detect a leitmotivic foundation – this time Golaud's royal theme, first heard as he identified himself as the son of Arkel – but the reference is overshadowed by the mode of presentation, lost in sonority and timelessness.

A not dissimilar trumpet 'intrusion' appears in the first interlude of Act I (example 3.5). Here the question of leitmotivic reference takes another twist. There is no doubting the reference to the music that immediately followed Golaud's 'royal' theme as he referred to Arkel in Scene 1, but it is a motif that ultimately eludes any attempt to pin it specifically to Arkel, or indeed to any fixed dramatic concept. It seems, in other words, to defy the embrace of the stage's symbolic web. Again the trumpet seems to sound from nowhere, but here it gradually, almost imperceptibly emerges through a dense texture to soar briefly over the

---

[65] Ibid., p. 103.
[66] Roger Nichols, 'Synopsis', in Nichols and Langham Smith, *Claude Debussy: 'Pelléas et Mélisande'*, p. 70.

Example 3.5   Debussy, *Pelléas et Mélisande*, Act I (p. 25)

rest of the orchestra. In the context of a ponderous, march-like episode (marked 'très accentué') the trumpet is lyrical and graceful, and in the midst of thick, *Parsifal*-like orchestration, the trumpet represents a single, distinctive voice. It is a victory for an individuality of timbre within a mass of sound. And again the moment is arresting, a moment, indeed, that signals an end to the interlude, as if nothing more could be said.

Recovering the material

Could these intrusions in the discourse be read as parallels to the narrative effects we detected in *A Village Romeo and Juliet*? They might, in this reading, construct a conflicting point of view, one that challenges the Golaud-dream interpretation and opens a space, briefly but memorably, for other subjects from within the diegesis, or perhaps for a meta-diegetic figure like Delius's narrator or the composer figure in *Feuersnot*. But they surely demand to be considered beyond questions of narrative. Where so much of the musical discourse in *Pelléas* seems caught up in the web of dramatic association, these moments seem to offer an immediacy that defies signification in any familiar sense. There is a vividness of musical presence here that evokes that transgression through materiality that Kristeva identifies with the semiotic. Is the mystery of destiny's 'wordless operations' to be found here in the *jouissance* that marks the entry of the semiotic and its 'musicalised' Other?

The problem with Kristeva's use of music as a metaphor for the semiotic is that it re-enacts a familiar characterisation of music as beyond ordinary meaning and therefore beyond the social and historical. How, we might ask, can we seek the semiotic in music if its traces are to be found in musicalisation? Lawrence Kramer, for example, finds much of interest to musicology in Kristeva's theory, but balks at this particular analogy:

Real music ... *musica practica*, stands apart from this figurative deployment (something Kristeva herself fails to recognise). Music is, after all, a cultural practice.[67]

Kristeva is in fact aware of the limitations of her music metaphor. After citing music as a possible example of an 'exclusively semiotic' signifying system, she adds a qualification:

This exclusivity is relative, precisely because of the necessary dialectic between the two modalities of the signifying process, which is constitutive of the subject. Because the subject is always *both* semiotic *and* symbolic, no signifying system he produces can be either 'exclusively' semiotic or 'exclusively' symbolic, and is instead necessarily marked by an indebtedness to both .[68]

But in some ways the damage is done. Music has too often found itself a prop used to illustrate the collapse of the signifiable, and Kristeva's characterisation forces us to reclaim music from its enforced exile, to read the semiotic as an *effect* that music, like language, can generate, and not something intrinsic to it.

The passages analysed here in terms of the semiotic are constructions of music – they *signify* what they present as beyond signification. They align music with a remoteness – call it destiny, mystery, the unknowable – that positions it as Other, while drawing on sensual, grounded means that embrace the body instead of 'transcending' it. These moments might in fact be read as Debussy's response to Mallarmé's reservations about music and its role in the theatre. Focusing on Wagner, Mallarmé claims that music drama reduces music to accompaniment, to announcement, to illustration; it is a 'stage music' whose identity is defined by the enshrouding character of the leitmotif: 'deity costumed in the invisible folds of a tissue of chords'.[69] Wagner's music 'penetrates and envelops Drama by awe-inspiring will', but 'its very principle escapes Music'.[70] Ultimately, Mallarmé sees language as the medium of

[67] Kramer, *Classical Music and Postmodern Knowledge*, p. 19.
[68] Kristeva, *Revolution in Poetic Language*, p. 24.
[69] Mallarmé, 'Richard Wagner: Rêverie d'un poète français', cited in Philippe Lacoue-Labarthe, *Musica ficta (Figures of Wagner)*, trans. Felicia McCarren (Stanford: Stanford University Press, 1994), p. 70.
[70] Ibid., pp. 69–70.

this music – 'I know, they want to limit the mystery of Music when writing lays claim to it'[71] – but perhaps Debussy is here reclaiming the mystery that Mallarmé so misses in music drama, investing his opera with the non-representational quality that Mallarmé seeks. Perhaps this is what made the interludes indispensable, and encouraged Debussy to preserve them in their expanded form. Perhaps they offered a means of voicing what would otherwise remain silent.

But Debussy had added much more than that unnecessary violin part to which Mallarmé referred in his review of Maeterlinck's play, and could these moments in the interludes really compensate for the thoroughly post-Wagnerian spirit that pervades the opera? As repressed content, the semiotic suggests parallels with the dream analogy, with the notion that the interludes trace the most volatile, fractured, and therefore repressed material of Golaud's dream. If the semiotic offers a resistance to the symbolic order, then equally the tension and conflict characteristic of the interludes stands for a distance from the conscious – Kristeva, indeed, views the (unconscious) primary processes as critical to the organisation of the semiotic. The dream-like implications of the interludes suggest music's privileged access to the unconscious, while the semiotic reinforces a reading of music as unrepresentable and inaccessible to ordinary discourse. But these are arguably the very qualities that define the construction of music in late Wagner. There the idea of the musical unconscious allows the orchestra to assume a mastery of interiority (= knowledge) while the music's uncanny effects become signs of its unique immediacy (= truth), characteristics that are construed as part of music's mysterious essence. Perhaps, then, the occasional blatant Wagnerisms in Debussy's interludes should be taken as hints of what is actually a more profound debt to the spirit of Bayreuth.

Equally problematic in this context is Kristeva's reading of the impact of the semiotic. Since it dismantles the thetic unity central to signification, the semiotic is seen to fracture the unity of the subject position. If there is no unified pairing of signifier and signified, then there can be no unified subject to take up a position in relation to an object. To identify with the 'music' of the semiotic is to take up a subject position that is always 'on-trial/in-process' and not unified.[72] In this sense the semiotic can be seen to open the way to a decentred subjectivity, altering our engagement with the symbolic order. But this process implies a textual openness to difference, to heterogeneity, to a kind of self-exposure that is willing to question its own terms of engagement, and this is something

---

[71] Mallarmé, 'Le mystère dans les lettres', in his *Variations sur un sujet*, in Mondor and Jean-Aubry (eds.), *Oeuvres complètes*, p. 385, cited in Lacoue-Labarthe, *Musica ficta*, p. 44.

[72] Kristeva, *Revolution in Poetic Language*, p. 181.

that post-Wagnerian opera tends to resist, preferring to present itself as whole and complete. Here the interludes become pivotal: for all their resemblance to the fractured forms of the primary process, the interludes also have a transitional/introductory/commentating/reflective role as part of the totality of the opera. Certainly their tendency to divert from the path established by the staged scenes, to fracture the discourse, to concentrate some of the most highly charged material, seems to characterise the interludes in terms of difference, but the links with the scenes nevertheless remain. Counterbalancing the dislocations and gaps are transitions and bridges, and the teleological character of the whole is not seriously challenged. The interludes release themselves from their surroundings, but only teasingly.[73]

They also encourage identification within a larger framework in that they exclude the visual and verbal discourses, leaving gaps that the spectator 'fills'; invisible and silent characters seem to leave strangely vacated subject positions that the spectator can assume, and in this sense the music becomes both external and internal, heard and dreamt. In this fantasmatic setting the liberating effects of the semiotic might be seen as subverted to serve the purpose of total illusion. If there is a liberating experience to be had here, it is based on a subjectivity that is not so much decentred as self-estranged in a way that implies pleasure in escapist identifications and loss of self. In other words, *Pelléas* can be seen to fall far short of the radical reorientation of subjectivity that Kristeva detects in Mallarmé, but its musical impressions of immediacy and uncanniness might lend themselves to a different kind of self-alienation. Associated with popular cinema, this is a mode of engagement that has polarised theoretical responses, from the concerns voiced by critical theory over captivation and seduction in mass culture, to a legitimisation in cultural studies of new forms of spectatorship. Either way, post-Wagnerian opera needs to be seen as part of the debate. If it lacked the popular appeal of cinema, it nevertheless offered cinema a possible model for audience engagement and identification. It is in this thoroughly ambivalent, modern, and post-Wagnerian sense that we might identify with Golaud's words: 'Je suis perdu aussi'.

---

[73] Katherine Bergeron identifies a similar point of release in the last song of Debussy's *Cinq poèmes de Baudelaire*, relating it to notions of *jouissance*. She grants this 'momentary liberation' considerable power, but perhaps with some justification: positioned strategically at the very end of 'La mort des amants', it arguably figures much more prominently in the context of the song, or even the collection as a whole, than do the semiotic intrusions of *Pelléas* in relation to the whole opera. See 'The Echo, the Cry, the Death of Lovers', *Nineteenth-Century Music* 18/2 (1994), especially 149–51.

4

'Sympathy with death'

In one sense the Wagnerian ideal of complete audience absorption and identification represents an extension, perhaps an intensification, of theatrical experience. When Wagner anticipated the Bayreuth audience entering a dream-like state, he articulated a view of spectatorship centred around a maximum suspension of disbelief. It was to this ideal, for example, that Friedrich Klose (whose *Ilsebill* Rudolf Louis had so praised) appealed when he wrote of the need for scene changes to avoid provoking an 'alienated' or 'sober' attitude that he equates with the reading of fiction.[1] But any appeal to belief of this sort is also inherently political – profoundly so; it opens up the possibility for a dissemination, reinforcement, and legitimisation of values, attitudes, and desires. By taking pleasure in musical drama – by identifying with the musical and dramatic subjects it constructs – the spectator is to a certain extent positioned in relation to (as part of) a particular set of cultural norms. How the process of identification might be theorised and elucidated, and the role orchestral interludes might play in this process, are the questions to which we shall now turn. And, as with *A Village Romeo and Juliet*, we shall be confronted with an absolutist aesthetics that insists on musical autonomy from what exists beyond its 'own sphere'.

In *Reflections of a Nonpolitical Man* Thomas Mann relates a conversation with Hans Pfitzner between performances of *Palestrina* at its Munich premiere in 1917. He quotes Pfitzner as saying 'in *Palestrina* everything tends toward the past; it is dominated by sympathy with death'. The phrase 'sympathy with death', writes Mann, had a striking effect on him:

It was my expression. Before the war I had begun to write a little novel, a type of *Bildungsroman*, in which a young person, landed in a morally dangerous locale, found himself between two equally quaint educators, between an Italian literary man, humanist, rhetorician and man of progress, and a somewhat disreputable mystic, reactionary, and advocate of antireason – he had the choice, the good

[1] Friedrich Klose, *Meine Lehrjahre bei Bruckner: Erinnerungen und Betrachtungen* (Regensburg: Gustav Bosse Verlag, 1927), p. 334.

youngster, between the powers of virtue and of seduction, between duty and service to life and the fascination of decay, for which he was not unreceptive.[2]

Written during the war, *Reflections* is Mann's attempt to come to terms with nationalism, the threat to German culture, and the question of taking a political stand in Germany's defence. At times a fierce indictment of the democratic, liberal values Mann associated with his brother Heinrich, at others a warning against Germany's infatuation with potent leader images and conservative militarism, the work unevenly, sometimes bafflingly, juxtaposes philosophy, political insight, literary criticism, and cultural analysis in an ambivalent and often tortured dialogue. In his discussion of Pfitzner, it is the conservative Mann who speaks, and here he resigns himself to 'sympathy with death' almost affectionately. Here he could well identify with his hero's fascination for decay. If the idea of democracy and progress, equated by Germany's enemies with 'health' and 'virtue', means renouncing pessimism and the past, then he could have no part in it: 'Not everyone is suited by nature for the blessed pact with the times and with progress; democratic health is not exactly for everyone.'[3]

Palestrina and its composer presented Mann with a particularly vivid image of something he detected in himself, something he saw as integral to German culture. It is an attitude that emerges equally clearly in a number of operatic scenarios that, while thematicising death and the past on a quite literal level, seem to offer a gloss on the wider implications of Mann's (and Pfitzner's) phrase. In Berg's *Wozzeck* and Pfitzner's own earlier *Die Rose vom Liebesgarten*, the death of the protagonist is followed by an orchestral interlude that, like the *Trauermarsch* in *Götterdämmerung*, laments and eulogises. Death here becomes an invitation to reconstruct a life, to revisit the past, but in a way that deliberately undermines any comfortable assumptions about the source of the eulogy. Who sings/speaks/writes these eulogies? There seems to be no single answer. It is within this disorientation, this sleight of hand, that a mere sympathy with the dead begins to touch on the broader and more ominous political implications of a 'sympathy with death', and it is here that the ideal realm of 'absolute music' reveals its secret groundedness in subtle, compromising ways.

Images of mourning

Four years after their collaboration on *Der arme Heinrich* (1894), Pfitzner persuaded James Grun to write a second libretto for him. At one time a

---

[2] Thomas Mann, *Reflections of a Nonpolitical Man* (1918), trans. Walter D. Morris (New York: Frederick Ungar, 1983), pp. 311–12.

[3] Ibid., p. 314.

student with Pfitzner at the Frankfurt Conservatory, Grun had become a
poet and mystic philosopher described by Pfitzner as a 'sectarian, a pen-
itent, a wandering monk [who] followed his trade of a world reformer
and benefactor'.[4] Grun drew his initial ideas for the new libretto from the
paintings of Hans Thoma, a close family friend who had painted Grun
and illustrated a collection of his poems. The most obvious source is
Der Wächter vor dem Liebesgarten (1890), which, with its idealistic, chival-
ric imagery, suggests parallels with Symbolist painting. In her memoirs,
Grun's sister described it as

very well known and of richly coloured beauty. Before the dark columns of the
entrance stands tall and solemn the armour-clad figure of the guardian, a mighty
lion lying near him in the shadows.[5]

Thoma's image finds theatrical form in a series of tableaux contrasting the Eden of the *Liebesgarten* – Pfitzner repeatedly referred to it as
a 'Germanic paradise'[6] – with an outside world of mountains, dark
forests, and deep caves. Populated by a *Parsifal*esque religious order
dedicated to a Star Maiden and Sun Child (virgin and child figures),
the *Liebesgarten* is surrounded by a wall that protects it from an assort-
ment of dwarfs, giants, and forest dwellers familiar from nineteenth-
century German folk tales. Both the settings and the plot they threaten
to overshadow represent a rather incongruous mixture of Wagnerian
and biblical themes, of Rosicrucian mysticism and *Märchen* imagery.

In a lengthy prologue, consisting of little more than a static series of
visually sumptuous rituals, we are introduced to the inhabitants of the
Liebesgarten. The purpose of the ceremonies is to choose a guardian of
the gate to the *Liebesgarten*, and it is ultimately the young knight Siegnot
who is chosen and granted the rose that symbolises the reign of love
in the garden. No sooner does he take up his responsibilities, however,
than he finds himself smitten by Minneleide, an Undine-like creature
who reigns over the forest outside the gate. Certain that she will be
happier in the paradise of the *Liebesgarten*, he accompanies Minneleide
through the gate, but she is blinded by the light in the garden and flees in
terror. At that moment she is abducted by the Night Sorcerer – a demonic
creature who seems to personify Minneleide's Otherness – and taken to
his subterranean domain. Act II chronicles Siegnot's heroic attempt at

[4] Hans Pfitzner, *Sämtliche Schriften*, vol. IV (Tutzing: Hans Schneider, 1987), p. 587, trans.
in John Williamson, *The Music of Hans Pfitzner* (Oxford: Clarendon Press, 1992), p. 13.
[5] Walter Kreuzburg (ed.), *Hans Thoma und Frances Grun: Lebenserinnerungen von Frances
Grun* (Frankfurt am Main: W. Kramer, 1957), p. 26, trans. in Williamson, *The Music of
Hans Pfitzner*, p. 14.
[6] Hans Pfitzner, *Die neue Ästhetik der musikalischen Impotenz*, in *Gesammelte Schriften*, vol. II
(Augsburg-Benno Filser, 1926), p. 212, trans. in Williamson, *The Music of Hans Pfitzner*,
p. 214.

rescue, as he journeys, rose in hand, to the cave of the Night Sorcerer. But his plan is thwarted by Minneleide herself; much as she loves Siegnot, she fears re-entering the *Liebesgarten* and hesitates to go with him. Siegnot's response is to assume responsibility, Christ-like, for the sins of Minneleide and win her soul for the *Liebesgarten*. He calls upon the Star Maiden, and brings down the cave around him, killing the Night Sorcerer and himself. Minneleide is grief-stricken, but Siegnot's sacrifice has given her courage, and she sets out to return Siegnot's lifeless body and the rose itself to the *Liebesgarten*, even if her role in Siegnot's death puts her life in danger there. The new guardian confronts her at the gate, but Minneleide calls on the Star Maiden, and before the guardian can strike her she falls lifeless to the ground. Minneleide's renunciation of life redeems her, and both she and Siegnot are raised to the Star Maiden's side as the walls of the garden collapse and spring reigns over the world outside.

The central themes of the plot – the noble hero who harbours a death wish, the temptation of 'woman', redemption through renunciation – are familiar enough from Wagner, but it is the central role of visual imagery that ultimately defines the opera. Peppered throughout the score are detailed scenic descriptions that situate the opera's quasi-Symbolist imagery within typical nineteenth-century operatic settings – caves, forests, idyllic pastoral surroundings – described in language typical of traditional naturalistic concepts of stage design. But the descriptions also include scenic features that seem to conjure a different aesthetic: the white marble balustrade that dominates the *Liebesgarten* in the opening scene; the *Liebesgarten*'s 'blue-steel walls towering towards the sky'; a gloriously kitschy shower of white blossoms (the so-called *Blütenwunder* that celebrates Siegnot's selection); and the twilight of the Night Sorcerer's cave, 'illuminated by thousands of glittering, many-coloured precious stones'. The self-conscious decorativeness of these scenic details points towards *Jugendstil* as a source of imagery and aesthetic values: like *Jugendstil*, the opera seems to foreground unapologetically its 'design' element and the self-advertising, sometimes highly ornate 'constructive' quality of its visual forms and materials. Writing to a stage manager prior to a 1937 production of the work, Pfitzner observed that 'in the *Rose* the stage picture and the scenic as a whole play a very important role, much more important than in all my other operas'.[7] Pfitzner's assessment is difficult to question, but lurking behind this seemingly straightforward observation is one of the central polemics outlined in his theoretical writings. For Pfitzner, the self-professed disciple of Schopenhauer, the visual belongs to the 'world of appearances', and therefore fails to meet music on its own terms, as immediate copy

---

[7] Letter to Erik Wildhagen, 27 January 1937, in *Sämtliche Schriften*, vol. IV, p. 771.

of the Will itself.[8] In opera music cannot be forced 'to serve another art or non-art through illustration or accompaniment'.[9] Rather, the relationship must result from a convergence of the 'spirit' of the music with that of the other discourse. It is above all in the *Wort-Ton-Verhältnis* (word–note relationship) that Pfitzner detects the possibility of a true interaction. Appealing to the tradition of the *Lied*, he shifts the terms of the music–stage relationship away from the scenic and theatrical and towards the verbal. Even here, he warns, the temptation towards word-painting must be resisted.

The alternative, demonstrated repeatedly in opera and *Lied*, is what he calls 'illustrative non-music'.[10] He traces the origins of this tendency in Wagner's *Ring* and its culmination in the 'cinema style' of Strauss and other post-Wagnerians:

For what is the cinema other than a theatre that highlights the visual, while the displayed proceedings are accompanied by music to which we scarcely listen, if at all, but which we don't want to be without?[11]

In his own operas, by contrast, he sees the triumph of music that is genuinely dramatic without sacrificing its independence, its 'self-justification'.[12] Here, in what he calls 'musicalised opera', is music whose material is generated from within itself, whose origins lie only in 'musical inspiration, a theme, a musical idea'.[13] Might Pfitzner's admission of the importance of the visual in *Die Rose vom Liebesgarten* then represent a challenge to his own theoretical position, a chink in his absolutist armour?

Judging by Paul Bekker's 1910 review of the opera, the question admits of no simple answer. On the one hand Bekker is quick to distance Pfitzner's music from the accompanying function against which the composer's theoretical writings are directed:

There is no particular virtuosity of psychological detail in Pfitzner, no naturalistic tone-painting, no illustration of the text or external events.[14]

But Bekker also draws attention to the 'shadowy', 'fantastic' images that dominate the libretto, and which resound in Pfitzner's music:

To these [images] he lends the strongest, most profound music that resounds in him; for them he exhausts the sources of his creative power. The plot, around which these surroundings group, and which is actually the reason for all the magical atmosphere, he puts up with as an unavoidable addition. To this end the musician even disrupts the uniform effect of the stage, distracting the listener's

---

[8] Hans Pfitzner, *Die Oper* (1942), in *Sämtliche Schriften*, vol. IV, p. 99.
[9] Ibid., p. 98.   [10] Ibid., p. 102.   [11] Ibid., p. 103.   [12] Ibid., p. 98.
[13] Ibid., p. 99.
[14] Paul Bekker, '*Die Rose vom Liebesgarten*', *Neue Musikzeitung* 31 (1910), 249.

attention from the progress of the action itself with theatrical decorative effects and interspersed lyrical intermezzi.[15]

If Pfitzner had avoided illustration on the immediate level, then, he had, in a broader sense, given his music over to it. Visual imagery, Bekker suggests, is not a surface feature of this music. It is, rather, its underlying motivation in a very profound sense. By allowing that the music avoids localised illustration, Bekker might be seen to play into the hands of Pfitznerian theory. Pfitzner would no doubt argue that his music never 'serves' the visual imagery, but merely conveys it as a by-product of the convergence of libretto with his own entirely self-sufficient 'musical idea'.[16] Bekker's other observations, however, seem to challenge Pfitzner's argument for the 'self-justification' of his music, replacing it with a music that is, as Bekker describes it elsewhere in the article, 'awakened' by the visual imagery of the libretto, and 'far from any end in itself'.[17] From this perspective visual imagery is the ultimate goal of Pfitzner's music. It is associated, according to Bekker, with Pfitzner's 'strongest, most profound music', even if the result is a static, decorative quality that distracts from the 'progress of the action itself'.

Both positions could be applied with equal relevance to the *Trauermarsch* that links Act II with the Epilogue. Here, on the one hand, is an example of Bekker's 'lyrical intermezzi', a static 'image' removed from the thrust of the narrative. Here an orchestral eulogy for the dead hero, Siegnot, is presented in the context of traditional musical images of a funeral (a minor-mode march, muffled percussion, heavy, chorale-like textures). But Pfitzner might counter that in the *Trauermarsch* he most successfully avoids the 'accompaniment' function that he criticises in the 'cinema style'. By drawing a curtain over the 'actual' visible and conveying the imagery through music that avoids the merely 'illustrative', Pfitzner could claim to have substituted the mere world of appearances with the idea behind them, while maintaining the integrity of music's 'autonomy'. What draws the two perspectives together is a sense that the scene, the image of mourning, is somehow displaced into a realm removed from the 'reality' of the staged action. Whether conceived as the 'idea' behind the mere visual imagery of the stage – and therefore, in Schopenhauerian terms, actually closer to the ultimate reality of the Will itself – or as what Bekker calls a 'distraction' from the staged action, the realm occupied by the *Trauermarsch* is one marked by difference. It is a realm in which a scene is presented without scenery, in which a funeral passes with an invisible and silent procession, in which death is mirrored by total darkness. Even when the curtain rises for the Epilogue (revealing the new guardian at the gate of the *Liebesgarten*), the only

[15] Ibid., 252.   [16] Pfitzner, *Die Oper*, p. 103.
[17] Bekker, '*Die Rose vom Liebesgarten*', 249.

sounds are those of an invisible chorus of mourners ('Weh' uns, weh!') ushering in the approaching funeral procession. The *Trauermarsch* exemplifies the 'removed' quality (*Entrücktheit*) that both Bekker and Pfitzner identify in the opera.[18] 'All the images are shadowy', writes Bekker, 'the characters delicate children of a fantasy, who cannot endure the glaring light of day and only let their fire glow in the darkness of night.'[19]

Acoustic hallucinations

Bekker's description, with its fantasies and darkness, recalls Wagner's account of the interior design of the Festspielhaus at Bayreuth:

> Between [the spectator] and the image in view there is nothing plainly visible, merely a floating atmosphere of distance ... The scene is transported, as it were, to the remote world of dreams, while the ghostly music emanating from the 'mystic abyss', like vapours rising from the holy womb of Gaia beneath the Pythia's tripod, inspires him with a clairvoyance in which the scenic picture seems to become the truest image of life itself.[20]

It is towards this regressive condition, this twilight state between waking and sleeping, that the Bayreuth theatre, with its invisible orchestra and darkened auditorium, directs itself. The spectator is to enter a state in which theatre resembles reality, paradoxically, because it is rendered dream-like. It is the same 'impression of reality'[21] that Metz identifies in cinema when the spectator 'hallucinate[s] what was already there, what at the same time he in fact perceived: the images and sounds of the film'.[22] In this reading the cinema becomes a twilight space that mobilises the ambiguous territory between perception and imagination.

As Friedrich Kittler has pointed out, it is above all the 'acoustic hallucination'[23] that comes to the fore in Wagner, a world in which, to use Nietzsche's words, all things animate and inanimate desire an 'existence in sound' and listening becomes paramount.[24] 'I hear you', sings Hagen, as Alberich appears to him in his sleep. 'Do I alone hear this melody?' asks Isolde, as the dead Tristan's 'voice' wells up from the orchestra pit. And when Isolde imagines that the sound of Mark's horns has given way to a 'murmuring spring', the orchestral sound transforms magically, while the stage direction indicates that 'Isolde listens'. In a

---

[18] Pfitzner, *Die Oper*, p. 108. [19] Bekker, '*Die Rose vom Liebesgarten*', 249.

[20] Richard Wagner, 'Das Bühnenfestspielhaus zu Bayreuth' (1873), *SSD* vol. IX, p. 338.

[21] Metz, *The Imaginary Signifier*, p. 66. [22] Ibid., p. 104.

[23] Friedrich Kittler, 'World-Breath: On Wagner's Media Technology', in David Levin (ed.), *Opera through Other Eyes* (Stanford: Stanford University Press, 1993), p. 224.

[24] Friedrich Nietzsche, 'Richard Wagner in Bayreuth', in his *Untimely Meditations* (1876), trans. R. J. Hollingdale (Cambridge: Cambridge University Press, 1983), p. 289.

sense Wagner's interludes represent the apex of this world of hearing, totalising it, absorbing the verbal and visual discourses of the stage into sound. The 'floating atmosphere of distance' that Wagner sought for the Bayreuth stage is pushed one step further: into darkness itself. Now the visual gives way entirely to hallucination, brought to life in sympathetic surroundings by an almost equally fantasmatic music. It is this tradition of acoustic illusion from which Pfitzner's *Trauermarsch* stems. Here a hidden music transposes a visual image – an image of mourning – into a disembodied, sightless realm. It is an image that is both represented and not represented at the same time; it is given shape in the darkness by music, and yet the music itself seems to come from nowhere. The source of music and image seems, as we saw in our *Pelléas* dream analogy, both 'outside' and 'inside', real and imagined.

Analysed in terms of psychoanalytic theory, the *Trauermarsch* would seem, like the cinema, to re-enact the conditions of the Lacanian imaginary. Of course, as film theory has recognised, the spectator addressed within the cinema's imaginary inhabits the symbolic order, a term whose connotations in Lacan's theory are not dissimilar to its connotations in Kristeva's. Initiated by the mirror stage and shaped by the Oedipus complex and the acquisition of language, the entry into the symbolic order teaches the subject that difference and lack are the order of the day, that the fluid boundaries of the self must give way to what Lacan calls 'the armour of an alienating identity'.[25] Yet it is precisely the possibility of experiencing the imaginary, if only from within the symbolic, that may be seen to account for the lure of the cinema. Cinema allows us to re-animate the fantasies of the imaginary order. It is capable of providing a flood of pleasurable fantasies, but it also provides a space in which we can safely expose ourselves to fantasies that the symbolic order would seek to contain and repress.

What, then, are the fantasies to which the *Trauermarsch* might give rise? Bekker's reference to 'lyrical intermezzi' provides a starting point, recalling as it does Pfitzner's appeal to the tradition of the *Lied* and pre-Wagnerian Romantic opera as a model for the revitalisation of opera. The opening theme in the *Trauermarsch*, an extended solo for trombone, does indeed suggest a song, a *Klagegesang* (example 4.1). The suggestion is made explicit after the rise of the curtain when Minneleide takes up the theme, *in toto*, as her own expression of grief:

> He who died for you,
> whose blood won you peace,
> carry him now to the gateway of his homeland.

---

[25] Jacques Lacan, *'Ecrits': A Selection*, trans. Alan Sheridan (New York: W. W. Norton, 1977), p. 4.

Example 4.1   Pfitzner, *Die Rose vom Liebesgarten*, *Trauermarsch*

The effect is, in a sense, to mirror Pfitzner's own aesthetic of the *Lied* with its *Wort-Ton-Verhältnis* that seeks to distance music from any dependence on poetic imagery:

[The music] is not born wearily from the spirit of the poem; it must come from its own domain and in its own way independently conjure up the same atmosphere which the poem expresses; this can happen *entirely* independently, *before* knowledge of the poem, or gently touched by it, as with a divining rod.[26]

Minneleide's song is almost an afterthought, heard only as an echo of the shattering climax of grief that precedes it. It is the wordless, invisible song of the *Trauermarsch* which takes precedence. If Minneleide can be heard in retrospect as the 'singer' of the *Trauermarsch*, it is only as a ghost that sings wordlessly through the lamenting trombone, itself carefully concealed in the orchestra pit. Here Minneleide truly becomes one of Bekker's 'children of the night'; her fear of the light in the *Liebesgarten* finds a mirror in this song sung in the darkness.

But if this opening portion is a wordless song, it is a short-lived one. As soon as the trombone gives way to full orchestra, the *Klagegesang* is dispersed, never again heard in the *Trauermarsch* as a complete entity or as a solo voice. At letter B+3 an abbreviated statement of the *Klagegesang* in solo horn is imitated canonically at the fourth in flute and oboe, while the theme's concluding cadential gesture is passed to the first violins. Elsewhere the theme is reduced to fragments and merged with already familiar material, including leitmotifs. One bar before letter A a series of fluid scalar passages in the woodwind recalls the *Blütenwunder* scene of the Prologue (example 4.2). But built into the upper melodic line (flute) and echoed by strings and bassoons (letter A+4) is the opening triad of the *Klagegesang*, a melodic pattern not found in the *Blütenwunder* scene. From letter A+10 the violins seem to break the *Klagegesang* down into characteristic melodic intervals, isolating them rhythmically and drawing attention to them. The ascending minor sixth at the climax of the *Klagegesang* is presented at letter A+12, but it is the falling minor

---

[26] Pfitzner, *Die neue Ästhetik der musikalischen Impotenz*, p. 212, trans. in Williamson, *The Music of Hans Pfitzner*, p. 214.

Example 4.2   Pfitzner, *Die Rose vom Liebesgarten, Trauermarsch*

Example 4.3   Pfitzner, *Die Rose vom Liebesgarten*, Prologue

second that is emphasised, dramatising its relationship with the motif associated with Siegnot's name (example 4.3). At letter C+8 a motif – or, rather, a theme – first heard as Siegnot pledged his life to the service of 'die Minne' (Prologue, figure 7+8, example 4.4) is shown to have a strong melodic affinity with the ascending sequence of the *Klagegesang*. And in the final climax of the *Trauermarsch* (five bars before letter F), a theme which had accompanied the bestowal of the guardian's sword on Siegnot (example 4.3, bars 1–4) is presented almost unaltered. Now the triad of its opening bar turns out to be merely a retrograde version of the opening triad of the *Klagegesang*, a connection reinforced by the accompanying rolled percussion and string tremolo that characterised the opening of the *Klagegesang*. At letter F+2, too, we find the minor-sixth leap that forms the climax of the *Klagegesang*.

Example 4.4   Pfitzner, *Die Rose vom Liebesgarten*, Prologue

In the context of the *Trauermarsch* these interconnections might be interpreted in terms of the impact of the *Klagegesang* on the opera's leit-motifs, as if nothing could remain the same after Siegnot's death. Yet for all the clarity with which fragments of the *Klagegesang* seem to resurface in this material, their impact on the motifs is almost negligible. The effect is rather to suggest that the *Klagegesang* evolved from the motifs, that it represents a synthesis of musical fragments drawn from the opera's past. In a sense it has always been there, fragmented and concealed in Siegnot's motifs like a premonition of death. Its refragmentation during the *Trauermarsch*, then, suggests that the synthesis is a fragile one, quickly dismantled and dispersed. It is as if the *Klagegesang* has dissolved back into the motivic material from which it emerged, and can now only be heard, as it were, by proxy. Only with the physical re-appearance of Minneleide – only with her re-embodiment – is it restored to its original form.

A song broken into fragments and a singer dispersed through an orchestra: the *Trauermarsch* speaks of nothing if not the Lacanian fantasy of the fragmented body, a fantasy illustrated in his account of the mirror stage. The gratifying image of completeness that confronts the child in the mirror is only the final outcome of a series of potential fantasies:

The mirror stage is a drama whose internal thrust is precipitated from insufficiency to anticipation – and which manufactures for the subject, caught up in the lure of spatial identification, the succession of phantasies that extends from a fragmented body-image to a form of its totality that I shall call orthopaedic.[27]

The fantasy of fragmentation presents the child with a dispersal rather than a consolidation of body parts, a failure to co-ordinate and control limbs and extremities, which seem to detach themselves and erode any sense of a single, centred subjectivity. Lacan presents his mirror stage as a specular drama, but it is equally applicable, as Guy Rosolato and Kaja Silverman have shown, to sound.[28] The 'acoustic mirror', too, can centre or fragment the subject.

Pfitzner's *Trauermarsch* presents the spectator with a double image of fragmentation, an acoustic hallucination of dispersal. On the one hand a song is sung not by an embodied voice, but by a hidden, apparently disembodied source. And, on the other, the song itself is dispersed through the orchestra, as if divided up among the fragmented body parts of the singer. It is an auditory image that decentres the subject, that threatens to break down the fragile fortifications of the ego. But there is another image here, too – that of Siegnot himself. For the *Trauermarsch* is above all a musical eulogy, and as such sets itself the task of 'remembering' the dead hero.

Rose-coloured glass

The taboo against insulting the memory of the dead is nowhere more strongly manifest than in the inherently uncritical assessment of a life that is the eulogy. Clearly, since eulogies are delivered by those who feel affection and loyalty towards the deceased, criticism will never be high on the agenda. Yet there remains a falsifying aspect here, an unwritten law that frowns even on negative thoughts, not to mention public criticism. The eulogy, on one level simply an appreciation, is also a shared lie. It seeks to remake the image of the deceased in a way that knowingly suppresses the truth of that individual, omitting or glossing over attributes and deeds that are not remembered with affection. It is as if the collective memory of the individual, as it stands, will not do. It

[27] Lacan, *Ecrits*, p. 4.
[28] See Guy Rosolato, 'La voix: entre corps et langage', *Revue Française de Psychanalyse* 38/1 (1974), and Silverman, *The Acoustic Mirror*.

must be reconstructed publicly, so that an official, and homogenised, version prevails. It must steer a course between complete fiction on the one hand and the harsh truth on the other. Meanwhile the audience for the eulogy, subject to the social norms of mourning, believe and invest in that version, partly as a reflection of their own affectionate feelings, but also perhaps as a means of keeping criticism at bay.

It is this eulogistic shaping of memory that underlies Mann's characterisation of the *Götterdämmerung Trauermarsch*. For Mann, the traditional 'operatic *pompe funèbre*' would never have sufficed to mourn what Wagner called 'the most noble hero in the world'. But by drawing on the history acquired by his web of leitmotifs, Wagner would be able to transform the lament into

a veritable feast of associations, a whole universe of brilliant and profound allusions, a structure of musical remembrance so magnificent that nobody would be able to hold back tears of enthusiasm – the same enthusiasm that he himself felt at the very idea of it all. It would be an overwhelming celebration of thought and remembrance.[29]

Typically dripping with irony, Mann's commentary highlights Wagnerian grandiloquence, but he follows Wagner's lead when he characterises the *Trauermarsch* as a series of what he calls 'sublime reminders'. According to Cosima's diaries, Wagner compared his orchestral eulogy to the chorus in Greek tragedy,

but a chorus which will be sung, so to speak, by the orchestra; after Siegfried's death, while the scene is being changed, the Siegmund theme will be played, as if the chorus were saying: 'This was his father'; then the sword motif; and finally his own theme; then the curtain goes up.[30]

Wagner's appeal to the Greek chorus is a familiar theme in his own writings, an analogy that seeks to incorporate into the orchestral role the idea of the chorus as representative of the *polis*: the orchestra comments on the action on behalf of the people. Mann undermines this notion when he relates the audience's 'tears of enthusiasm' to Wagner's own reaction to his work. The implication here is that of a sleight of hand by which a response built into the work is presented as though it belonged to the audience.

At the same time, Mann echoes Wagner when he suggests that the impact of the *Trauermarsch* is a result of its conjunction of *pompe funèbre* with memory, with a leitmotivic 'feast of associations'. Like Wagner in

---

[29] Thomas Mann, 'Richard Wagner and *Der Ring des Nibelungen*', in Allan Blunden (ed. and trans.), *Thomas Mann: Pro and Contra Wagner* (London: Faber and Faber, 1985), p. 188.

[30] Diary entry for 29 September 1871, in Gregor-Dellin and Mack (eds.), *Cosima Wagner's Diaries*, p. 325.

Cosima's quotation, he reads the *Trauermarsch* as a parade of leitmotifs with definite and stable references to the past. For Adorno, the linear presentation of the leitmotif represents one of the contradictions at the core of the music drama: 'Beneath the thin veil of continuous progress Wagner has fragmented the composition into allegorical leitmotifs juxtaposed like discrete objects.'[31] For all Wagner's appeal to symphonic continuity, Adorno argues, the leitmotif 'calls a halt to the sheer flow',[32] replacing continuity with a thoroughly undynamic series of moments. It is a criticism that applies only too well to the *Trauermarsch*, as Wagner and Mann implicitly concede. Here, above all, the orchestral discourse bases itself on the linear succession that is at the heart of Adorno's criticism. The result is that the process threatens to become a parody of itself. Like self-contained musical units, the leitmotifs parade before us, reviewing aspects of Siegfried's life like some badly written biography (or eulogy): these were his parents . . . and this was his sword . . . and this was his beloved.

Less convincing, at least in the context of Wagner's orchestral eulogy, is Adorno's characterisation of the leitmotif as a static, rigid 'picture', a 'particle of congealed meaning' that refuses to adapt itself to new contexts.[33] Where Mann invests the leitmotif with a stability that allows it to become a 'sublime reminder', Adorno sees total inflexibility in which 'the supposed psychological variations' of the leitmotifs 'involve only a change of lighting'.[34] Although Mann makes some attempt to characterise the presentation of the leitmotifs in the *Trauermarsch* – the 'vast rhythmic cadences' of Siegfried's horn call, for example – it is ultimately their role as triggers of memory that he values, an approach that lends weight to Adorno's 'change of lighting' charge. Yet for all the linear, parade-like quality of their presentation in the *Trauermarsch*, many of the leitmotifs are transformed here in a manner that finds no precedent throughout their long history in the *Ring*. They are recognisably linked to the past, and yet they are, in a sense, radically reconstructed. It is as if all their previous incarnations were merely stages in an evolution towards this triumphant form. Now they assert their presence with overwhelming force, demanding attention that was previously shared with the stage. If their effect is to construct an image of Siegfried, then it is not the bullying lout of *Siegfried* or the all too gullible hero of *Götterdämmerung*. In the *Trauermarsch* Siegfried truly becomes the 'greatest hero in the world', a figure who exceeds all doubt, all resistance. The eulogy that unfolds in the *Trauermarsch* has served the memory of Siegfried well – perhaps we might call it 'the greatest eulogy in the world'. But perhaps Wagner's music glorifies too much. Perhaps, in the blatant contrast between what we know of the living Siegfried

[31] Adorno, *In Search of Wagner*, p. 48. [32] Ibid., p. 37. [33] Ibid., p. 45. [34] Ibid.

and what Wagner's eulogy attempts to 'reconstruct', there emerges a sense of doubt and an unwillingness to identify with what we perceive as false. In that case the *Trauermarsch* merely throws light on the contribution of the figure who delivers the eulogy, a virtual author figure who now attracts unwelcome attention. The Greek chorus is in danger of losing its mandate to represent the people.

In contrast to the ecstatic glorification of Siegfried's memory, Pfitzner's Siegnot is mourned in terms of nostalgia. Far from reconstructing his image, the *Trauermarsch* seems to preserve it, as though eager to bring time to a standstill and revive the past. If the *Klagegesang* suggests a fragmented body, the leitmotifs which ultimately absorb it preserve Siegnot with an antithetical wholeness. In this context Adorno's characterisation of the leitmotif as static picture takes on a new relevance. In fact, what Bekker and others have labelled 'motifs' in *Die Rose vom Liebesgarten* might be better described as themes, restated as complete musical entities with harmonic setting, rhythm, and phrasing intact. Letter D+6, for example, quotes almost verbatim from a passage in the Prologue in which Siegnot pledges his life in the service of love, promising to 'rise victorious, be it through suffering and death' (one bar before figure 7, example 4.4). Even the *fortissimo* setting for full orchestra in the *Trauermarsch* is merely an echo of the past, in this case figure 10+11 of the Prologue, where the opening portion of the theme was presented (in the major mode) in a similarly full texture. Likewise, the final four bars of the *Trauermarsch* (four bars before letter F, example 4.5) merely

Example 4.5   Pfitzner, *Die Rose vom Liebesgarten, Trauermarsch*

Example 4.6   Pfitzner, *Die Rose vom Liebesgarten*, Prologue, *Blütenwunder*

represent a transposed and very slightly modified version of figure 53+7, itself an extension of the 'Siegnot' motif. Thus, in its final gesture before the human voice returns in the form of the invisible chorus of mourners, the orchestra seems to call out Siegnot's name, vainly summoning the hero from beyond death. There is no triumph here, no transfiguring celebration of his redeeming sacrifice – merely a morbid nostalgia that negates time, seemingly in an effort to disavow Siegnot's death.

It is an attitude that is presaged in the *Klagegesang* portion of the *Trauermarsch* when the fragmented portions of the song are presented in a setting strongly reminiscent of the *Blütenwunder* scene. Typical of the decorative, visual quality emphasised by Bekker, the gentle rain of blossoms had been characterised musically by arpeggiated harp and winds organised into contrasting sonorities that suggest a *Klangfarbenmelodie*. Superimposed on these shifting sonorities is a flowing ostinato pattern of parallel thirds in strings, orchestrated in a way that surrounds the winds with a halo of sweet, high violins and magisterial organ pedals in the cellos and basses. It is a thoroughly Delian image of pleasurable immersion in a static nature, reflected in a kaleidoscope of musical colour, an unhurried harmonic rhythm, and an emphasis on harmonic drift rather than goal-directedness[35] (example 4.6). This is the texture and sonority that returns one bar before letter B in the *Trauermarsch*, an echo reinforced with a modulation to E flat minor, an appropriately funereal reflection of the G flat major of the *Blütenwunder*

[35] Perhaps this reminder of Delius's sensual appeal suggests another way in which Pfitzner's music might undermine his absolutist position.

Example 4.7   Pfitzner, *Die Rose vom Liebesgarten, Trauermarsch*

(example 4.7). As woodwind and horns exchange fragments of the *Klagegesang*, upper woodwind recall the interlocking arpeggios of the *Blütenwunder* scene, while first violins provide a thin, seemingly half-hearted echo of the string halo. It is as though the orchestra were attempting to call forth the rain of blossoms as a symbol of happier times.

With its emphasis on a nostalgic recall of the past, the *Trauermarsch* avoids the alienating exaggeration of Wagner's interlude. The image of Siegnot it presents rings true because it suggests a oneness with the living Siegnot we saw and heard on the stage. It is an image, moreover, that is possessed of an impressive wholeness in contrast to the fragmented subjectivity that dominates the first half of the *Trauermarsch*. While the identity of the *Klagegesang* becomes increasingly precarious, the leitmotifs emerge as something complete, barely altered from their original form. It is a contrast illuminated by the drama of dispersal in which the last vestiges of the *Klagegesang* seem to resound in the leitmotifs, as if absorbed into them. And if Minneleide is the imagined singer of the *Klagegesang*, then the fragmentation of her song, and its absorption by the image of Siegnot, represents the redefinition of her 'self' within Siegnot's image.

For Lacan, as for Freud before him, the process that leads away from the fantasy of fragmentation and towards the unified ego rests on a fundamental narcissism. The 'lure' Lacan ascribes to the mirror image depends on a misrecognition (*méconnaissance*) in which the subject sees in/projects onto the image an identity that is more satisfying and complete than that which it experiences in its own body. Reflected back upon the subject, that image provides a flood of narcissistic pleasure. It is precisely this narcissistic drive from 'insufficiency to anticipation'[36] that is captured in the drama of subjectivity that lies at the heart of the *Trauermarsch*. On the one hand it engages with fantasies of fragmentation and decentring, but it simultaneously holds up the mirror image that offers the possibility of refortification. The subject discovers in this acoustic image an ideal ego which, introjected by the subject, satisfies its narcissistic drive towards completion. In 'Group Psychology and the Analysis of the Ego', Freud theorises the ideal ego as an object of desire that corresponds to a position of imagined superiority within the ego that he terms the ego ideal:

[T]he object serves as a substitute for some unattained ego ideal of our own. We love it on account of the perfections which we have striven to reach for our own ego, and which we should now like to procure in this roundabout way as a means of satisfying our narcissism.[37]

Introjection, in other words, is a process in which 'the object has been put in place of the ego ideal'.[38] In the *Trauermarsch* this 'idealisation' is magnified by the fantasmatic juxtaposition of a fragmented subjectivity with a wholeness and perfection that offers to heal the wound.

But there is a price to be paid here. To identify with that wholeness is to surrender, like Minneleide, to an impossibly preserved fragment of time. The leitmotifs in the *Trauermarsch* represent a preoccupation with images of the past, preserved like relics. Writing on Wagnerian narratives, Adorno observes that they

call a halt to the action and hence, too, to the life process of society. They cause it to stand still so as to accompany it down into the kingdom of death.[39]

Pfitzner's *Trauermarsch* also turns its glance backwards, exempting itself, as Bekker points out, from the 'progress of the action'. In the wake of Siegnot's death, Minneleide renounces her desire for life. Accompanied by echoes of the *Trauermarsch*, she reveals herself to be a worthy successor to Isolde:

O agony of longing, o painful wound!
Never will my heart's remorse end!
In death my love becomes one with you!

Like the phantom Tristan of Isolde's *Liebestod*, who lives only as a fantasy projected by the orchestra, Siegnot lives on in music. And like Tristan, he offers fulfilment only in death. The fetishistic preservation of Siegnot is an expression of the death drive, for death is the object around which

---

[36] Lacan, *Ecrits*, p. 4.

[37] Sigmund Freud, 'Group Psychology and the Analysis of the Ego' (1921), in Strachey (ed. and trans.), *The Standard Edition*, vol. XIV, pp. 112–13.

[38] Ibid., p. 113.   [39] Adorno, *In Search of Wagner*, p. 60.

this fantasy revolves: it is the 'highest bliss' towards which the negation of time points. To follow Minneleide is to attain wholeness only through self-annihilation; it is to identify with a nostalgia rooted in the desire for death.

Covering our ears

The experience of Pfitzner's *Trauermarsch* has been characterised in terms of absence and a subsequent compensation for that loss. The combination of Minneleide's 'hidden' body and the dispersal of her *Klagegesang* was seen to stand for a fantasy of fragmentation that was answered later in the *Trauermarsch*, as Siegnot was eulogised by musical images of consolidation and wholeness. But orchestral interludes can equally centre on excess, on an overwhelming flood of musical immediacy. Sound, by its very nature, calls into question the borders of the body. Unlike sight, it penetrates the body, resisting attempts to shut it out. As Friedrich Kittler puts it,

Sound . . . pierces the armour called Ego, for among all of the sensory organs, the ears are the hardest to close.[40]

Kittler's observation is directed specifically towards the Wagnerian music drama, and what he calls the 'amplifier' function of the orchestra. 'The all-pervasive power of sound,' he argues, 'sustains Wagner's artistic imperialism.'[41] For Kittler Wagner renounced music as such, and replaced it with 'pure dynamics and pure acoustics'[42] which have the effect not of persuading, but of overwhelming the subject. Mann conveys a sense of this quality in *Reflections* when he describes an outdoor performance of the *Götterdämmerung Trauermarsch* in Rome:

I shall never forget how the Nothung motif welled up for the second time, amidst the cries of 'Evviva!' and 'Abbasso!', unfolding its mighty rhythms above the bawling factions, and how, when it reached its climax in that shattering dissonance that precedes the twice-repeated C-major chord, a great howl of triumph broke forth, engulfing the helpless, broken opposition, and cowing them into discomfited silence for some considerable time.[43]

Even without the technical miracle of Bayreuth, the sheer mass of sound has the effect of shock. It presses in upon the body, overwhelming and 'shattering' subjectivity.

In Berg's *Wozzeck* acoustic shock reaches a new level of brutality. The whole idea of music as shock is condensed into the interlude that follows the death of Marie in Act III, Scene 2. In keeping with the unifying principle of the scene ('Invention on a Note'), melody is abolished in favour of

---

[40] Kittler, 'World-Breath: On Wagner's Media Technology', p. 222.   [41] Ibid.
[42] Ibid.   [43] In Blunden (ed. and trans.), *Thomas Mann: Pro and Contra Wagner*, p. 57.

a sustained B natural that forms the basis for two extraordinary crescendos for full orchestra, the first on a single unison B without percussion, the second in octaves with percussion. Beginning *ppp*, each crescendo builds gradually, adding instruments as it goes, and reaching a climax on a terrifying *fff*. Here music becomes sound in the truest sense, a wave of noise that challenges the listener not to cover his/her ears. And, as if the effect needed any heightening, the final *fff* gives way abruptly to an out-of-tune piano and the rising of the curtain on the following tavern scene. Here shock as noise is supplemented by rapid and unexpected change, a bombardment effect that Walter Benjamin detected in cinema. In 'The Work of Art in the Age of Mechanical Reproduction' he argues that the effect of shock 'should be cushioned by heightened presence of mind', but cinema, with its barrage of images and sounds, promotes a state of 'distraction'; it suggests a deliberate exposure to shock that represents an 'adjustment to the dangers' of industrialised society.[44] With its rapid succession of brief scenes, *Wozzeck* can be read in very similar terms. Shock as noise potentially alienates the subject, forcing us to recoil and cover our ears. But shock as bombardment catches the subject unawares, 'penetrating the armour called ego'. 'How much is added,' wrote critic Arthur Jacobs, 'by the fact that the crescendo takes place in the darkened theatre, with the curtain down, and that the piano's entry coincides with the raising of the curtain on the populated interior of the shabbily-lit tavern!'[45]

Respite

It is in the aftermath of this experience, compounded by the rush of events that culminate in Wozzeck's suicide, that the curtain finally descends for what Berg called an 'Epilogue'. To quote the last of the *Altenberg Lieder*, 'Here is peace, here I pour out my tears.' Here in the lyrical D minor opening, with its rich post-Wagnerian harmony and string-dominated texture, is a musical trope of mourning, a call to lament the dead. For Berg it represented

a confession of the author who now steps outside the dramatic action on the stage. Indeed, it is, as it were, an appeal to humanity through its representatives, the audience.[46]

Certainly the Epilogue is vividly marked by difference. One of these differences is a sustained and unambiguous tonal centre in contrast to

[44] Walter Benjamin, 'The Work of Art in the Age of Mechanical Reproduction' (1935), in Hannah Arendt (ed.), *Illuminations*, trans. Harry Zohn (New York, Schocken Books, 1969), p. 238.

[45] Arthur Jacobs, 'An Expectation Fulfilled', *Musical Times* 93 (March 1952), 127.

[46] Alban Berg, 'A Lecture on *Wozzeck*' (1929), in Douglas Jarman (ed.), *Alban Berg: 'Wozzeck'* (Cambridge: Cambridge University Press, 1989), p. 169.

Example 4.8   Berg, Piano Sonata in D minor and *Wozzeck*, Epilogue

the fleeting tonal references throughout the remainder of the opera. Tonality surfaces repeatedly in *Wozzeck*, but only here is a single key clearly stated, departed from, and re-established so unambiguously.[47]

Another difference lies in the apparent motivic independence of the opening material of the Epilogue from the remainder of the opera. The first nineteen bars of the Epilogue are in fact based on the opening of an abandoned Piano Sonata in D minor, one of a series of sketches dating from Berg's apprenticeship with Schoenberg.[48] It is possible, indeed, to align the first seven bars of the Epilogue on an almost note-for-note basis with bars 2–8 of the Sonata (example 4.8). Nor do the opening fifteen

[47] When Emil Petschnig suggested in *Die Musik* that 'the tonality of the interlude is not up to much' and that 'after two pages the flat is completely cancelled (it apparently being unnecessary)', Berg responded, rather defensively, that the interlude is a 'three-part structure in D minor . . . the middle section which follows this cancellation leads back to the main key, in which the piece now continues and in which the adagio finishes as clearly as it began'. See Emil Petschnig, 'Creating Atonal Opera', *Die Musik* 16/5 (February 1924), trans. in Jarman (ed.), *Alban Berg: 'Wozzeck'*, p. 146, and Berg, 'The Musical Forms in My Opera *Wozzeck*', *Die Musik* 16/8 (May 1924), trans. in Jarman (ed.), *Alban Berg: 'Wozzeck'*, p. 151.

[48] The sketch for the Sonata (housed in the Austrian National Library) is reproduced in facsimile in Jarman (ed.), *Alban Berg: 'Wozzeck'*, p. 91.

bars make any *overt* leitmotivic reference. In this they stand out; there are few other passages of similar duration – and certainly none in the interludes – that so pointedly lack leitmotifs. It is as if the opening of the Epilogue is advertising its difference – it wants us to believe that it is independent from the diegesis.[49]

Unlike the ambiguous extradiegetic voices that we noted in *Götterdämmerung* and *A Village Romeo and Juliet*, then, Berg's virtual author insists on difference from the diegesis: it confesses, as Berg put it. And if the effect in *Götterdämmerung* is an unintentional alienation, the Epilogue achieves a calculated reversal that, in effect, alienates itself from alienation. In other words, it substitutes the consistently alienating and shocking effect of the opera as a whole with a contrasting position that invites reflection and identification. After the fragmenting experience of shock that has characterised the fourteen cinematically brief scenes, a subject position emerges that seems to take stock. Joseph Kerman characterises the effect in terms of a 'sanity and relief in warm contrast to the hysterical world of the stage, from which the audience has just been rescued'.[50] Where the diegesis had seemed to offer no single, stable subject position, bombarding and buffeting the spectator, the subject of the Epilogue represents a desirable respite from shock and a healing unity. Partly a bystander, partly a mourner, and insistent about its remoteness from the action, this compassionate subject is perfectly placed to encourage identification. From the fragmented position(s) of the exhausted spectator, it amounts to an ideal ego.

No sooner has this appeal been established, however, than an ambiguity sets in. Beginning at bar 335, references to Act I, Scene 2, begin to undermine the emphatic independence of the Epilogue's subject. A

[49] Allen Forte has extracted from the opening of the Epilogue a number of pitch-class sets which function, he claims, as recurring motifs 'beneath the surface', each with a specific dramatic association. The implication, then, is that Berg, consciously or unconsciously, developed some of the musical material of the opera out of these bars, and that this development was based on *unordered* collections contained within it. Berg's own analysis, true to Schoenberg's teaching, reveals an acute awareness of motivic pregnancy based on the most minute details of a motif's intervallic content: see, for example, his 'Die musikalische Impotenz der "neuen Ästhetik" Hans Pfitzners', *Anbruch* 2/11–12 (June 1920), in which he subjects Schumann's *Kinderszenen* to detailed analysis as a response to the concept of compositional inspiration (*Einfall*) laid out in Pfitzner's *Die neue Ästhetik der musikalischen Impotenz*. Even if we accept Forte's argument, however, the 'surface' independence of the opening remains. Allen Forte, 'Berg's Symphonic Epilogue to *Wozzeck*', in David Gable and Robert Morgan (eds.), *Alban Berg: Historical and Analytical Perspectives* (Oxford: Clarendon Press, 1991).

[50] Joseph Kerman, *Opera as Drama* (New York: Alfred A. Knopf, 1956; rev. edn. Berkeley: University of California Press, 1988), p. 187.

quotation of Andres's hunting song, 'Das ist die schöne Jägerei', repeats almost literally its appearance in the interlude following Act I, Scene 2; there, as now, it was scored for two horns 'as if in the distance', an obvious reference to the hunting imagery of the song. Now the Epilogue seems only too anxious to stress its relationship with – or perhaps knowledge of – the diegesis. Indeed, most of the remainder of the interlude is saturated with motivic reference, a 'veritable feast of associations', as Mann described the *Götterdämmerung Trauermarsch*. Like a eulogy the motifs review the characters and events of Wozzeck's life 'eins nach dem andern': the Captain, the Doctor, the Drum-Major, the sexual encounter of Marie and the Drum-Major (although not Marie herself!), Wozzeck's 'Wir arme Leut' motif, and his theme from the triple fugue in Act II, Scene 2. And like Pfitzner's *Trauermarsch* the quotations seem to be based on literal fragments of the past. The canonic treatment of the Captain's motif (bars 349ff.), for example, recalls its repeated contrapuntal manipulation as the first theme of the triple fugue in Act II, Scene 2, but particularly bar 322 of that scene, when the Captain taunts Wozzeck about Marie's infidelity (example 4.9). In both cases the motif is harmonised in thirds and successively imitated canonically at the fourth.

Example 4.9   Berg, *Wozzeck*, Act II, Scene 2

If these literal quotations recall Pfitzner's *Trauermarsch*, with its nostalgic reminiscences, do they then represent a (perverse) nostalgia for the shock atmosphere of the diegesis? For Adorno the answer is quite the opposite. He characterises the leitmotif in Berg as an effective 'medium for shock absorption'.[51] Citing in particular a demisemiquaver motif associated with Wozzeck himself (Epilogue, bar 345), Adorno argues that 'the more openly it appears in the course of the opera, the more willingly does it renounce its claim to be taken literally: it establishes itself as a vehicle of expression, and repetition softens its effect'.[52] By renouncing the succession of ever-new, ever-unfamiliar material, then, Berg blunts the force of shock. In contrast to the 'rapidly revolving pictures' that Adorno perceives in Schoenberg, *Wozzeck* grants musical ideas a history that imparts a comforting familiarity. From this perspective the Epilogue's careful imitation of previous motivic incarnations would be indicative of a desire to distance it further from the diegesis. Far from plunging us back into a state of shock, it would permit a second look, a re-examination, as it were, in the light of day.

Shifting terms of engagement

But perhaps all is not so simple, for there is something here that seems calculated to dispel any complacency. As much as the various motivic quotations carefully preserve the past by imitating pitch and rhythmic values, there is a decided shift in terms of sheer quantity and intensity of sound. These are not fine adjustments of sonority or orchestral balance, but rather an amplification that suggests Kittler's 'pure dynamics and pure acoustics'. The Doctor's leitmotif, for all its many appearances in Act II, Scene 2, as the second theme of the triple fugue, has been presented almost always with soft dynamics for soloists or small groups of instruments. The only exception was its very first appearance at bars 562–4 of Act I, Scene 4, when it was heard in *forte* first violins. But nothing anticipates its *furioso*, *fortissimo* incarnation for two trumpets at bar 345 of the Epilogue.

As for the canonic Captain's motif, in Act II, Scene 2, it was presented respectively by solo violin, cellos, violas, and second violins, all *pianissimo*. And an earlier, albeit less closely related canonic arrangement (bars 307–9) is scored for *forte* solo trumpet, horn, and bass clarinet. But in the Epilogue the canon begins with *forte* full upper strings followed by *fortissimo* horns and trumpets. The real amplification, however, is saved

---

[51] Theodor W. Adorno, *The Philosophy of Modern Music* (1949), trans. Anne G. Mitchell and Wesley V. Blomster (New York: Seabury Press, 1973), p. 30.

[52] Ibid, p. 31.

Example 4.10   Berg, *Wozzeck*, Epilogue

for the 'Wir arme Leut' motif. The canonically imitated melodic line, originally presented by Wozzeck (supplemented by three trombones) and first violins, and building dynamically from *piano* to *fortissimo*, is rescored for four trombones and twelve woodwind that *begin* the motif *fortissimo* and build from there. Meanwhile, the twelve-tone simultaneity that concludes the motif (example 4.10) threatens to rival the crescendo interlude of Act III in its effect. In its original form the chord omits trumpets and all percussion except for timpani, while violas and second violins refrain from joining the crescendo, instead holding a C major triad (*sempre pp*) that spills over into the subsequent episode. In the Epilogue they all rejoin, and it is rather the bass-clef instruments that are omitted. The resulting treble-dominated crescendo lacks the sheer power of the full orchestra in the crescendo interlude, but it more than compensates with the dissonance of its pitch content. Even the hexachord that culminated the first crescendo on the unison B at the end of Act III, Scene 2, is no match for the excruciating dissonance of the Epilogue's twelve-tone chord, a simultaneity that is only partly softened by its arrangement as superimposed thirds. And unlike the *sfffz* hexachord of the crescendo interlude, this dissonance becomes louder and louder. Thus the threat of continual amplification implicit in the B natural crescendos is given renewed power in the form of dissonance. Throughout this 'B' section, it is as if the potentially comforting effect of familiarity is balanced by a technique of magnification that depends on the shock potential of sound itself.

Perhaps, then, the treatment of Adorno's 'Wozzeck' motif at bars 342–5 represents the inauguration of this process, an attempt to counter the cushioning effect of repetition through successive acceleration and dynamic intensification. Adorno argues that Berg's music ultimately confounds the cushioning effect of familiarity through a process of disintegration:

Wozzeck negates its own point of departure precisely in those moments in which it is developed. The impulses of the composition – alive in its musical atoms – rebel against the work proceeding from them. These impulses do not permit lasting resolution.[53]

No sooner do the leitmotifs form themselves, then, than they are subjected to a form of atomisation that breaks them down into their constituent parts. But the Epilogue suggests quite the reverse. It rebels against the cushioning effect of the leitmotif not through fragmentation, but through acoustic amplification. Shock effect is restored through an inflation that allows no comfortable terms of engagement.

By restoring the shock atmosphere of the diegesis, the Epilogue, as suggested before, risks re-alienating the spectator. But just when the compassionate subject of the Epilogue seems furthest away, it reasserts its presence. As the twelve-tone chord reaches its climax it is cut off, not by a curtain, but by the A – D dyad that opens the D minor theme, now intoned *fff* by all the bass-clef instruments (example 4.10). It reminds us – reassures us – that we can identify with this subject, that this is not the alienating world of the diegesis. At the moment we feel compelled to turn away, we are drawn back. Now the subject absorbs the accumulated shock-energy into its D minor voice of compassion. Wozzeck's theme from the triple fugue is now given its most overpowering incarnation (bars 365ff.), but it is harmonised as a chord stream based on the same ninth chord that accompanied the D minor theme during its initial presentation. Meanwhile, a rhythmically augmented version of the theme's first four bars is presented as a kind of *cantus firmus*, dying slowly until it cadences on the ninth chord in its familiar quiet dynamic. Only with the raising of the curtain is the Epilogue's subject left behind, as the alienation of the diegesis returns, embodied in the cruel objectivity of children and a cool, remote, *perpetuum mobile* musical setting.

Sleight of hand

The effect of this final reassertion of the D minor theme adds a twist to something that Metz has attempted to account for in cinema. Incorporating the psychoanalytic concept of disavowal, Christian Metz argues that voice-overs represent the 'ramparts of disbelief':

The distance [they] establish between the action and ourselves comforts our feeling that we are not duped by that action: thus reassured (behind the rampart), we can allow ourselves to be duped by it a bit longer.[54]

[53] Ibid.   [54] Metz, *The Imaginary Signifier*, p. 73.

In this way the voice-over builds into the film the double quality that is associated with disavowal: the subject both acknowledges and denies what he/she perceives. Although he outlines the Freudian definition of disavowal as a reaction to the castration anxiety invoked in the infant male subject by the site of the female genitalia, Metz ultimately turns to a Lacanian reading in which disavowal comes to stand for the 'splittings of belief' that both characterise and constitute subjectivity even before the establishment of sexual difference.[55] In this sense disavowal as applied to the cinema revolves around the tension between the fantasmatic plenitude that it foregrounds and an awareness of the underlying lack of the object, a knowledge which originates within the imaginary but which is fundamental to the symbolic. Disavowal reminds us that the ascendancy of the imaginary in cinema is something that occurs to a subject who has already entered the symbolic order, one who can never fully resubmit to the imaginary.

But Berg's extradiegetic commentary differs in that it is also the very voice that persuades us to believe. On the one hand it insists on its separation from the diegesis, because only then can it encourage belief/identification in the first place. At the same time, however, it attempts to avoid becoming too remote from the action – and thus irrelevant – and so it establishes a relationship to the diegesis with musical reminiscence combined with a revival of its shock atmosphere. But the two attitudes risk becoming two solitudes: a compassionate and inviting subject remote from the action, and a perspective so closely related to the action that it becomes alienating. Kerman, for example, questions the ability of the Epilogue's 'emotional' character to 'adhere' to the action, viewing it rather as 'self-indulgence after the shattering experience to which the audience has found itself subjected'.[56] The solution reveals itself in bar 364, for here the two find a powerful synthesis. By intersecting the shocking effect of the twelve-tone crescendo, the A–D dyad re-establishes the inviting compassion of the Epilogue's subject and its comforting distance from the diegesis. But it only does so by meeting the crescendo on its own terms; it subdues only by matching its power, by pounding out *fff* dynamics of its own. And it shows, in its presentation of Wozzeck's triple fugue theme, that it can match the amplified motifs of the previous section with some inflation of its own. The implication is far-reaching, for it suggests the possibility of a slippage in the gap between compassion and shock, between identification

---

[55] Silverman welcomes what she perceives as a certain 'deconstructive potential' in Metz's position *vis-à-vis* feminist film theory. By stressing those Lacanian 'splittings which precede the Oedipal juncture', she argues, Metz opens up the possibility of conceiving disavowal beyond the limits of sexual difference, of 'dislodging woman from the obligatory acting out of absence and lack'. Silverman, *The Acoustic Mirror*, p. 14.

[56] Kerman, *Opera as Drama*, p. 189.

and alienation. The compelling voice of the D minor subject proves capable of sliding into shock effect without losing its identity, which is another way of saying that shock can be both unleashed and concealed at the same time. Through a conflation that is as cunning as it is deceptive, Berg's Epilogue creates the conditions in which the very force that threatens to fragment the subject presents itself in the guise of an ideal ego. The result is that the subject willingly yet unwittingly exposes itself to shock. It is here that we find an echo of Pfitzner's *Trauermarsch*. Just as identification with Pfitzner's ideal ego meant identifying with a death-rooted nostalgia, so Berg's spectator comes to identify, perversely, with the fragmentation of his/her own subjectivity.

Perhaps from one perspective these perverse reversals could be interpreted as revelatory, even liberating. Both potentially expose the process of subject formation for the *méconnaissance* that it is. They reveal how easily the narcissistic desire for completion can lead the subject into the most paradoxical of identifications, even to the demise of that which it seeks in the first place. But there nevertheless remains a sense of something highly calculated, to the point of manipulation. It is difficult not to see in these clever reversals, conflations, and concealments some trace of the techniques of propaganda. Particularly relevant is the idea of making subjects recognise as their own decision what has actually been dictated to them. This sleight of hand begins with the cultural trope of mourning and its appeal to a community united in grief. For Durkheim,

the foundation of mourning is the impression of loss which the group feels when it loses one of its members. But this very impression results in bringing individuals together, in putting them into closer relations with one another, in associating them all in the same mental state.[57]

Drawing this sense of unity into the theatre, these operatic laments equate the dead characters with the lost member of the community and the audience with the community itself. They are, as Berg describes them, 'representatives of humanity'.[58] Positioned as unified mourners, they accede willingly to the orchestral eulogist and identify with his/her image of the deceased (Pfitzner) or with the compassion of the eulogist him/herself (Berg).

Lacan relates the formation of subjectivity to the question that he sees as central to Freud's work: 'What is a Father?' Freud's answer, according to Lacan, is: 'It is the dead Father.'[59] What determines the subject more than the real father is the symbolic, law-giving Name-of-the-Father, an

[57] Emile Durkheim, *The Elementary Forms of the Religious Life* (1912), trans. Joseph Ward Swain (London: George Allen and Unwin, 1915), p. 401.
[58] Berg, 'A Lecture on *Wozzeck*', in Jarman (ed.), *Alban Berg: 'Wozzeck'*, p. 169.
[59] Lacan, *Ecrits*, p. 310.

authority that is only enhanced in death, from where demands cannot be questioned or reasoned with: the ghost of the dead Father speaks with absolute authority. What the Oedipus complex does is to trace the process by which the subject gives up competing with this symbolic authority and identifies with it, assuming the position occupied by the dead Father.[60] Lacan sees this Oedipal identification as straddling the boundary between the imaginary and the symbolic, and he maps this onto the distinction between ideal ego and ego ideal. Where (primary) identification in the imaginary is characterised by an aggressive tension between the wholeness of the projected image (ideal ego) and the fragmented experience of the body, symbolic (secondary) identification involves an introjection (ego ideal) that internalises the image of what preceded the subject, namely the Father. It suggests an internalisation of, and adaptation to, the symbolic order (the order of the Law and of the Father). There is, in other words, a normalising and conforming function to Oedipal identification, and Lacan relates the Father to the 'pacifying function of the ego ideal'.[61] Not that these two levels of identification happen in sequence: rather, they continue to interact. For Lacan, any identification will always partake of and depend on the imaginary, even if its ultimate effect is to move beyond the imaginary to the symbolic. Applied to orchestral eulogies, this might mean that the two registers work simultaneously, that we encounter an imaginary environment that encourages identification, while the images of the mourned dead take on the symbolic role of dead Fathers. Identification finds fertile ground in the darkened theatre with its hidden musicians, and for the spectator beset by fantasies of fragmentation, whether the scattered body images in *Die Rose vom Liebesgarten* or the shock effects in *Wozzeck*, the musically constructed subject that emerges seems to offer a particularly ideal ego. This orchestral subject assumes, like the dead Father, a position of authority and perfection, a position unattainable for the living, all too imperfect staged subjects that it now 'remembers'. It takes up a position of authority within the ego, standing, as Freud argued, for 'the perfections we have striven to reach for our own ego'.

---

[60] Lacanian theory emphasises the impossibility of simultaneously 'being' and 'thinking'. The 'I' of language and thought is a substitution that stands in for my being, but it is always a substitution: my being is elided the moment the signifier 'I' stands in for it, so that Lacan reads the Cartesian *cogito* ('I think therefore I am') as 'I am not where I think and I think where I am not'. Lacan stresses that the ghost of the dead Father does not know that he is dead: the survival of his symbolic role depends on this. My 'I' emerges precisely when I substitute myself for the dead Father, assume that role for myself, so that, like him, I am unaware of my 'self': 'Being of non-being, that is how "I" as subject comes on the scene, conjugated with the double aporia of a true survival that is abolished by knowledge of itself, and by a discourse in which it is death that sustains existence.' Ibid., p. 300.

[61] Ibid., p. 22.

Artificial regression

It was to Freud's theory of group psychology that Adorno turned when he attempted to theorise the mechanisms of fascist propaganda:

What happens when masses are caught by fascist propaganda is not a spontaneous, primary expression of instincts and urges but a quasi-scientific revitalization of their psychology – the artificial regression described by Freud in his discussion of organized groups. The psychology of the masses has been taken over by their leaders and transformed into a means for their domination.[62]

It is precisely this 'artificial regression' that characterises the strategies encoded in these interludes. If operatic representations of mourning seem a long way from mass indoctrination and fascist leaders, there nevertheless remains a similarity between the manipulative effects we have detected here and the carefully presented persuasion that lies at the heart of the propaganda deployed by fascism.

It is in this disguised suppression of the individual will that a sympathy with the dead can be seen to touch on one of the ramifications of a 'sympathy with death'. With the 1925 publication of the 'little novel' – *The Magic Mountain*, actually Mann's longest – Mann demonstrated that the ambivalence underlying *Reflections*, if not resolved, had certainly taken another step towards an acceptance of democratic, liberal values. Mann's stance alienated the conservative nationalists who had once considered him an ally, among them Pfitzner, who signalled his displeasure in a strangely confrontational birthday greeting.[63] Mann responded:

The modest hero of my last novel is occasionally called a 'problem child of life'. All of us artists are life's problem children, but we are children of life all the same, and whatever the romantic license of the musician may be, a literary artist who in such a moment of European history as the present did not choose the party of life and the future as against the fascination of death would truly be an unprofitable servant.[64]

Confronting the rise of an official fascism, Mann insists that a 'sympathy with death', something to which he had once resigned himself, now

---

[62] Adorno, 'Freudian Theory and the Pattern of Fascist Propaganda', in J. M. Bernstein (ed.), *The Culture Industry*, trans. Andrew Arato and Eike Gebhardt (London: Routledge, 1991), p. 130.

[63] Pfitzner wrote: 'So I would like to say what you have probably felt for some time, that your recent public "political" (to use a not quite applicable word) declarations have sadly estranged me from you.' Letter to Thomas Mann, 18 June 1925, in Bernhard Adany (ed.), *Hans Pfitzner: Briefe* (Tutzing: Hans Schneider, 1991), p. 405.

[64] Letter to Hans Pfitzner, 23 June 1925, in Richard Winston and Clara Winston (eds. and trans.), *Letters of Thomas Mann, 1889–1955* (New York: Alfred A. Knopf, 1971), p. 145.

reveals itself as the seed of a nationalism in which the individual will might find its true antithesis.

Not that *Die Rose vom Liebesgarten* or *Wozzeck* were ever to find an audience under National Socialism (*Götterdämmerung*, of course, is another matter). *Die Rose vom Liebesgarten* all but disappeared from the repertoire long before the rise of National Socialism, but it is unlikely that it would have fared well under Nazi cultural policy, which was never able comfortably to embrace Pfitzner and the qualities of 'romantic pessimism'[65] he seemed to embody. Meanwhile, *Wozzeck*, like all Berg's music, fell victim first to *de facto* then to official suppression. Besides, *Wozzeck* would seem to question the very kinds of authoritarian brutality on which National Socialism was based. The point, rather, is to understand how opera, and specifically music, might reflect and participate in the formation of fascist attitudes, not merely in their overt political form, but, as Jeremy Tambling has persuasively argued, as ideological undercurrents of culture.[66] It is to understand how these orchestral interludes, because they play a role in the construction and legitimisation of identities, might function ideologically in ways that extend and even contradict the values of the drama in which they are embedded.

One of the issues at stake here is the idea of aesthetic autonomy, the perceived ability of art – above all, music – to transcend the merely fashionable, the material, the contingent, and the political. This is a question raised by the novelist Soma Morgenstern, one of Berg's closest friends. In his collection of memoirs, *Alban Berg und seine Idole*, Morgenstern describes an exchange with Berg over Schoenberg and what Morgenstern felt was the latter's outdated and uncritical reverence for the figure of the heroic, misunderstood Romantic artist. For Morgenstern, Schoenberg had held on to the Romantic concept of 'shocking the bourgeoisie' in an era characterised by 'powers more alive and dangerous than the bourgeoisie ever were',[67] while his uncompromising modernism had rendered his music not so much shocking as irrelevant.[68] Berg, he writes, ultimately agreed that his teacher might be out of step, although he had added wryly that he would avoid presenting the argument to Schoenberg himself. What was not discussed, according

---

[65] Heidegger uses the phrase to describe Wagner. See Martin Heidegger, *Nietzsche*, 2 vols., trans. David Farrell Krell (New York: Harper and Row, 1979), vol. I, *The Will to Power as Art* (1961), p. 133, cited in Jeremy Tambling, *Opera and the Culture of Fascism* (Oxford: Clarendon Press, 1996), p. 69.

[66] Tambling analyses opera in terms of the 'nostalgia for power it can give its listeners' and relates this tendency to fascist attitudes in late nineteenth- and early twentieth-century European culture. Tambling, *Opera and the Culture of Fascism*, p. 5.

[67] Soma Morgenstern, *Alban Berg und seine Idole: Erinnerungen und Briefe* (Lüneburg: zu Klampen, 1995), p. 321.

[68] Ibid., p. 322.

to Morgenstern, was the broader question of art's political and social relevance:

In my conversations with Alban I never called into question the holiness of art. I myself had not yet gone that far (or perhaps not yet sunk so low – depending on one's perspective).[69]

How much more acute the problem when the subject is music, with its history of absolutist isolation. Mann articulates the problem when he distinguishes his political responsibilities as 'literary artist' from those of Pfitzner 'the musician', as though music might not participate in the struggle of ideas. Perhaps it is this very impression of music's 'romantic license', of its remoteness from the real world, that allows it to become such a powerful ideological tool in the first place.

[69] Ibid., p. 324. Berg uses the phrase 'holiness of art' in the article 'Two Feuilletons', reprinted in Willi Reich, *Alban Berg*, trans. Cornelius Cardew (New York: Vienna House, 1974), p. 219.

5

'A torrent of unsettling sounds'

One peculiarly Viennese realisation of the tensions generated by the 'absolute music' debate is to be found in Berg's obvious ambivalence towards opera and music drama. The appeal in *Wozzeck* to the forms of instrumental music, for example, can be read as an attempt to bridge the uncomfortable gap between the daunting Viennese classical heritage, embodied for Berg in the imposing figure of Schoenberg, and what appeared to be, in comparison, the popular and grossly theatrical character of opera.[1] And the alienating effect of so much of the opera is certainly at odds with the kind of total engagement and communal sympathy imagined by Wagner. Nevertheless, the effect of the Epilogue – occupying, as it does, such a pivotal role in the opera – is to (re)situate the opera very much within operatic, and specifically Wagnerian, tradition. *Wozzeck* appears to re-evaluate the genre, only to fall back on familiar gestures.

Quite the reverse is true of Berg's contemporary and fellow Viennese, Franz Schreker. Here is a figure whose operas at first glance represent a more orthodox Wagnerism, who was in fact hailed as Wagner's successor by Paul Bekker.[2] Rejecting the idea of *Literaturoper* (operatic settings, like Berg's, of more or less intact plays), Schreker followed Wagner in writing his own dramatic texts, which tend to combine the fantastical, the idealistic, and the sensual in a not un-Wagnerian manner. His music, too, possesses an emotionally charged, intoxicating, palpable quality that had always been central to the success of Wagnerian music drama, even if it had not always been acknowledged (and here Schreker found himself at odds with the Viennese legacy, for these were the aspects of the Wagnerian heritage most inimical to classical values).[3] But, as we shall see from Schreker's most popular opera, *Der Schatzgräber*, these

---

[1] In his 1929 lecture on *Wozzeck*, for example, Berg is anxious to distinguish between the 'vague self-sufficient sonorities' characteristic of 'impressionism' and his own impressionistic effects, which have 'more to do with the building of a whole musical structure according to rigorous principles'. In Jarman (ed.), *Alban Berg: 'Wozzeck'*, p. 169.

[2] Paul Bekker, *Franz Schreker: Studie zur Kritik der modernen Oper* (Berlin: Schuster and Loeffler, 1919), p. 20.

[3] Berg illustrated the fault lines of Viennese culture when he reported to Schoenberg on Schreker's dramatic reading of the libretto of *Die Gezeichneten*, describing it as 'a bit

Wagnerian qualities mask a deeply embedded critique of the whole premise of music drama and its appeal to magic and metaphysics. Once again an orchestral love scene plays a vital musical and dramatic role, and it is arguably within that scene that the terms of the critique are most clearly articulated. As in our earlier love scenes, too, the intersection of a musical self-referentiality and a narrative of desire has important implications for constructions of gender and sexuality. But unlike the *Liebesszene* of *Feuersnot*, Schreker's scene refuses to align itself unambiguously with any polarising configurations of gender or music. Rather, it seems to highlight the open-ended nature of the questions it poses.

In his review of *Der Schatzgräber*, Bekker encapsulated his reading of the opera in a few words:

> Out of music a fairy-tale dream emerges and loses itself again in music. That is really all; the rest is scenic parable that lures the imagination away from the sensually representable, conceptually graspable and towards the distant regions of dream-life.[4]

Music in the beginning and music at the end – this, for Bekker, is the core of Schreker's opera, perhaps of all his operas. Following Bekker, we might trace the imaginary source of music in *Der Schatzgräber* (*The Treasure-Digger*) to the folk-style ballads that recur throughout the opera. These fairy tales, sung by the opera's principal characters, seem to beget the opera in which they are embedded. Each is a *mise-en-abyme*, a mirror of its surroundings, as if plot, setting, and music all emerged from song. The timeless, magical world of the ballads becomes the fairy-tale kingdom of the opera, while their *völkische Ton* lends the opera a lyrical simplicity and clarity unexpected from the composer of the complex sound-worlds of *Der ferne Klang* and *Die Gezeichneten*. It is a ballad, too, that brings *Der Schatzgräber* to a close, as if the opera were returning to its source, 'losing itself again in music'. Elis, the treasure-digger of the title, accompanies his songs with a lute that resounds magically when treasure is near, and it is the sound of the lute, represented by harp and celeste, that mediates between music heard and unheard. It both resounds literally as music and represents music allegorically, a sonorous trace of a fantasised music that is always just beyond our reach, like the distant sounds of celebration evoked by Elis in his last fairy tale:

> Do you hear the trumpets and cymbals and harps, the jubilation and rejoicing and happy piping?

kitschy'. Letter of 8 May 1912, in Juliane Brand, Christopher Hailey, and Donald Harris (eds. and trans.), *The Berg–Schoenberg Correspondence: Selected Letters* (New York: W. W. Norton, 1987).

[4] Paul Bekker, '*Der Schatzgräber*', *Frankfurter Zeitung*, 21 January 1920, in his *Klang und Eros* (Stuttgart and Berlin: Deutsche Verlags-Anstalt, 1922), p. 48.

This music seems to beckon from beyond the 'sensually representable'; it is a distant sound that, to quote Adorno, 'comes from nowhere and returns to the same place'.[5]

Yet, as both Bekker and Adorno are quick to point out, this 'distant sound' has a double quality. For Adorno, it is 'separated from empirical reality by a heaving abyss, and yet it is essentially sensuous'.[6] Bekker observes that, for all its 'intangibility and immateriality', it is a 'vital impulse capable of inviting both beauty and disaster', a 'seductive, intoxicating sensual power that shapes the emotions and creates them anew'. It is a 'manifestation of extreme subjectivity . . . charged with creative energy and the most marked strivings of our personality'.[7] In Lacanian terms, the distant sound traces desire, pointing the way to that ever-elusive fantasy object that promises to make good all lack. In this sense, far from transcending the body, the distant sound returns precisely to the body, inseparable from the subject's material, erotic impulses.

But the erotic is also given a very different musical representation in *Der Schatzgräber*, one that we might term an 'all too near sound'. Here the orchestra relocates the distant sound as a relentless, overwhelming tide of music that presses in upon the subject (in this case, Elis). This is a music that stresses immediacy and impact; it seems to come from inside rather than from the distance. We hear its deafening roar as though we were listening with the subject's ears. And yet these waves of orchestral sound speak of the same sensuality as does Elis's lute – the difference seems to lie not in the meaning and nature of the sound itself, but in how the subject hears it. The relationship between these ways of hearing lies at the heart of *Der Schatzgräber*, configured in Schreker's music as a conflict that offers no resolution.

Nowhere is the conflict more vividly represented than in the third-act love scene with its duet followed by an orchestrally depicted night of passion. Actually two interludes separated by a brief vocal interjection, this orchestral sex scene, like Strauss's, is performed with the curtain open, but again the stage is discreetly darkened as the moon sinks beneath the horizon. Here the gulf separating the longing for an elusive object from a flood of immediacy is dramatically demonstrated. And it is here that Bekker and Adorno are most at odds. Bekker views the scene as one of the highlights of the opera:

A musical work of an intoxicating sonic splendour, a melodic eloquence of such sweetness and tenderness, an expansive structure of such power – we say it

---

[5] Theodor W. Adorno, 'Schreker' (1959), in *Quasi una fantasia* (1963), trans. Rodney Livingstone (London: Verso, 1992), p. 134.
[6] Ibid., p. 138.   [7] Bekker, *Franz Schreker*, pp. 26–7.

calmly, without in any way approaching too closely and without pronouncing a comparison – as has not been written since *Tristan*.[8]

Adorno, never comfortable with the *Sinnlichkeit* of Schreker's music, sees it as a moment of overindulgence:

[I]n the over-long orchestral interlude in Act III, the erotic centrepiece of the work, the emotional surge becomes a splurge, the representation of inarticulacy itself becomes inarticulate.[9]

But perhaps Adorno's aversion to this aspect of Schreker's music blinds him to the critical force of the scene. Far from simply indulging in an uncontrolled display of musical eroticism, Schreker deliberately problematises the issue of musical sensuality by relating it to the question of music's idealisation. What happens, he seems to ask, when the sensual is renounced in favour of the idea?

Schreker began work on *Der Schatzgräber* in the summer of 1916 and dated its completion '12 November 1918 (on the day of the declaration of the German-Austrian Republic and the union with the German Reich!)'. By the time of its Frankfurt premiere on 21 January 1920, anticipation among critics and audiences had reached fever pitch. The postwar revival of theatrical life had produced the beginnings of the *Schreker Welle* (Schreker wave) as theatres throughout Germany and Austria clamoured to produce *Der ferne Klang* and *Die Gezeichneten*. Judging by attendance and critical reaction, the new opera did not disappoint. In the thirteen years from its premiere to the beginning of the Nazi suppression of Schreker's work, *Der Schatzgräber* was presented on fifty different stages, more than *Der ferne Klang* and *Die Gezeichneten* put together.[10]

Bekker's reaction to the love scene, although in some ways extreme, gives some indication of the kind of enthusiasm with which *Der Schatzgräber* was greeted. The critic of the *Badische Landeszeitung* characterised Schreker's orchestra as 'the most magical instrument any musician has ever mastered',[11] while the *Leipziger Tageblatt*, echoing one of the recurrent themes of Bekker's criticism, hailed Schreker's attention to melody:

And this time Schreker has conquered our hearts more than ever. And what is the reason? Certainly because he, whom over-zealous prophets of his fame had seen in the land of the futurists, remains among us on firm ground, with strong hands and the clearest senses, and because he loves melody. And yet his music is modern in the best sense of the word.[12]

[8] Bekker, '*Der Schatzgräber*', trans. in Christopher Hailey, *Franz Schreker, 1878–1934: A Cultural Biography* (Cambridge: Cambridge University Press, 1993), p. 103.

[9] Adorno, 'Schreker', p. 141.

[10] Matthias Brzoska, *Franz Schrekers Oper 'Der Schatzgräber'* (Stuttgart: Franz Steiner Verlag Wiesbaden, 1988), p. 145.

[11] Trans. in Hailey, *Franz Schreker*, p. 100.   [12] Ibid.

The suggestion here of a conservative retreat from the earlier operas, of a more popular appeal, is a common theme in the *Schatzgräber* criticism, and may help to account for the extraordinary reception the work enjoyed. But just as important for many critics was the unpretentious appeal of Schreker's *Märchen* plot. This was a factor stressed by Bekker:

> There is no constructed principle, no logically defined 'idea' in the vulgar sense, no philosophy, no consciously emphasised 'meaning'. And yet – and this is the artistry – the dramatic events provoke and compel, drawing the spectator under the spell of the action.[13]

In fact, as we shall see, the simplicity of Schreker's plot is deceptive, concealing rich and sometimes contradictory layers of meaning that echo through words, action, scenery, and music. It is to this plot that we must first turn our attention in order to place the love scene in context.

Es war einmal . . .

Described in the list of characters as a 'roaming singer and scholar', Elis emerges as something of a cross between the romanticised notion of the minstrel and Robin Hood. His lute, partly an accompaniment for his songs, also magically seeks out hidden treasure, which Elis distributes to the poor. We first hear of him in the Prologue as the king seeks advice from his wily fool. The queen, it seems, has lost a collection of magic jewels which, she believes, have the power to bestow youth upon her. Deprived of their caress, she has withdrawn from the world and is 'losing her beauty day by day'. Most alarming from the king's perspective, she has withdrawn her sexual favours from him:

> And worst of all, fool, she keeps me at a distance, and when she does yield to me, she does so with sighs.

The fool suggests that Elis, with his magic lute, may be able to relocate the jewels, but the first challenge will be to find this elusive figure 'who travels about, this way and that, without a destination'.

Act I, set in a 'forest tavern', opens to find the innkeeper's daughter, Els, fending off an amorous advance from her fiancé. Els reminds her impatient lover that tomorrow is their wedding day, and that they will soon be together. But in the meantime, he must fetch her the wedding present for which she has asked: 'a gold necklace with five emeralds and a little crown'. Els tells him where he can find it and he sets off into the night. Left alone, Els bursts into an impassioned solo that reveals the

---

[13] Bekker, *'Der Schatzgräber'*, in his *Klang und Eros*, p. 48. Bekker was already familiar with the libretto before the premiere; Schreker had sought Bekker's advice during the drafting of the libretto, as their correspondence demonstrates. See Brzoska, *Der Schatzgräber*, pp. 181ff.

true nature of her plans. The jewellery she desires is in fact part of the queen's collection, and her fiancé is only one of a series of lovers who have been duped into retrieving it for her, piece by piece. Before they could return to claim their 'reward' they have been murdered by Els's servant, Albi, who in turn awaits promised sexual favours. Once again Els dispatches Albi and, while awaiting his return, turns her attention to the next potential victim, the smitten local bailiff.

It is at this point that Elis enters, tired and thirsty after a long journey. His fellow drinkers demand a song, and Elis obliges by recounting his experiences on his journey to the inn. Roaming through the forest his lute had begun to sound, leading him to a tree on which was hung a necklace with five emeralds. He produces the necklace and Els realises that it is the same one she has sent her fiancé to fetch. Noticing Els's astonishment, Elis offers it to her; he is interested not in 'trinkets', but in the 'great treasure of life, the goal of all longing'. Els begs Elis to stay with her, and confesses that his song has made her fall in love with him. Overwhelmed by Els's display of emotion, Elis declares that he shares her feelings and agrees never to leave her. But events intervene: the dead body of Els's fiancé has been discovered, and Elis, with his unlikely story of jewels in the forest, is an obvious suspect. The bailiff sees an opportunity to dispose of a rival suitor, and arrests Elis on a charge of murder.

Act II opens to reveal Els gazing at the gallows on which her lover will shortly meet his end. The fool enters, still unsuccessful in his search for the elusive Elis. Unaware of the fool's quest, Els asks him if he will help free an innocent man. As they converse the fool gradually realises the identity of the condemned man and resolves to return with forces from the king to free Elis. As Elis is led to the gallows, Els instructs him to try to delay the proceedings until the royal forces arrive. Elis sings a rambling song in which he declares that the role of selfless redeemer no longer has any meaning for him. Els's love has opened his eyes to the possibility of his own happiness, and it is to the pursuit of that happiness that he will now devote himself:

I know but one command, a supreme command: Life for myself, joy for myself!

Just when it seems that Elis has run out of time, the royal party arrives and frees him, with the proviso that failure to retrieve the queen's jewels will result in his being publicly flogged and exiled. As Elis is led off to assume his royal mission he promises that he will visit Els the following night. Els immediately realises her predicament: love compels her to assist Elis in his quest by handing over the jewels, but Elis's lute will expose her treasure and take the gesture right out of her hands. The only answer is to steal the lute, and the ever-hopeful Albi is summoned to commit the deed.

Dreams of longing

The third act opens in Els's room at twilight, as Els awaits the arrival of Elis. Schreker's scenic description concludes:

The room is furnished not without a feeling for splendour and luxurious living: Arabic and Oriental influences are to be seen.

In her opening solo Els reveals a very different side to her personality. Here scheming and passion give way to a childlike vulnerability as Els recalls her mother's tender lullaby. Her reverie is brought to an abrupt halt as a distraught Elis enters with the news that his lute has been stolen. Els consoles him with a tantalising promise: she cannot bring his lute back, but she may be able to give him the jewels. Elis is dumbfounded, but Els asks him to make a promise:

Never to ask me how it all happened. Never to torment me with mortifying suspicion. Only to take what my heart gives you from purest, overflowing love?

Elis eagerly consents and Els leaves the room, promising to return in a moment. It is here that the love scene can be said to begin.

Left alone, Elis finds himself bewitched by the setting. His words are worth quoting at length:

Night secretly announces its approach. A torrent of unsettling sounds draws near like waves of misty veils. It sounds like the song of murmuring choirs wafting from distant islands, blissful abodes of earthly happiness. Sweet fragrances envelop me, rock me gently in dreams of longing, dreams in which ancient songs, once sung, die away.

We, too, seem to hear those 'murmuring choirs' as a wordless chorus envelops Elis's solo. Sounding from 'far away behind the scene', the chorus is as elusive to us as it is in Elis's fantasy. As Elis turns to dreams of 'ancient songs', it is the orchestra that echoes the fantasy sound, gently evoking a fragment of a lullaby. But these images of distance are contradicted by a sense of nearness, of being surrounded. Elis's references to sounds that 'draw near' and breezes that 'envelop me' are echoed as he develops his fantasy:

Is it her breath that hovers around me? Or is it a whisper of magic to beguile me, to ensnare me, to dissipate the anxious question that quivers on my lips? What secret does this room conceal? What horror hovers over the form of the bewitching woman who soon will lovingly embrace me?

What emerges is a sense, on the one hand, of Elis as passive recipient, caught up in a field of sounds that enfolds him. But at the same time those sounds remain tantalisingly beyond his reach, demanding that he listen – that is, that he act. And the contradiction goes further, for the experience is presented as both seductive and threatening, pleasurable and horrific. The fantasy space that he has already managed to construct around Els represents something irretrievably alien, but something which he must enter, must hear. Like Esclarmonde's island or Diemut's basket, Els's room is an Other space that invokes fear, and yet there is no question of turning away from it and opting for safety; Elis is compelled by desire to submit and to listen. The position he takes up in his fantasy is never stable, hovering between active and passive, subject and object. In a sense the love scene has begun before Els has even arrived.

The entry of Els, dressed only in diaphanous veils and the queen's jewels, complicates the fantasy question all the more. On the one hand she seems to embody Elis's fantasy image, but on the other attempts to ground that image. Having overheard Elis's last words, she responds:

No horror, my friend! It is the spirits of longing who bewitch you. It is your ardour for me that bewilders you.

But Elis will hear none of it. He continues to indulge his fantasy unabated, addressing Els as a 'goddess from vanished times'. Now that he has found Els, he declares, his former quest seems like nothing more than a delusion:

My foolish striving seems feeble to me. What are the treasures of the whole world, what is the lustre of this poor earth?

The melody to which these words are set (example 5.1) outlines a mode whose prominent augmented seconds connote a characteristically 'Eastern' sound (echoes of Els's decor?). The futility that Elis now attributes to his quest is reflected in what seems to be a deliberately clichéd musical trope of longing, a sound full of Eastern promise but ultimately empty. Els, not some endlessly postponed treasure, is now the object of his desire.

But, as Els realises, the real object of Elis's desire is what he fantasises as Els. Again she tries to confront him with reality:

I am no phantom, my sweet love, no shape from dreams and visions.

This time she begins by appropriating Elis's 'Arabian' mode, as if to incorporate its connotation of falseness. And this time it seems that Elis has heard her, as he joins her in an anticipation of sexual union that allows little room for half-heard sounds and fantasmatic visions:

Ah, vibrant, red, tempestuous blood surges in raging waves! Burn yourself out in fevered veins, glow in wild, consuming flames! Engulf us, world! Absorb us, night! Ah, take possession of us, night!

Here the delicate, shadowy solos and chamber textures that had evoked Elis's visions are engulfed in a torrent of vocal and orchestral sound,

Example 5.1   Schreker, *Der Schatzgräber*, Act III, *Liebesszene*

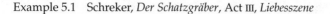

building towards a frenzy that threatens to challenge inhibition and repression. It invokes that 'fear of throwing off all restraint' that Adorno identifies as the 'goal of [Schreker's] best music'.[14] But just as the duet reaches its height, signalled by the indication 'orgiastic' in the score, the momentum dissipates and Elis's fantasy reasserts itself as vividly as ever:

Ah, can you feel it, my love: distant music, the scent of roses, heaven, Eden!

Here the music of the duet becomes a shadow of itself as the surging orchestra gives way to a delicately scored passage for solo violin accompanied by strings, harps, and cor anglais, an ensemble characteristic of Elis's fantasy visions (example 5.2).

As night descends and darkness obscures the stage, the first of the two interludes begins, dominated at first by the sound of distant music. But *Steigerung* is in the air, summoned literally by Schreker's direction 'Mehr und mehr gesteigert', but also evoked through dynamics, *accelerando*, an increasingly restless juxtaposition of material from the duet, and a chromatic harmonic ascent in the bass. Finally, the distant music is all but swept away as the orchestra brings the scene ever closer to a powerful climax. The passion is brought to a halt as Els once again seeks her lover's assurance that he will never ask 'how it all happened'. The interruption seems to trigger the distant sound (solo violin and woodwind) yet again, but now the impression is that Elis is only too eager to return to the 'all

[14] Adorno, 'Schreker', p. 133.

137

Example 5.2   Schreker, *Der Schatzgräber*, Act III, *Liebesszene*

too near' sound. As Els's words echo in his unconscious (three offstage female voices doubling muted trumpets),[15] an agitated Elis assures his lover that he will respect her wishes:

Never, never, I swear to you! Do not think about it! I love you, I love you, for ever, for ever!

Finally, just as they had called upon it to do, night 'takes possession' of the lovers. In the darkness the orchestra makes it quite clear that Elis has given up on his distant sounds, allowing himself to be swept up in the immediate pleasure that Els has promised him.

Maintaining a distance

How, then, are we to interpret Elis's initial stubborn resistance to the immediate pleasure that Els offered? Why did he continually displace and fantasise? In Lacanian terms the drives associated with desire (scopic, invocatory) are distinguished from those of demand (anal, oral) precisely by their dependence on distance. Metz's observations on the scopic drive might equally apply to Elis's distant sounds:

The voyeur is very careful to maintain a gulf, an empty space, between the object and the eye, the object and his own body . . . The voyeur represents in space the

---

[15] In the score Schreker indicates that 'the singers (definitely soloists!) should be positioned near the trumpets, unobserved by the audience, so that it will be difficult to tell whether it is actually being sung in the orchestra, or whether the vague sound is deceiving our senses'.

fracture which forever separates him from the object; he represents his very dissatisfaction (which is precisely what he needs as a voyeur), and thus also his satisfaction . . . To fill in this distance would threaten to overwhelm the subject, to lead him to consume the object . . . to bring him to orgasm and the pleasure of his own body, hence to the exercise of other drives, mobilizing the senses of contact and putting an end to the scopic arrangement.[16]

Distance, then, is the very condition by which the scopic and invocatory drives are activated. The gap between subject and object – the lack – that lies at the heart of desire is replayed through the distance of the viewed or heard object.

In Elis's case that distance is continually challenged, and desire threatens to collapse into orgasm. His response, motivated by the preservation of desire, is to fantasise distance, to stave off the collapse of desire by 'relocating' the object. This fantasmatic distancing, however, is always under siege, hence the images of 'closing in' and 'surrounding' that haunt Elis's fantasies. And, as Jacqueline Rose has observed in her critique of Metz, there is more than distancing here – there is also externalisation.[17] This is the positioning that Laplanche and Pontalis emphasise when they characterise fantasy as a *mise en scène* of desire. Elis projects himself as an active subject who *listens* for sounds in the distance. But he also takes up a position as object of the soundscape – not so much listener as involuntary *hearer* of sounds that press in upon him. Eventually he can maintain the distance no longer, and the result is indeed orgasm, something about which Schreker's music leaves no doubt. These fantasmatic transformations of the object of desire recall the Freudian concept of idealisation. Unlike sublimation, in which 'the accent falls upon deflection from sexuality', idealisation 'aggrandises' and 'exalts' the object of desire without necessarily affecting the 'libidinal instincts'.[18] As we have seen, far from deflecting desire the distance of the sound is its very support.

But how does this relate to Elis's intellectual/spiritual quest, his 'idea'? Can we detect here an extension of the idealisation responsible for Elis's aural and visual projections, and does this imply a deflection of sexuality that touches on Freudian sublimation? Schreker's own commentary on the opera, published in the programme of the Frankfurt Opera, can be seen to both affirm and question the complicity between body and mind/soul.[19] Schreker describes Elis as a kind of 'missionary . . . who brings redemption to the unredeemable'. Until he meets Els

---

[16] Metz, *The Imaginary Signifier*, p. 120.

[17] Jacqueline Rose, *Sexuality in the Field of Vision* (London: Verso, 1986), p. 196.

[18] Freud, 'On Narcissism: An Introduction', *Standard Edition*, vol. XII, p. 94.

[19] Franz Schreker, 'Der Schatz – seine Hüter und sein Orchester', in Emil Pirchan, *Das Werk der Staatsoper: Der Schatzgräber* (Berlin: F. Gurlitt, 1922), reprinted in Brzoska, *Der Schatzgräber*, p. 204.

his commitment is above all to his idea: 'he will find the treasure, redeem the queen, accomplish his mission'.[20] But the love scene represents a turning point for Elis. In Schreker's words, Elis experiences an 'unconscious awakening' of 'every great emotion that any man experiences when he can bring his sensual urges into harmony with his highest idea'.[21] That moment of 'harmony' is signalled immediately after the night of passion when Elis awakens to find Els laying the jewels at his feet. Content with what she has already given him, Elis is reluctant to take the gift, but Els insists:

I beg you with all my heart, oh take it, it is deliverance for me.

Here Elis and Els redeem each other: sexual pleasure is complemented by a 'higher' satisfaction. On the one hand Schreker seems reluctant to give up on the notion of the genius who summons inspiration from a place that is remote from sensuality. His characterisation of Elis's experience as a 'harmony' of idea and sensuality suggests a temporary co-existence, a fortuitous convergence, rather than any deep interdependence. Schreker presents Elis's pleasure as stemming from the simultaneous satisfaction of impulses that remain separate from each other. At the same time, however, the flood of emotion that Schreker attributes to this convergence hints at the stakes involved here. It suggests that idea and sensuality should indeed converge, that they were always meant to be in harmony.

It is the latter possibility that seems to underpin the opera itself. If Elis's idea – his role as redeemer – is symbolised by his ongoing quest for the 'great treasure of life', then his lute represents what Schreker calls his 'power' and 'genius'.[22] It is the mediator between Elis and his idea, the means by which the idea realises itself to him. But the lute's musical representation, a distant sound, suggests that, like Elis's fantasies, his idea is a quest for an elusive object, an object that remains desirable because of its very elusiveness. Compare, for example, the orchestra's evocation of the lute at bars 176ff. (example 5.3) to one of Elis's fantasy visions ('Sweet fragrances envelop me, rock me gently in dreams of longing') (example 5.4). More telling still is Els's assurance (bars 285ff.) that Elis himself is the source of the sounds and visions ('It is the spirits of longing who bewitch you. It is your ardour for me that bewilders you'). Here her words are accompanied not only by the sounds of the lute, but by the treasure motif, musical symbol of Elis's idea (example 5.5).

Musically aligned with his aural fantasies, Elis's idea emerges as a fantasy itself, a deferral of the material and sensual in the interests of a 'higher' purpose. The implications for the artist are clear: the 'genius' of Elis the musician – his artistic idea – is ultimately a sublimation of

[20] Ibid.   [21] Ibid.   [22] Ibid.

Example 5.3   Schreker, *Der Schatzgräber*, Act III, *Liebesszene*

sensuality, but it is only through sublimation that sensual experience is recognised as 'art' in the first place. In this sense sublimation is both a distortion and an obligation. Overindulged, it runs the risk of losing sight of sensuality altogether, of obscuring the material, embodied foundations on which all art rests. Its absence, however, raises the spectre of the inability to meet what Adorno called the 'demands of culture', a problem with which Schreker was all too familiar.[23] As an 'artist' accused of failing to satisfy the demands of 'art', Schreker was fully caught up in the cultural struggle born of sublimation. But, as Schreker's ambiguous positioning in his article suggests, this struggle also manifests itself internally. The idea of the aesthetic, inherited from the nineteenth century and reinforced by modernism, is something to which Schreker maintained allegiance, even as 'he consciously desert[ed] to the realm which culture has distanced itself from and consigned to the vulgar'.[24] His is a vision of music that, to quote Peter Franklin, 'maintains the highest ideals while being eagerly complicit with the shady and even shocking motives of opera librettists and Hollywood film producers alike'.[25]

[23] Adorno, 'Schreker', p. 143.   [24] Ibid.
[25] Peter Franklin, 'Distant Sounds – Fallen Music: *Der ferne Klang* as "Woman's Opera"?', *Cambridge Opera Journal* 3 (1991), 172.

Example 5.4   Schreker, *Der Schatzgräber*, Act III, *Liebesszene*

Example 5.5   Schreker, *Der Schatzgräber*, Act III, *Liebesszene*

It is the inability to come to terms with the relationship between the idealistic and the pleasurable that Bekker identifies as the 'tragedy' of Schreker's male characters. Summarising the operas prior to *Der Schatzgräber*, he identifies what he calls the 'irresolvable conflict between the natural law and genius'.[26] In *Die Gezeichneten* Alviano is driven to madness by the horrific consequences of that conflict when his island paradise, a manifestation of his genius, proves to be the source of an intoxicating sensuality that gives rise to debauchery and ultimately claims his beloved Carlotta. And in *Der ferne Klang* Fritz acknowledges the sensual truth of his creative impulse only when disavowal has already taken a fatal toll on him. Is tragedy then in store for Elis? His moment of 'harmony' certainly represents no realisation about the true nature of his idea, merely a temporary simultaneity of what for him are two solitudes.

In fact Schreker seems to break from the pattern established in the earlier operas. Act IV returns to the king's palace where Elis is the subject of much royal praise. Asked to explain his discovery of the jewels, Elis relates the events of Act III as a ballad in which Els's identity is carefully disguised. But his anger at seeing the jewels in the queen's hands instead of Els's gets the better of him, and he rebukes the king and queen for wasting the jewels, demanding that they be returned. Elis finds himself in grave danger of being put to death for his insult, when suddenly the bailiff enters with Albi in custody. Albi has revealed all, and Els stands accused of murder. Scarcely able to believe his ears, Elis pleads with Els to tell him that it is all a 'bad dream', but Els can only justify her actions by assuring Elis that what she did 'was done from love'. The fool steps in to save Els's life by claiming her as the bride he had been promised for his part in the recovery of the jewels. Elis, however, can find no forgiveness within him; as Els holds out her hand pleading for his understanding, he turns his back on her and walks away.

When, in the Epilogue, he responds to the fool's plea to visit the now dying Els, he is a transformed man. As Schreker puts it:

In the end Elis has found his way again. He is free of all feelings of sensuality, but remains a friend, redeemer, [a] kind, understanding man.[27]

The suggestion here is that Elis has turned his back not only on Els but on his sexuality. Like a Wagnerian hero, Elis seems to have engaged in an act of renunciation, an outcome that seems entirely at odds with the message of Schreker's early operas. Granted, the revelations of Els's past come as a tremendous shock to Elis, but they fail to explain his apparently total sacrifice of sensuality on the altar of the idea.

---

[26] Bekker, *Franz Schreker*, p. 43.   [27] Schreker, 'Der Schatz', p. 204.

'It gleams and sparkles'

In many ways Elis's victory over himself suggests the asceticism proposed by Otto Weininger as the only means for man to overcome the feminine, sexual aspects of his nature and aspire to the higher existence that is his alone:

Since the absolute female has no trace of individuality and will, no sense of worth or of love, she can have no part in the higher transcendental life. Some sort of relation to the idea of supreme value, to the idea of the absolute, that perfect freedom which he has not yet attained, because he is bound by necessity, but which he can attain because man is superior to matter; such a relation to the purpose of things generally, or to the divine, every man has.[28]

Weininger's psycho-sexual pathology seeks to characterise the traits of the absolute male and female, and although he is quick to point out that any individual will fall between these absolutes, his conclusions suggest a rigid sexual differentiation founded on biological essentialism (notice, for example, how Weininger begins with the 'absolute female', but ends with 'every man').

Elis's 'highest idea' would seem to correspond to Weininger's 'idea of supreme value' with its suggestion of longing for something not yet attained. Schreker, indeed, suggests that his male characters, in contrast to his women, are characterised by the 'pursuit of some definite deed'.[29] The genius, writes Weininger, represents 'man in his highest form'; he should devote himself either to 'the highest worth of existence, in which case he is a philosopher', or to 'the wonderful fairyland of dreams, the kingdom of absolute beauty, and then he is an artist'.[30] In the Epilogue of *Der Schatzgräber* Elis the artist-genius constructs just such a world. Els, now deprived of both jewels and Elis's love, is fading towards death, and Elis, ever the redeemer, comforts her in song. Accompanying himself on the lute, he sings of the 'return to fairyland of the prince and princess, Elis and Els, both children of the dream-king's grace'. Perhaps, too, we can detect something of Weininger's thought in Elis's persistent displacement of Els into a fantasy-world:

Love of a woman is possible only when it does not consider her real qualities, and so is able to replace the actual psychical reality by a different and quite imaginary reality.[31]

These words, as we shall see, have more profound implications for *Der Schatzgräber* than might appear.

[28] Otto Weininger, *Sex and Character*, trans. unidentified (London: Heinemann, 1944), p. 284.
[29] Schreker, 'Der Schatz', p. 205.   [30] Weininger, *Sex and Character*, p. 286.
[31] Ibid., p. 249.

Bekker had already traced the impact of Otto Weininger's best-selling *Sex and Character* in Schreker's earlier operas, but there is something more explicit and self-conscious about its presence here. This is particularly true in the case of Els's character: Schreker actually describes her as a 'kind of child-woman who might be traced, not without justification, to the influence of Weiningerian thought'.[32] Perhaps the most obvious of these traces is to be found in Els's relationship to the queen's jewels. Unlike Elis, whose treasure-seeking is always motivated by his idea, Els demands to hold and touch the jewels, to feel them next to her body. After she has sent her fiancé on his ill-fated mission, Els bursts into a barely controlled fit of anticipation:

Ah! Ah! But I shall have it, it will be mine, this last piece . . . It gleams and sparkles in the room. Already its magic is working: Els is becoming more beautiful, Elschen is more lovely every day.

Her words bring an unprecedented vocal and orchestral outburst of densely chromatic music characterised by sudden juxtapositions of material and short, choppy phrases.

A similar, though more subdued, outburst is to be found in the Epilogue as a delirious Els realises she no longer has the jewels. Just as the outburst begins, Schreker's stage directions indicate that Els 'starts up, feeling her body with trembling fingers as if searching for something'. Nor is Els alone: in the Prologue the king describes his wife's infatuation with the jewels in terms of a similarly physical response:

She dreams about it, that glittering finery, as if it were a lover.

Theirs is an entirely sensual, material attraction to the jewels. There is nothing of Elis's idealisation here, nothing of the distance sought by the scopic and invocatory drives. What they seek is material presence. Weininger offers a similar analysis of women:

A woman's thought is superficial, and touch is the most highly developed of the female senses . . . Touch necessitates a limiting of the interest to superficialities; it is a vague effect of the whole and does not depend on definite details.[33]

And in a discussion of their contributions to the arts, Weininger explains why he believes women have achieved more in painting than in drawing:

The sensuous, physical element of colour is more suitable for them than the intellectual work of formal line drawing, and hence it is, that whereas women have acquired some small distinction in painting, they have gained none in drawing.[34]

---

[32] Schreker, 'Der Schatz', p. 205.   [33] Weininger, *Sex and Character*, p. 191.
[34] Ibid., p. 120.

It is in the love duet and the orchestral night of passion that follows that touch and materiality are foregrounded. It is here that Els seems to experience pleasure capable of rivalling the sensual rewards of the jewels. The onset of this sensuality is signalled above all by music, by the gradual displacement of Elis's distant sounds at the beginning of the love duet with bolder, more immediate sonorities, more forceful dynamics, and a latent energy and momentum. Clearly set in contrast to Elis's music and coinciding with Els's entries, this new impetus seems to originate with her. The association with Els is further reinforced with prominent metallic sonorities (tambourine, triangle, xylophone) that suggest the jangling of the jewels that adorn her body. At the height of the invisible love scene (bar 521), for example, a battery of ten percussion instruments reinforces the crescendo towards the climactic bar of the interlude.

Clearly, then, an opposition is established between the immediate sensuality of Els's music and the fantasmatic distant sounds of Elis's world. Hers is a feminine music that overwhelms the male subject, that foregrounds sound as material, embodied experience and casts aside repression. What it seems to represent is a corollary to the logic of desire outlined by Metz, a rejection of the distance characteristic of the scopic and invocatory drives. What is also striking about the attitude of Els and the queen to the jewels is the level of their investment in the object. Temporarily deprived of her jewels, the queen withdraws from the world, while Els, who gives them up permanently, actually ages and dies as a result. For Weininger, women fail to develop an 'intelligible ego' and so must

get their sense of value from something outside themselves, from their money or estates, the number and richness of their garments, the position of their box at the opera, their children, and above all, their husbands or lovers.[35]

This last point bears particular relevance to Els, for the opera hinges precisely on her renunciation of the jewels in favour of Elis. In Weiningerian terms, she exchanges one ego substitute for another.

We can detect traces of this idea in the Freudian theory of identification. Fuelled by (narcissistic) ego libido rather than object libido, identification is seen as the earliest form of emotional tie with an object. Here the subject has yet to encounter the distance associated with desire because objects seem to meet its demands with a total sufficiency that belies any separation. The operative drives here are those of demand with their emphasis on consumption and incorporation. But, as we saw in the previous chapter, the collapse of this imaginary sufficiency (the entry into Lacan's symbolic) does not spell the end of identification. The residue of that infantile narcissism compels the mature subject to

---

[35] Ibid., p. 202.

identify with objects that compensate for the deficiencies of the ego, as we have seen in Freud's theory of the introjection of an ego ideal. And, as in Weininger, Freud's theory is marked by sexual difference, for it is above all women with whom he associates narcissism:

Women, especially if they grow up with good looks, develop a certain self-contentment which compensates them for the social restrictions imposed upon them in their choice of object. Strictly speaking, it is only themselves that such women love with an intensity comparable to that of the man's love for them.[36]

In this reading, the jewels would provide Els with an ego ideal that ensures narcissistic pleasure, while Elis's desire for her would reinforce that pleasure.

If the exchange between the jewels and Elis's love begins to occur when Els first finds herself transfixed by Elis's strange ballad in Act I, it is completed only at the end of Act III, when a pantomime depicts her release from the spell of the treasure. As the frenzy of the orchestral night of passion gradually fades into post-coital slumber, the sun begins to rise and cast light once more on Els's room and the garden outside. Woodwind depict a chorus of bird calls not unlike the dawn chorus in Act III of *Der ferne Klang*, although the naturalistic effects of that scene are replaced here by something much more impressionistic. Embedded in the middle of the bird calls is a quotation of a portion of the famous *Tristan* progression – a trope of unfulfillable longing? – altered to create a symmetrical and more dissonant effect. Els rises from the bed and begins to remove the jewels from her body, placing them one by one at the feet of the still slumbering Elis.

Her renunciation is not without its price, however, as Schreker's stage direction indicates:

This is done slowly, piece by piece, with ardent, expressive sympathy which increases in accordance with the beauty of the individual pieces, and manifests itself in gestures of admiring, often childlike joy, then again in obvious grief, even despair.

As she removes the last piece from her head, the sun's rays catch it and make it 'sparkle wondrously'. The orchestra responds with a huge crescendo capped by the most forceful climax of the opera, an *fff* rendition of the treasure motif replete with suitably prominent percussion (example 5.6). In a draft version of the score Schreker had noted at the climax, 'Struggle between the treasure and love'.[37] Here the visceral appeal of the treasure asserts itself in the most forceful terms, refusing to renounce its hold on Els. But the moment of greatest temptation marks

[36] Freud, 'On Narcissism: An Introduction' (1914), in Strachey (ed. and trans.), *The Standard Edition*, vol. XII, pp. 88–9.

[37] Brzoska, *Der Schatzgräber*, p. 47.

Example 5.6   Schreker, *Der Schatzgräber*, Act III, *Liebesszene*

Example 5.7   Schreker, *Der Schatzgräber*, Act III, *Liebesszene*

the decisive turning point, for the treasure motif is supplanted by an equally convincing statement of the *Liebesthema*, marked 'mit größtem, innigstem Ausdruck' ('with the most intense, heartfelt expression') (example 5.7). Heard here for the first time as a *fortissimo* statement for full orchestra, the *Liebesthema* is presented in canon, as if to reinforce the completeness of its victory over the jewels. It is only after Els's inner battle that Elis awakes to find the treasure at his feet.

The brief exchange that closes the act centres on Elis's reluctance to deprive Els of the jewels, to which Els responds, as we have seen, by insisting that it would represent 'redemption' to her. What also emerges is the shadow of deceit. Els, after all, refuses to reveal how she acquired her collection, and her 'gift' has been made possible only by the theft of Elis's lute. She warns Elis that 'a time will come . . . when it will be hard for you to believe in me'. Perhaps it is this shadow that truly explains the *Tristan* reference during the dawn chorus: it paints the love of Els and Elis as something riddled with deceit and treachery, just as Tristan and Isolde deceive themselves and betray Mark. Support for this reading is to be found in Act II, when Els promises a 'reward' to the bailiff if he

Example 5.8   Schreker, *Der Schatzgräber*, Act III, *Liebesszene*, Tristan quotation

will allow her a few moments with the condemned Elis. Accompanying her words is a fleeting quotation (at pitch) of the *Sehnsucht* motif as it appears in Act II of *Tristan* when Tristan kisses Isolde in front of Mark. Els, of course, has no intention of fulfilling her promise – the bailiff's longing will never be anything more than that – and a link is established between the *Tristan* music and Els's deceiving ways.[38]

Diaphanous veils

There is, however, another trope of deception hidden within the pantomime music. One of the standard readings of the *Tristan* chord is as a French sixth chord delayed by an appoggiatura in the top voice. If Schreker's *Tristan* quotation preserves the melodic shape of the upper voice in the *Tristan* progression, it sacrifices both the spelling and harmonic context of the original in favour of a symmetrical motion of melody and bass around two static inner voices (example 5.8, bars 551–2). Tonally, only one note separates the *Schatzgräber* chord from its *Tristan* model – F–G–C sharp–F sharp instead of F–G–C sharp–A sharp – but the dissonant effect of the semitonal clashes renders the chord almost unrecognisable. Meanwhile, the final chord of the progression, a dominant seventh in the original, becomes a French sixth here. It is really only voice leading that recalls the *Tristan* progression

---

[38] Another quotation of the *Tristan* chord, this time unaltered, appears in the harp accompaniment at bar 415 (on A flat) and bar 416 (on F). There are *Tristan* chords, too, in Schreker's earlier operas. In *Die Gezeichneten*, in the Act III encounter between Carlotta and Tamare (anticipated in the overture), the chord is presented as B–F–A–D with an added C sharp in the bass that ultimately draws it towards V7 of F sharp. And in *Das Spielwerk* it is heard at the opening of one of the major themes of the opera (see Prelude, letter A).

(notice, for example, how the mirror motion of the bass voice simulates both the melodic and rhythmic character of the chromatic descent that precedes the *Tristan* chord, as if the whole motif were compressed through juxtaposition). What, then, is the meaning of the distortion? Is it influenced by the music that surrounds it? Certainly the A minor arpeggio of bar 550 (a bar that is similarly set apart from the bird chorus and that seems to introduce the *Tristan* quotation) picks up on the prominent A major tonal centre of the opening bars of the bird chorus, and the tonal configuration of the *Tristan* quotation does return in the bars following the quotation. But otherwise the quotation and its introductory bar seem quite isolated. A more telling clue is to be found by comparing the quotation to an earlier event. The opening F–F sharp clash in the outer voices is 'resolved' through symmetrical motion around the static inner voices. If we read both pitches as chromatically inflected appoggiaturas (the F sharp resolving up a semitone to G and the F down a semitone to E) the remaining pitches of bars 550–2 comprise the 'Elis' mode beginning on C sharp (i.e. C sharp–D sharp–E–G–G sharp–A–B sharp). This accounts not only for the *Tristan* quotation but the A minor–C sharp superimposition that precedes it.[39]

The implication of this combination of two tropes of deception is not necessarily that Els is a figment of Elis's imagination (her appearances in the earlier acts lack the kinds of narrative and stage devices that would make her seem imaginary in the sense that the Flying Dutchman in Wagner's opera seems to emerge from his own portrait). What it does suggest is the ambiguous identity of that which is desired. Els stands before Elis, but, as Hepokoski observes of the seductions in *Don Juan* (see chapter 2), what she actually 'is' is unknowable, dependent on perspective and shrouded in veils of fantasy. Everything in this scene is presented through the filter of Elis's subjectivity, seen through his eyes, heard through his ears. We have already seen that Elis almost manages to initiate the erotic encounter before Els has even arrived. Her appearance, dressed only in the jewels and diaphanous veils, becomes in this context a staged projection of Elis's words. It is a sight that seems calculated to call attention to its fantasmatic support. Els's words, too, seem to beckon from the depths of Elis's desire, even as she attempts to ground the fantasy. 'I am no phantom,' she insists, 'no shape from dreams and visions'. In this context the reality check she provides only serves to reinforce the credibility of the fantasy. Immediately she contrasts this elusive, dream-like imagery with the 'reality' of her body:

[39] The passage is in fact only one of a whole series in the love scene that can be read in relation to the same collection or close derivatives of it. Some of the collections feature a greater chromatic density, but they all share augmented-second gaps framed on either side by semitones.

You should hold me and embrace me, kiss me and drink me in!

But then comes a line that recasts her as the disturbing product of a misogynist fantasy:

You should press me tight, beat me and, if you wish, kill me tonight.

If this invitation can be justified in dramatic terms as a manifestation of Els's guilt, it nevertheless provides a horrifying twist to the scene, particularly in the context of the distant sounds and visions that have dominated the proceedings to this point. And what is the musical setting for Els's words? While the vocal line suggests, as only the voice can, a hysterical cry, the orchestra seems to underline the violent imagery of Els's words with syncopated, staccato 'blows' from percussion and brass. But the passage's tonal origins remain rooted in the Elis mode, highlighting the ambiguous juxtaposition of sensuality and idea, object and subject.

Though he knows nothing of Els's guilt, Elis is not shocked by her death wish. He is, in fact, aroused all the more:

Ah, how you speak! I am losing my mind!

Els's masochistic desire for punishment, it seems, represents the next step in Elis's sexual fantasy, and the trigger that initiates the orchestrally depicted act of love. The shocking brutality of its imagery also seems to reinforce the transparency of the scene as fantasy, projecting ever more taboo desires onto the stage and further eroding any comfortable distinctions between fantasy and reality.

Another musical suggestion of this slippage from reality emerges immediately prior to the love scene, as Elis, awaiting Els's return, gives his imagination free rein:

Sweet fragrances envelop me, rock me gently in dreams of longing, dreams in which ancient songs, once sung, die away.

Elis's words are given an appropriately gentle, lyrical setting (example 5.4), highlighted by a theme that will soon develop into the principal *Liebesthema*. But the melodic contour of the theme seems vaguely familiar. In fact it recalls one of the most prominent phrases from Els's lullaby at the beginning of the act. Framed as a closed number 'im Volkston', the lullaby's three stanzas each feature a version of this phrase as their melodic highpoint. The connection is reinforced at the end of Elis's line (bar 264), when hushed clarinet and strings recall the lyricism of the lullaby, with its simple diatonicism and pedal harmonies. The descending phrases in canon, meanwhile, suggest the gentle closing bars of the lullaby. What the orchestra implies is that we have shared Elis's aural imagination, that we, too, have heard one of those 'ancient songs'. What had seemed like a fleshing out of Els's character – another side to the driven, demonic figure of the first two acts – is cast here in a different light. The touching vulnerability she reveals in the lullaby emerges as a prop in Elis's fantasy, a manifestation of the 'child-woman' to which Schreker refers in his article.

In the aftermath of the love scene, the objective 'identity' of Els is further veiled. Relating the encounter to the king in Act IV, Elis recalls:

It was a night such as there had never been. Dreams spun strangely into life, a fragrant tissue of softly luminous veils.

Here Elis almost suggests that dreams had indeed spun their way into life, that it was indeed a night that never was. More telling still is Els's demise in the Epilogue. Physically weakened by the absence of the jewels, she no longer possesses the strength even to fantasise. Once she had dreamed of a prince who would take her to a fairy-palace, but now Elis must construct her fantasy for her, singing to her and playing his lute. Els loses herself, literally, in Elis's song, returning to the fairy tale from which she emerged; the end of Elis's story is the end of Els.

'Only fiction'

The overlapping of fantasy and reality that Els represents suggests a Schrekerian critique of music drama, a gesture that amounts to a form of self-critique. Schreker begins his article on *Der Schatzgräber* by drawing attention to the implications of Elis's final song. In contrast to Elis's previous lyrical outpourings, Elis here seems to have detached himself from his material. The song represents a deliberate act of fiction in which he no longer believes, a symbol of the loss of his investment in the fantasy. It is a loss signalled in music. As Schreker points out, Elis *sings* the treasure motif for the first time when he evokes the 'beautiful glass fairy-palace', the 'goal of our longing'. No longer hidden in the fantasmatic realm of the orchestra (the realm of the love scene), the treasure surfaces to the 'conscious' level of the voice. 'After all,' writes Schreker, 'the treasure is accessible to humankind only within longing, only as a dream of joy and redemption.'[40] In other words the motif in the voice symbolises Elis's conscious recognition of the fairy-palace/treasure as a goal of longing (a fantasy object) in contrast to the vital (unconscious) impulse that it has represented for him until now. Only within the transparently fictional confines of his fairy tale can Elis 'reach' the treasure.

The implications for music theatre are clear. The cloaking of opera in the metaphysics of Wagnerian music drama represents an illusion

---

[40] Schreker, 'Der Schatz', p. 204.

that puffs up theatrical representation and credits it with the capacity to touch on the absolute, the will, the idea. By revelling in that illusion, in that falseness, Schreker's music theatre seeks to celebrate, rather than enshroud, its falseness. The excess that characterises every aspect of the opera can be read precisely in terms of this celebration. From the fantasmatic flavour of the settings (Els's Arabic-Oriental decor) to the spilling-over of Elis's *Märchen* imagery outside the diegetic frame of his songs (dwarf characters and dark forests) to the magic of the treasure itself: everything calls attention to its own falseness. In his interpretation of the treasure, Schreker turns, not surprisingly, to music as a metaphor:

For this treasure is really nothing other than that to which, at bottom, any musical work of art aspires: the symbolic linking of events. If you like, only fiction, but in the same sense that life's great longing is only fiction. One thinks it away, and every impulse is extinguished.[41]

Like the pursuit of the fantasy object, then, listening to music is an act of investment, of belief. For the listening subject, music may seem to suggest Truth, reaching beyond empirical reality to convey the idea. But it is never more than an illusion, what Schreker calls 'fiction'. It depends on the subject's investment in order to be meaningful, just as the impact of the *Liebesszene* for Elis depends on his investment in *his* vision of Els.[42] In this context Els's raw, uninhibited, sensual music might go beyond the typical alignment of femininity with the bodily and sensual. Elis the artist-genius who repeatedly relocates music into the distance is also implicated as the subjective source of a music of barely controlled ecstasy. His distant sounds emerge here as the product of the same libidinal drive that fuels the 'raging waves' of blood. The 'demands of culture' – the need to idealise and sublimate – emerge here as nothing more than a manipulation and reinterpretation. For Bekker, Schreker's operas convey the message that 'the urge is not a sin, but the highest law, dictated by nature'.[43] Elis follows the cultural imperative to idealise, but his efforts are unmasked from within as a self-deluding resistance to the 'highest law'.

The truth of deception

If Schreker's concern for artistic idealism and his characterisation of eroticism in terms of a coursing, indiscriminate urge represent a

---

[41] Ibid., p. 204.
[42] Lawrence Kramer makes the important point that music in which we find ourselves unable to invest 'counts, literally and figuratively, as noise'. *Classical Music and Postmodern Knowledge*, p. 24.
[43] Bekker, *Franz Schreker*, p. 38.

holdover from prewar cultural debates, then the unprecedented success of *Der Schatzgräber* would suggest that these questions continued to hold relevance for postwar audiences. But the opera's popularity in the years immediately after its premiere testifies all the more dramatically to the stark reversal of fortune suffered by Schreker's operas during the later 1920s. In the period 1920–5 *Der Schatzgräber* was performed 354 times; from the following year to 1932 it was given no more than thirty-one performances.[44] Part of the reason for the decline might be attributed to the huge expense involved in the production of Schreker's operas with their elaborate scenarios and large casts and orchestras. Yet they thrived through the postwar years of economic crisis and began to drop out of the repertoire in mid-decade, a period of relative stability. The much discussed sensuality of Schreker's music also met with a strange and contradictory reception history. On the one hand it was subjected to criticism on moral grounds, much of which attests to the influence of fascist aesthetic ideology long before the official Nazi suppression of Schreker's work. In some ways *Der Schatzgräber* might be seen to anticipate some of these moral objections. If the love scene offers a musical sensuality of a directness that is rare even for Schreker, then Elis's act of renunciation might be interpreted as a crucial counterbalance, a kind of moral olive branch. If this is the case, however, it failed to impress critic Alfred Heuss, who used his *Schatzgräber* review as an opportunity to launch a vicious attack against Schreker. Responding to Bekker's observations on the erotic in Mozart, Wagner, and Schreker, Heuss declared indignantly:

To consider the eroticism of Mozart and Schreker in the same breath – one could laugh about it if we lived in a more or less healthy age with surer instincts.[45]

The operas after *Schatzgräber* suggest that attacks like these left their mark. Beginning with *Irrelohe* (1924), Schreker seems to have broadened his moral compromise, retreating to a representation of eros that challenges the 'demands of culture' less openly.

On the other hand, this was a culture experimenting with new forms of sexual freedom and more frank representations of sexuality. It seems inevitable that Schreker's elaborate erotic symbolism would appear increasingly dated, that Els's 'diaphanous veils' would quickly become old-fashioned. This is certainly the sense that emerges in Bekker's review of *Irrelohe*, in which the critic adopts a somewhat defensive tone

---

[44] Brzoska, *Der Schatzgräber*, p. 146. The performance statistics were compiled by Christopher Hailey.

[45] Alfred Heuss, 'Über Franz Schrekers Oper *Der Schatzgräber* – seine Geschäftspraxis, die Schreker-Presse und Anderes', *Zeitschrift für Musik* 88/22 (1921), 568, trans. in Hailey, *Franz Schreker*, p. 179.

in his assessment of the composer's contemporary relevance.[46] For Christopher Hailey, 'Schreker's treatment of the dilemmas of sexual passion was irrelevant to an era in which sexual license had revolutionised morals and mores.'[47] A complex picture emerges, then, in which increasingly tolerant attitudes co-exist with (perhaps provoke) a strident conservativism, leaving Schreker's operas vulnerable to attacks from both directions.

The question of irrelevance also raises the broader issue of cultural change. To what extent did the demise of Schreker's operas stem from the cultural trends of the later 1920s, from an erosion of the post-Wagnerian, Weiningerian ethos in which operas such as *Der Schatzgräber* have their origins? The answers to such questions often raise more problems than they address. An elaborate *Märchen* centred on idealism and music's intoxicating sensuality would certainly seem to fall prey to the very conscious rejection in Weimar culture of the legacy of Romanticism and the *fin de siècle*, and yet we oversimplify the process of change drastically if we fail to acknowledge the possibility of diversity. If, for example, *Der Schatzgräber* succumbed to a growing distaste for *Märchen* and sultry *fin-de-siècle* eroticism, then we might ask why operas like *Hänsel und Gretel* and *Salome* continued to flourish. And could Schreker's operas really have become that irrelevant that quickly?

What is more certain is that the period witnessed a re-evaluation of the metaphysical foundations of music drama, a project to which Bekker dedicated himself. Writing in 1924, he characterised Schreker's theatre as a return to what theatre had always really been,

even when it was taken to be a moral institution or a temple of regeneration: the great pleasure-house that meets the public demand for art, a place where the appearance of art is deceptively inflated to the status of art, so that deception becomes the truth of the moment.[48]

Schreker's operas, then, acknowledge the truth of their deceptive core. From this perspective, no-one is more implicated by the critique in *Der Schatzgräber* than Schreker himself. As an opera composer in the post-Wagnerian tradition, Schreker submits opera to a critique, as it were, from the inside; his music relies on the metaphysical magic of Bayreuth even as it seeks to expose it. With its hidden orchestra, its music sounding in the darkness, and its voices of the unconscious emanating from the pit, the love scene clearly places itself within the tradition of the post-Wagnerian orchestral interludes that we have already examined. Yet it also serves to shift the ground beneath that tradition, to make

[46] Paul Bekker, 'Irrelohe', *Anbruch* 6/4 (April 1924), 132–5.
[47] Hailey, *Franz Schreker*, pp. 193–4.
[48] Paul Bekker, 'Schreker und das Theater', *Anbruch* 6/2 (February 1924), 53.

the magic transparent. Perhaps, then, part of the opera's undoing stems from the acutely historical sensitivity of its terms. What may have appeared from one perspective to be a finely balanced dialectic could easily be dismissed from another as a kind of aesthetic waffling, or, worse still, a fatal contradiction. Responding to Bekker's thesis that the sincerity of Schreker's theatre lies in the consistency of its deception, Gerhard Tischer quipped: 'With the same logic the devil may also be made to become God.'[49] And in *Irrelohe*, Adolf Weissmann could only find 'the very Wagner who was supposed to have been surpassed by Schreker'.[50] Poised delicately at the edge of a critical reassessment of music drama, Schreker's operas found themselves dismissed as superficially altered heirs to an older and more sympathetic post-Wagnerianism.

Collapsing the Other

If the passage of time has permitted only a partial restoration of Schreker's reputation, it has surely proved that the issue at the heart of *Der Schatzgräber* – the battle between 'idea' and 'sensuality' – does not belong on some scrapheap of historical debates. Inherited and sustained by Hollywood, the conflict underpins the all too familiar fantasy in which woman, object of the male gaze, is projected as inviting the gaze; she, not masculine desire, is author of her erotic appeal, what Laura Mulvey calls her 'to-be-looked-at-ness'. The male hero meanwhile devotes himself to the important business of 'making things happen', regarding her as a pleasurable (or threatening) distraction from his quest.[51] Certainly this is the gender ideology underlying Schreker's article. When Schreker grounds the metaphysics of the idea in human 'longing', he means masculine longing. Only Elis engages in 'the pursuit of some definite deed', while the most to which Els can aspire, meanwhile, is a 'certain artistic tendency' that drives her to seek beauty and love.[52]

But what of the love scene itself? Is it not possible that, in the course of characterising fantasy *as* fantasy, the love scene uncovers this projection of the feminine *as* projection? Does it not potentially cast a light where darkness is preferred? Rendered transparent, Elis's fantasy would then

[49] Gerhard Tischer, 'Franz Schreker: *Irrelohe*: Uraufführung im Kölner Opernhaus am 27. März 1924', *Rheinische Musik- und Theater-zeitung* 25/13–14 (5 April 1924), 70–1, cited in Matthias Brzoska, liner notes for audio recording of *Der Schatzgräber* (Capriccio 60010–2), p. 16.
[50] Adolf Weissmann, 'Schrekers *Irrelohe*', *Berliner Zeitung am Mittag*, 28 March 1924, trans. in Hailey, *Franz Schreker*, p. 193.
[51] Laura Mulvey, 'Visual Pleasure and Narrative Cinema', in John Caughie and Annette Kuhn (eds.), *The Sexual Subject: A 'Screen' Reader in Sexuality* (London: Routledge, 1992), pp. 27–8.
[52] Schreker, 'Der Schatz', p. 205.

lose what Rose calls 'its elevation to the status of truth'.[53] Following Lacan, Rose interprets the phallic notion of the feminine in terms of a fantasy object that

gets transposed onto the image of the woman as Other who then acts as its guarantee . . . The absolute 'Otherness' of the woman, therefore, serves to secure for the man his own self-knowledge and truth.[54]

For Lacan this 'Otherness' is defined in two ways:

On the one hand, the woman becomes, or is produced, precisely as what he is not, that is, sexual difference, and on the other, as what he has to renounce, that is, *jouissance*.[55]

In *Der Schatzgräber* we can detect the excess that characterises *jouissance* in the seething sensuality of the love scene. Elis fantasises Els as the bearer of that sensuality; he renounces it onto her. Els then becomes the sensual/feminine 'Other', his complement who satisfies his sense of what Weininger calls 'his real higher self'.[56] The persistent suggestion in the love scene and later in the opera that the identity of Els is bound up with fantasy proves, in this context, to be a decisive critical turn: the status of the Other is seen to collapse back into the fantasy that is its source.

Or perhaps it would be more accurate to say that the Other is *heard* to collapse, for it is in music that Els's ontological status is most radically redefined. And this critical turn says much about music when it returns the Otherness of Els's orchestral torrents to Elis. There is a passage in Weininger that touches on this issue:

This subjection to waves of feeling, this want of respect for conceptions, this self-appreciation without any attempt to avoid shallowness, characterise as essentially female the changeable styles of many modern painters and novelists. Male thought is fundamentally different from female thought in its craving for definite form, and all art that consists of moods is essentially a formless art.[57]

What must Schreker have thought of Weininger's gendered art? Surely his own music, and particularly the love scene, is implicated here. What does Schreker open music up to if not 'waves of feeling'? Adorno voices similar doubts, as we have seen, when he characterises the love scene in terms of 'inarticulacy' and an 'emotional splurge'. Schreker's response seems to be to reclaim so-called feminine music for the male artist, not by appropriating it, but by questioning the terms of the debate. Partly this depends on Schreker's approach to the relationship between music

[53] Rose, *Sexuality in the Field of Vision*, p. 75.   [54] Ibid.

[55] Jacques Lacan, 'Le séminaire, livre XVIII: D'un discours qui ne sera pas semblant, 1970–1971' (unpublished typescript), pp. 6, 9–10, trans. in Rose, *Sexuality in the Field of Vision*, p. 73.

[56] Weininger, *Sex and Character*, p. 243.   [57] Ibid., pp. 190–1.

and gender. Elis's distant sounds, for example, have a delicate, shimmering quality that invites traditional associations with femininity, and the immediate sensuality of the Els music is climax-oriented in a way that fits a common view of the masculine in music. But, more importantly, Schreker's music suggests that the gap between music as sensual, embodied experience and music as transcendental idea maps onto gender only in fantasy. It suggests, indeed, that the gap is itself a fantasy. The conclusion is that there is no masculine and feminine music, merely a masculine and feminine projection and listening; that there is no transcendent idea, merely a fantasy object.

Of course it is once again Schreker who potentially provides a prime target for this unmasking. In female characters such as Grete, Carlotta, the Princess, and Els herself, Schreker arguably does more to reinforce Weiningerian-style stereotypes of woman as amoral, sexual being than any critique could ever hope to unmask. Again and again it is 'their' music that is dominated by 'waves of feeling', that seems compulsive and irrational, that most provokes what Adorno called a 'fear of throwing off all restraint'. Yet in the end we might locate the significance of a site such as the love scene not in the critical weight it carries but in the willingness to cast doubt at all. If, as Bekker suggests, *Der Schatzgräber* emerges from and returns to music, then the love scene is the moment when the opera stops to reflect upon the nature of that music. What is revealed is a music that resists uncomplicated alignments with notions of gender, a music that questions the idealising bid to distance it from the body.

6

Wagner and 'invisible theatre'

The doubt that permeates *Der Schatzgräber* becomes all the more apparent when we return to Wagnerian music drama and the origins of the traditions Schreker seems to question. Here every gesture is marked by a conviction that threatens to sweep away resistance in any form. Both in theory and in practice Wagner presents music drama in terms of a wholeness and seamlessness that is impervious to doubts, to gaps, or to self-questioning. But, as suggested in the introduction, the orchestral interludes (and preludes) may serve as a particularly instructive means of penetrating Wagner's armour on different levels. That the withdrawal of the stage should heighten the theatre experience, that mere transitions are often invested with pivotal musico-dramatic roles, that a palpably sensual music is credited with metaphysical transcendence, that the feminised realm of the orchestra would articulate a disgust for the feminine – these are some of the tensions that emerge in these orchestral 'scenes', pointing to the (unacknowledged) contradictions at the heart of music drama. Inherited and further complicated by post-Wagnerian opera, these are issues that return repeatedly, as we have seen, in both a latent and a consciously problematised form. Investigating the preludes and interludes, then, opens the way to a critical analysis of music drama, and this in turn offers to shed further light on some of the questions that have surfaced in our study up to this point.

Floating in music

Sleepless one night in Venice, I stepped out onto the balcony of my window overlooking the Grand Canal. Like a deep dream the legendary city of lagoons lay spread out in the shadows before me. Out of the breathless silence arose the powerful lamenting cry of a gondolier just awakened on his bark; repeatedly he cried out into the night, until from afar the same cry answered along the Canal... After a solemn pause the distant dialogue began again, and seemed finally to merge in unison, until at last the sounds from far and near died softly back to slumber. What could the sunlit, colourful, swarming Venice of daylight tell me of itself that this sound-dream of the night had not brought infinitely deeper into my consciousness?[1]

[1] Wagner, *Beethoven*, p. 74.

In this typically evocative anecdote, Wagner almost seems to offer a metaphor for the experience of the orchestral interlude. Introduced to illustrate the effects of what he calls a 'sound-world', it is a scene of invisible music-making, of sounds issued from beyond sight. Even when its source is visible, he argues, music has the ability to plunge the listener into a 'dream-like state' in which 'our eyesight is paralysed to such a degree ... that with open eyes we no longer intensively see'.[2] It is a state he compares, paraphrasing Schopenhauer, to 'hypnotic clairvoyance', a state that 'shuts us off from the outer world to let us gaze solely at our inner selves, and at the inner essence of all things'.[3] The sight of an orchestra performing is something that the 'spellbound listener' will dismiss, while for those 'untouched by the music' it will remain a distraction.[4]

Here, then, is the goal of Bayreuth's invisible orchestra. Rather than leave the 'paralysation' of the eye to chance – so that the sight of the performers may or may not distract – Wagner eliminates the problem for the audience. Not only is the orchestra hidden, but the auditorium is darkened so that the audience itself disappears. What is left is the image of the stage, and, as Wagner's 'invisible theatre' comment suggests, even this could be resented for its inability to aspire to the ideal heights of the music. The suggestion, of course, was made in a moment of frustration, and Wagner's begrudging sympathy with the theatre never allowed him to follow it through. Yet we might see the orchestral interludes, especially those presented before a closed curtain, as the closest manifestation of this tendency in Wagner's theory and practice. In the sympathetic setting of Bayreuth, music is briefly allowed to dispense not only with words and actors but occasionally with sight altogether. And where scenic effects remain (the steam clouds in *Das Rheingold* or the transformations in *Parsifal*) Wagner can still lay claim, as Pfitzner would later, to an ideal relationship in which the stage presents the outward appearance of things while music transcends to their inner essence.

That the revolutionary effects of Bayreuth made a deep impression on audiences is apparent from the reports of some of the early critics. Few failed to mention the darkening of the auditorium and the hidden orchestra. For Albert Lavignac the experience was totally engaging:

Suddenly darkness envelops the hall and there is perfect silence. The eye can distinguish nothing at first, then it gradually becomes accustomed to the feeble light produced by some lamps near the ceiling. From this moment one might hear a pin drop – everyone concentrates his thoughts and every heart beats with emotion. Then amidst the luminous and golden tone which arises from the depths of the 'mystic abyss' there mount warm, vibrant and velvety, the

---

[2] Ibid., p. 75.   [3] Ibid., p. 78.   [4] Ibid., p. 75.

incomparable harmonies unknown elsewhere and which, taking possession of your whole being, transport you to a world of dreams.[5]

Wilhelm Mohr, critic for the *Kölnische Zeitung*, was similarly struck by the effect of this uncanny sound:

> The whole theatre was plunged into a cellar-like darkness ... Out of the empty space behind the orchestra balustrade, deep beneath us, a mysterious impression surges upward and disperses across the simple red curtain.[6]

Reporting on *Parsifal* at the 1891 festival, Mark Twain drew particular attention to the darkness:

> All the lights were turned low, so low that the congregation sat in a deep and solemn gloom. The entire overture, long as it was, was played to a dark house with the curtain down. It was exquisite; it was delicious.[7]

Sir George Grove, unsympathetic to Wagnerian music drama, attributed much of the effect of Bayreuth to sheer novelty:

> The circumstances of the dark theatre, the hidden orchestra, the very prominent and brilliant stage, and the extraordinary stage effects and machinery – are all so new that of themselves they throw you off balance.[8]

Hanslick, who had received *Tannhaüser* warmly, found himself alienated by the *Ring* and the experience of Bayreuth:

> The mysterious heaving of the invisible orchestra gives the listener a mild opium jag even before the rise of the curtain; he is subjected to the enduring impression of a magically lighted fairy-tale scene before anyone on the stage has opened his mouth.[9]

Again and again these reactions turn to an effect that might be described as disorientation: dreams, opium, imbalance. With Wagner, it seems, it is no longer a question of music as such, but of a panoply of effects designed to establish a precisely regulated environment, one that overwhelms and seduces the spectator. Thanks to the technology

---

[5] Albert Lavignac, *The Music Dramas of Richard Wagner and His Festival Theatre at Bayreuth*, trans. Esther Singleton (New York: Dodd Mead, 1898), cited in Hartford (ed. and trans.), *Bayreuth: The Early Years*, p. 202.

[6] Wilhelm Mohr, 'Briefe eines baireuther Patronatsherrn', *Kölnische Zeitung* 14 August 1876, cited in Susanna Großmann-Vendrey (ed.), *Bayreuth in der deutschen Presse: Rezeptionsgeschichte Richard Wagners und seiner Festspiele*, vol. I (Regensburg: Gustav Bosse Verlag, 1977), p. 89.

[7] Mark Twain, 'At the Shrine of Wagner', cited in Hartford (ed. and trans.), *Bayreuth: The Early Years*, p. 150.

[8] George Grove, letter to Charles Wood, 15 September 1889, cited in Hartford (ed. and trans.), *Bayreuth: The Early Years*, p. 139.

[9] Eduard Hanslick, review in *Neue Freie Presse*, 18 August 1876, cited in Hartford (ed. and trans.), *Bayreuth: The Early Years*, p. 83.

of Bayreuth, the experience of music drama becomes a total immersion of the senses, leaving the spectator bereft of any normal resistance.

This, of course, is the core of Nietzsche's Wagner criticism, that he bullies and assaults his audience, seduces them with 'stimulants', appeals directly to the nerves. It is in this sense that he is the corrupter of music, the 'artist of decadence'.[10] And like the Bayreuth critics, Nietzsche addresses the unique experience of listening to Wagner's music in terms of a loss of bearing. 'Endless melody' he compares to

going into the sea, gradually relinquishing a firm tread on the bottom and finally surrendering unconditionally to the watery element: one is supposed to swim. Earlier music constrained one – with a delicate or solemn or fiery movement back and forth, faster and slower, to dance: in pursuit of which the needful preservation of orderly measure compelled the soul of the listener to a continual self-possession. Richard Wagner desired a different kind of movement of the soul: one related, as aforesaid, to swimming and floating.[11]

Nietzsche evokes a sensation not unlike those described by the Bayreuth critics, and particularly Lavignac's reference to 'taking possession of your whole being'. But whereas Lavignac addresses the Bayreuth setting, Nietzsche focuses directly on the effects of Wagner's music. Taken together, the observations might suggest that the darkened theatre and invisible orchestra serve to reinforce effects that are already intrinsic to Wagner's music. In attempting to describe the Bayreuth experience, Lavignac borrows the phrase 'world of dreams' from Wagner's 'Das Bühnenfestspielhaus zu Bayreuth' (1873, quoted in chapter 4), and it is interesting to compare it with a phrase attributed by Nietzsche to an Italian 'Wagnerienne': 'Come si *dorme* con questa musica' ('How one *sleeps* to this music').[12]

Both Bayreuth and Wagner's music, then, seem to promote a mode of behaviour that is regressive, to use the psychoanalytic term. Lacan characterises regression as 'the reduction of the symbolic to the imaginary',[13] a theme to which we have returned repeatedly in an attempt to understand the operations of fantasy and identification in orchestral interludes. It is a form of withdrawal that Wagner clearly understands when he writes of the 'retuning of the whole sensorium' ('Umstimmung des ganzen Sensitoriums')[14] and 'gaz[ing] at the innermost essence of

---

[10] Friedrich Nietzsche, *The Case of Wagner* (1888), in Walter Kaufmann (ed. and trans.), *Basic Writings of Nietzsche* (New York: Random House, 1966), pp. 620–2.

[11] Friedrich Nietzsche, 'Assorted Opinions and Maxims, 134', in his *Human, All Too Human* (1886), trans. R. J. Hollingdale (Cambridge: Cambridge University Press, 1986), p. 244.

[12] Friedrich Nietzsche, *The Will to Power* (1901), trans. Walter Kaufmann and R. J. Hollingdale (New York: Alfred A. Knopf, 1968), p. 442.

[13] Jacques Lacan, *Le séminaire, livre IV: La relation de l'objet, 1956–1957*, ed. Jacques-Alain Miller (Paris: Seuil, 1994), p. 355.

[14] Wagner, 'Das Bühnenfestspielhaus zu Bayreuth', p. 336.

ourselves and all things'. It is precisely this sense of self-deception, mis-recognition, and illusory immediacy (of the self, of the world around) that Lacan identifies as characteristic of the imaginary order. But what might psychoanalytic theory make of Nietzsche's images of floating and swimming? Freud turns to just such a sensation in *Civilization and Its Discontents* (1930). There he refers to a letter from Romain Rolland in which Rolland had described a recurring 'sensation of "eternity", a feeling as of something limitless, unbounded – as it were, "oceanic" '.[15] Unable to reconcile this 'oceanic feeling' with his own theories or to identify such a feeling in himself, Freud nevertheless attempts to come to terms with the implications of Rolland's suggestion. Glossing it as 'a feeling of an indissoluble bond, of being one with the external world as a whole', he relates it to the breakdown of the ego's sense of autonomy. Where the ego normally armours itself against external objects, striving towards a separation that allows it to establish itself as a separate unity, the oceanic feeling suggests the relaxation of those boundaries. What Freud seems to have in mind is not so much an erosion of the ego as a regression to an earlier form:

Originally the ego includes everything, later it separates off an external world from itself. Our present ego feeling is, therefore, only a shrunken residue of a much more inclusive – indeed, an all-embracing – feeling which corresponded to a more intimate bond between the ego and the world about it.[16]

Later Freud sees the sensation as seeking 'something like the restoration of limitless narcissism',[17] a characterisation that would again position it at an early stage of the ego's development. The emphasis on narcissism and oneness with the world around recalls the Lacanian imaginary, although Lacan stresses the role of narcissism in leading the subject away from this imaginary oneness (via the mirror stage) and towards the formation of the autonomous ego. Perhaps the oceanic feeling might correspond to the fantasy of fragmentation that accompanies ego formation in the mirror stage. It reminds us that Lacan does not present fragmentation as a necessarily negative experience: resistance to whole-ness and autonomy is also resistance to the *illusion* of wholeness and autonomy. What the oceanic feeling implies is a resistance based not on the image of breaking apart but on holding on to that 'unbounded' feeling of oneness with the world.

Wagner seems to offer his own take on the 'oceanic feeling' in the famous La Spezia vision, his account of the genesis of the prelude to *Das Rheingold*:

---

[15] Sigmund Freud, *Civilization and Its Discontents* (1930), trans. James Strachey (New York: Norton, 1961), p. 11.
[16] Ibid., pp. 15–16.   [17] Ibid., p. 20.

Returning home in the afternoon, I stretched out dead-tired on a hard sofa, to await the long-desired hour of sleep. It did not come; instead I sank into a sort of somnolent state, in which I suddenly felt as if I were sinking in rapidly flowing water. Its rushing soon represented itself to me as the musical sound of the E-flat major chord, which continually surged forward in a figured arpeggiation; these arpeggios appeared as melodic figurations of increasing motion, yet the pure E-flat major triad never changed, and seemed through its persistence to impart infinite significance to the element in which I was sinking. Feeling as though the waves were now roaring high above me, I awoke in sudden terror from my half-sleep. I recognised instantly that the orchestral prelude to *Das Rheingold*, as I had carried it about within me without ever having been able to pin it down, had risen up out of me; and I also quickly grasped how things were with me: the vital stream would not flow from without, but only from within.[18]

Not only do we have here the sense of limitlessness and unity with the surroundings, but a narcissistic element in which Wagner recognises himself as source and creator of this wonder. Again and again in Wagner's theoretical tracts music is associated with the depths of the ocean, and although we need not confine any search for traces of the oceanic feeling to literal ocean imagery, the prominence of these particular metaphors is striking. In *The Artwork of the Future* he writes of the 'sea of harmony':

Man dives into this sea ... His heart feels widened wondrously when he peers down into depths filled with unimaginable possibilities, depths whose bottom his eye will never fathom, whose measureless dimensions fill him with astonishment and a foreboding of the infinite.[19]

And in *Opera and Drama* the poet, armed with 'melody', no longer fears the depths of the sea of harmony:

[It] is no longer an object of dread, of fear, of terror – that strange and unknown element that had appeared in his imagination. Now, not only can he float on the waves of this ocean, but, endowed with new senses, he dives into its lowest depths ... Clear and sober, his senses penetrate right to the ocean's primal source. From there he sends the columns of waves rising to the surface to ripple gently in the rays of the sun, to splash softly in the west wind, or to rear in manly fashion against the north wind's storm. For the poet now commands the very breath of the wind.[20]

---

[18] Richard Wagner, *Mein Leben: Erste authentische Veröffentlichung*, ed. Martin Gregor-Dellin (Munich, 1963), p. 580, trans. in Warren Darcy, 'Creatio ex nihilo: The Genesis, Structure, and Meaning of the *Rheingold* Prelude', *Nineteenth-Century Music* 13/2 (1989), 79.

[19] Richard Wagner, *Das Kunstwerk der Zukunft* (1849), *SSD*, vol. III, p. 83.

[20] Richard Wagner, *Oper und Drama* (1851), *SSD*, vol. IV, pp. 146–7. On Wagner's definition of terms such as 'melody' and 'harmony', see Thomas S. Grey, *Wagner's Musical Prose: Texts and Contexts* (Cambridge: Cambridge University Press, 1995).

If Wagner's metaphors centre on composition, Nietzsche's reaction suggests that these images of submergence return in the act of listening to Wagner's music. Clearly, in the case of the prelude to *Das Rheingold*, such an impression represents a very calculated effect based on a combination of harmonic stasis, rhythmic layering, and almost hypnotic repetition. This is true, as well, of many of the nature portraits in the *Ring*: the storm prelude to *Die Walküre*, with its static tremolos and ostinato bass; the ascent from the depths of the Rhine after the first scene of *Das Rheingold*; sunrise in the *Götterdämmerung* Prologue; and 'Siegfried's Rhine Journey'. Nature is represented musically by a kind of elementality that depends heavily on repetition, rhythmic motion, and static blocks of sound that mutate almost imperceptibly (Mann spoke of the music being 'resolved into its primal elements').[21] But what is noticeable in examining the purely orchestral passages of the music dramas generally is that this elemental quality is in fact a recurring feature, whether or not the dramatic context suggests nature or water. Nietzsche's comparison of Wagner's music to a kind of immersion is obviously a general impression directed at Wagner's whole oeuvre, but his observation never seems more apt than when applied to the preludes and interludes. There is, in other words, something different about the music here, as though the regressive setting of these moments were mirrored by a regressive quality in the music.

Above all it is repetition and a constant flow of sound that emerge as the defining characteristics here. Clearly, given the role of features such as the leitmotif and sequence in music drama, repetition will feature prominently in the music for the staged scenes, too, and yet the presence of the vocal line seems to exert a pull away from the kind of static, hypnotic repetition of the orchestral passages and towards a more arioso-like musical prose. The gap is most noticeable in *Das Rheingold*, perhaps because the interludes there are very much nature portraits, characterised by that very conscious elementality that we see in the prelude. But it may also have to do with Wagner's approach to vocal setting, which in *Das Rheingold* tends towards an almost recitative-like sparseness that would later give way to a more dynamic flow of musical material – dare we say 'symphonic'? – as the tetralogy progressed. The final bars of the first interlude of *Das Rheingold*, for example, present the so-called 'Valhalla' motif, itself audibly and seamlessly developed from the 'Ring' motif of the first scene. Consciously primitive and pompous, its block chords are presented in square phrases and subjected to sequential repetition until they seem to relapse into an aimless two-chord alternation. In the nineteen bars of its initial presentation there is not a

---

[21] Mann, 'The Sorrows and Grandeur of Richard Wagner' (1933), trans. in Blunden (ed. and trans.), *Thomas Mann: Pro and Contra Wagner*, p. 108.

single beat's rest, and if we look back at the interlude and the conclusion of the first scene we discover that there has not been a beat of silence in seventy-four bars, a passage dominated by the repetition of a few motifs, like that associated with the waves of the Rhine. By comparison, the exchange between Wotan and Fricka is characterised by long stretches of recitative-like musical prose with frequent caesurae in the orchestral fabric and very sparse deployment of motivic material. Here the emphasis is overwhelmingly on the vocal delivery of the text, while the orchestra assumes a discreet, altogether secondary role. Only at certain points, and above all in the interludes, is it given free rein to release its flood of elemental music.

As much as this kind of contrast seems to be levelled out later in the *Ring*, there remains a uniqueness about the musical character of the interludes. The opening scene of Act III of *Siegfried* in many ways continues the motivic interplay and very un-prose-like 'flow' of musical material heard in the act's prelude. But even here the 'Valkyrie' figure that gives the prelude a *perpetuum mobile* feel is dropped, leaving a more open and varied orchestral texture that tends to weave around the vocal line. And when there is motivic repetition, such as the oft-restated 'Erda' motif, it tends to be balanced by melodic and rhythmic variety in the vocal line. The effect in the prelude, by contrast, is almost one of being caught up in an infinite play of slightly varied repetition, an unstoppable and hypnotic tide of music that is only brought to an end by the rising curtain.

If this kind of regressive sensation suggests the oceanic feeling, it also invokes the death drive, opposed in Freudian theory to the sexual drives, whose aim is the preservation of life. Freud sees its clearest manifestation in the 'compulsion to repeat', that is, a tendency to return again and again to certain thoughts and actions, even when they are not pleasurable (literally beyond the 'pleasure principle' that we encountered as the root of the primary process in dream theory).[22] Repetition, in other words, involves a resistance to change. Freud defines the death drive very much in biological terms, as the desire of all living things to return to an 'inanimate state',[23] and the cycle of birth and destruction traced by the *Ring* could be read in a similar way. Mann describes the *Ring* in terms of Wagner's compulsion 'to go back to the first source and origin of all things, the primeval cell, the first E flat of the prelude to the Prelude' and to create a 'musical cosmogony' that would offer a 'ringing pageant of the world's beginning and end'.[24] Between this beginning and end the death drive operates as a central thematic of the drama, finding its

[22] Sigmund Freud, *Beyond the Pleasure Principle* (1920), trans. James Strachey (New York: Norton, 1961), p. 32.
[23] Ibid.
[24] Mann, 'Richard Wagner and *Der Ring des Nibelungen*' (1938), trans. in Blunden (ed. and trans.), *Thomas Mann: Pro and Contra Wagner*, p. 180.

clearest manifestation in Wotan's yearning for 'das Ende'. In this sense the flames and flooding waters of the Rhine at the end of the cycle are symbols of the 'inanimate state' which life desires and an embodiment of the death drive in Wotan, Brünnhilde, and all the gods.

But Wagner's concept of the death drive is concerned with much more than the destruction of biological life – it is also about release from the symbolic order and its laws, pacts, and power structures. It is a recognition not simply of a need to return to the inorganic state from which life emerges, as Freud would have it, but of nullifying society in all its corruption. The *Ring*, Wagner writes, testifies to the

> necessity of recognising and yielding to the change, the many-sidedness, the multiplicity, the eternal renewing of reality and of life. Wotan rises to the tragic height of willing his own destruction. This is the lesson that we have to learn from human history: to will what necessity imposes, and ourselves bring it about.[25]

Together with this approach to death as a revolutionary, heroic act is the more resigned legacy of the failed Dresden uprising:

> Death ... is the destructive act that we can direct towards ourselves, since, as individuals, we cannot direct it towards the wretched conditions of this world that has us in its grip.[26]

Wagner characterises this self-destructive urge as a sign of human 'imperfection', one that might be better directed outwards to the existing order. But he sympathises with what he sees as a thoroughly justifiable longing 'towards a better land beyond – towards death'.[27] This is death as a desire to step out of the world, an attitude that recalls the regressive character of the preludes and interludes. In his earliest interpretation of the death drive (1938), Lacan reads it as a nostalgia for a lost harmony exemplified by the pre-Oedipal relationship with the mother (a phase he would later term the imaginary order).[28] In this sense it represents a profoundly regressive desire, one that would seek escape in an earlier and seemingly ideal stage of development.

Of particular interest here is the *Ring*'s most familiar image of world withdrawal, the Forest Murmurs scene, in which Siegfried reclines in the shade of the *Lindenbaum*, a familiar image of withdrawal and death in German culture. Here we see that nature, which Wagner had identified in *The Artwork of the Future* as a model for human existence ('Man will never be what he can and should be until his life is a true mirror of

---

[25] Wagner, letter to August Röckel, 25 January 1854, in Kesting (ed.), *Richard Wagner Briefe*, p. 283.

[26] Wagner, *Eine Mitteilung an meiner Freunde*, p. 332.   [27] Ibid.

[28] Jacques Lacan, *Les complexes familiaux dans la formation de l'individu: Essai d'analyse d'une fonction en psychologie* (Paris: Navarin, 1984), p. 35.

nature'),[29] can also be a locus of escapist fantasy. As Siegfried ponders dreamily on the identity of his parents and yearns to know his mother, the woods envelop him in a seductive, soothing blanket of sound. It is nature as daydream, as timeless, pastoral refuge from the world, and as mother. Amidst the sonorous landscape of tremolos, trills, and woodwind bird calls is that combination of harmonic stasis and motivic repetition familiar from the prelude to *Das Rheingold*. In the first thirty bars of a sustained E major, the only harmonic motion is an oscillation between tonic and subdominant (a harmonic image of stasis if ever there was one) while strings repeatedly arpeggiate, bringing the woods to life rhythmically while also confirming nature's circularity and constancy.

In *Parsifal* the Act III transformation thematicises death on an explicit level (the 'death rites' of Titurel), but both journeys to Monsalvat (Acts I and III) stand precisely as withdrawals from life into the death-obsessed brotherhood of the grail, and it is interesting to see how this theme of withdrawal spills over into Wagner's comments on the theatrical effect of these scenes. In his retrospective on the 1882 festival, Wagner describes how, with the help of the famous *Wandeldekoration*, the audience 'was to be led quite imperceptibly, as if in a dream, along the unmarked approaches to the Gralsburg, whose legendary inaccessibility to the non-elect was thus to be brought within the scope of dramatic representation'.[30]

Here the dream analogy characterises the journey as a regression from consciousness, framing it as an impossible fantasy space shut off from ordinary perception, and it is impossible not to think of Golaud's journey into the unconscious of the forest: both are journeys into a Music characterised as withdrawal. And, as Wagner makes clear, there is pleasure to be had in that withdrawal:

> [T]he effects of the surrounding visual and acoustic atmosphere on our whole perceptive faculty bore us away from the familiar world . . . Yes, *Parsifal* itself had owed its origin and evolution to escape from that world.[31]

It is interesting, too, that the repetitive, static, circular qualities observable in the preludes and interludes were unexpectedly brought to the fore in the 1882 staging. When it turned out that the roll of scenery in the *Wandeldekoration* was too long for Wagner's Act I transformation music, Engelbert Humperdinck, as assistant, provided additional bars as a temporary solution. Although only a nine-bar passage, Humperdinck's supplement, introduced at figure 90, allowed Wagner's music to loop back to figure 87, and to continue looping as long as was required. Here

[29] Wagner, *Das Kunstwerk der Zukunft*, p. 44.
[30] Wagner, 'Das Bühnenweihfestspiel in Bayreuth 1882' (1882), *SSD*, vol. X, p. 305.
[31] Ibid., p. 307.

repetition as practical necessity was made to blend seamlessly with repetition as stylistic principle, each united by the need to maintain that
'retuning of the whole sensorium' so central to the effect of Bayreuth.

It is in the *Götterdämmerung Trauermarsch*, however, that the Wagnerian
death drive identifies itself most clearly. For, as we saw earlier, repetition
in the *Trauermarsch* is met by amplification, and it is this combination of
returning and reconstructing that is key. Repetition engages nostalgia,
but it is not enough, as it is in Pfitzner's *Trauermarsch*, to suspend time.
Adorno characterises Wagnerian narratives as

call[ing] a halt to the action and hence, too, to the life process of society. They
cause it to stand still so as to accompany it down into the kingdom of death, the
ideal of Wagnerian music.[32]

But this narrative insists on more than suspension; it represents the
past's radical reconstruction as an infinitely desirable future. And if
we should harbour any ambivalence about the past, Wagner's music
compensates with sheer force, monumentalising with a conviction that
leaves little room for a plurality of perspectives. For all the compatibility
of Wagner's death drive with Schopenhauer's philosophy (in which the
desire for death constitutes a passive resistance to the ensnarement of
the Will), there is an aggressive, proactive core to Wagner's conception
that finds no counterpart in Schopenhauerian, or Pfitznerian, submission. It is a characteristic that seems to find solace in the mythical, the
monumental, and the heroic, as though only in these forms does the
death drive avoid becoming something weak and decadent. Standing
over Siegfried's body, Brünnhilde proclaims:

> for my own body longs
> to share the hero's holiest honour.

It is this Wagnerian combination of withdrawal and aggrandisement
that represents the truly Wagnerian take on that attitude that Mann and
Pfitzner would define with the phrase 'sympathy with death'.

Asserting the symbolic

Returning to Lacan's definition of regression as a renunciation of the
symbolic, of the signifiable, we might read the interludes in terms of an
attempt to position music outside language, to escape to a presymbolic
form of meaning. Wagner suggests just such an interpretation in *Opera
and Drama* when he equates the role of the orchestra with expressing the
'inexpressible'[33] – that is, what is beyond the reach of verbal and visual
signification. But the idea of a fissure between music and stage surely

---

[32] Adorno, *In Search of Wagner*, p. 60.   [33] Wagner, *Oper und Drama*, p. 174.

represents a threat to the *Gesamtheit* in *Gesamtkunstwerk*, something Wagner's sense of organic unity refuses to contemplate. His response is the leitmotif – the expansion of the traditional reminiscence motifs into what he calls, as we saw earlier, a 'tissue of principal themes'. The impact on the preludes and interludes of the music dramas is decisive, for there are very few bars in all of this music that do not feature motivic material related to the stage action. For Adorno, the effect of the leitmotif is an 'allegorical rigidity' in which 'the gesture becomes frozen as a picture of what it expresses'.[34] Music becomes parasitic on the staged action, with the result that it is deprived of its essential nature:

[B]ecause of its extra, interpretative function, [music] finds itself drained of all the energies that make it a language remote from meaning, pure sound, and so contrast it with human sign-language, a contrast by virtue of which its full humanity is made possible.[35]

Adorno thus affirms a fissure between language and music, and the leitmotif creates a bridge that is not only artificial, but damaging. Abbate similarly affirms the music–language rupture, although she doubts the ability of the leitmotif to maintain its linguistic association:

Wagner's motifs may … absorb specific meaning at exceptional and solemn moments, but unless they are maintained in this semiotic state, they shed their meaning and become musical thoughts. (The *Ring* is unique in that so much energy is used to keep the motives suspended against gravity, against reversion to pure music.)[36]

By constantly reinforcing the association between a motif and its dramatic counterpart, then, Wagner postpones the inevitable breakdown of the relationship. But the gap implied by Abbate and Adorno is persuasively undermined by poststructuralist accounts of signification, not by asserting music's ability to aspire to a linguistic capacity for meaning, but by questioning any privileged, uncomplicated status of linguistic signification itself. As Lawrence Kramer puts it:

Language cannot capture musical experience because it cannot capture any experience whatever, including the experience of language itself. Language always alienates what it makes accessible; the process of alienation, the embedding of a topic in supposedly extrinsic discourses, is precisely what produces the accessibility.[37]

In this view, meaning, far from embedding itself neatly within language, is always subject to deferral, to delay, to (mis)reading. For Lacan,

---

[34] Adorno, *In Search of Wagner*, p. 46.   [35] Ibid., p. 104.

[36] Carolyn Abbate, *Unsung Voices: Opera and Musical Narrative in the Nineteenth Century* (Princeton: Princeton University Press, 1991), p. 168.

[37] Kramer, *Classical Music and Postmodern Knowledge*, p. 18.

language is not a system of signs (in which signifiers bind themselves to signifieds), but, rather, a system of signifiers, each potentially attached to multiple signifieds and linked in turn to other signifiers. In other words, the implied stability of the sign, with its binary relationship, gives way to a plurality of possible meanings that are never stable. To the extent that musical meaning is difficult to pin down, to articulate, or to translate, it only affirms its participation in the play of signification that characterises language and the symbolic order as a whole. Musical meaning, like that of language, is plural and elusive, but while these qualities have been suppressed in language (partly in the interest of communicative effectiveness) they have often been celebrated and idealised in music, perhaps nowhere more so than in the Western art-music tradition.

This is a point that Wagner seems to demonstrate in the relationships that he constructs between musical motifs and libretto. Indeed, music drama might be seen as a metaphor for an interrelationship of music with language and narrative that confirms their equal participation in the symbolic economy. Wagner's theoretical explanations of this interrelationship tend to take a dialectical approach in which music and poetry are presented as complementary opposites whose full potential emerges only when they are brought together. This is a position that would seem to confirm the gap between music and language, but it can also suggest an affinity based on common features and goals. In *Opera and Drama* we find the idea expressed in yet another ocean metaphor in which poet and musician, having journeyed in opposite directions around the world, meet at the halfway point and share their experiences so as to prepare each other for the way ahead. Enriched with this knowledge, each finds the remainder of the journey more rewarding and fruitful: the poet is able to sail the ship built by the musician (i.e. the orchestra) and the musician journeys armed with the knowledge of the terrain that the poet has provided.[38] Here the contrast between poet and musician (they travel in opposite directions) is countered by their common intent and their capacity to interact on equal terms.

This is a relationship that can be seen to emerge in the *Ring*. Certainly, as long as we read the staged action as somehow primary and definitive, and the leitmotifs as deriving semantic power only from this association, then we will be left with a parasitic process that consigns music to the status of a linguistic echo. But Wagner's practice seems to suggest something much richer and more balanced. At issue here is not simply the unfortunate (and at times unavoidable) practice of leitmotif labelling, initiated by the thematic guides written by Hans von Wolzogen for the first Bayreuth festival. It is clear, for example, that the so-called 'Sword' motif, first introduced as Wotan enters Valhalla at the end of

[38] Wagner, *Oper und Drama*, p. 159.

Das Rheingold, is not simply about the sword that Siegmund will later pull from the ash tree; Wagner makes at least that much clear by introducing the motif in the course of Wotan's 'grand idea', when there is as yet no verbal representation of the sword. More importantly, if the eventual appearance of the sword on stage and the references to it in the dialogue between Siegmund and Sieglinde provide definitions for the motif which now accompanies them, then, equally, the motif provides definitions for what happens on stage. The motif, the stage prop, and the verbal references to the sword are signifiers, brought into a nexus and qualifying each other to create a wealth of possible signifieds. Those meanings have as much to do with the militaristic and heroic associations of the musical motif and its scoring (not to mention the deliberately grand, arresting mode of presentation) as they do with the verbal representations of the sword, or the prop (whatever form it takes) that represents it on stage. And just as the visual and verbal signifiers are altered (Wotan will later smash the sword) and presented in new contexts (the sword will become a symbol of Wotan's powerlessness when Siegfried uses it to break his spear), so the motif takes on new forms.

In the prelude to Act II of *Die Walküre* the motif is melodically altered to outline a series of arpeggiated chords, is contrapuntally combined with several other motifs, and is presented in a rhythmic guise that anticipates the famous 'Valkyrie' music. On the one hand, the appearance of the motif and its transformations is 'explained' (Wagner writes of 'foreboding') by the scene that follows: Wotan commands Brünnhilde to fly to Siegmund's side in his battle with Hunding. But the urgency with which the prelude invests the motif carries its own weight: it is as much explanation as anticipation. The prelude robs the motif of the grandiose, epic quality that has marked its previous appearances, and whereas the motif had once brought the musical discourse to a standstill so that it could resound triumphantly, it now finds itself in competition with other material, swept away by agitated echoes of the love music from Act I, and tightly framed by other motivic material. The prelude presents a musical trope of conflict, one that invests the 'Sword' motif with new meaning(s). And with what Lawrence Kramer calls 'reciprocal semiotic pressure',[39] those meanings potentially impact upon the effect of future returns of the motif, which in turn interact with further verbal and visual signifiers related to the sword.

It is true, certainly, that the staged scenes can encourage the perception of the leitmotif as parasitic: consigned to the invisible depths, the orchestra (source of most of the motifs) is always in danger of sliding into an accompaniment role at the feet of the primary business of the stage. A possible function of the leitmotif-laden preludes and interludes,

[39] Kramer, *Classical Music and Postmodern Knowledge*, p. 97.

then, would be to provide a space that balances the accompaniment impression by briefly foregrounding *musical* chains of signification. We have seen, for example, that the so-called 'Ring' motif , with its associations of power, wealth, and greed, 'gives birth' to a new motif that will become associated with Valhalla, with Wotan's power and his sense of his own authority. The link between the motifs exemplifies that process of slippage/deferral that Lacan identifies when one signifier attaches itself to another, and it potentially sets up an interrelationship based both on difference and on similarity. Despite the explicit melodic bond between the two motifs, harmonic ambiguity and syncopation give way to a march-like simplicity and squareness suggestive of assurance and mastery, a transformation that links the equivocal nature of the ring's power with Wotan's very identity and thus suggests something of the duplicity and self-deception lurking beneath his pride. This is a question that is developed in the libretto into one of the central themes of the cycle, but it is never clarified in a way that 'says' anything more than that initial musical transformation. The question always remains as to how much this underlying conflict represents a conscious self-awareness, how much Wotan recognises his own role in negatively empowering the ring through his theft and exchange.[40] The point here is that the transformation in the interlude is not somehow defined by the events on stage, but rather that both involve a potentially endless play of meaning; neither musical *nor* dramatic meaning submits to simple definition or reduction. Wagner can be seen, then, to construct a symbolic economy in which neither music nor language is privileged as a guarantor of meaning. By participating in this symbolic exchange, do the leitmotifs then stand as a kind of defence against that regressive quality we identified in the interludes? Do they, in a sense, de-idealise music by resisting that imaginary, presymbolic element, that 'world of dreams', to which music drama seems to point?

Constructing metaphysics

Let us assume for the moment that without continual reassociation with word and scene the leitmotifs would revert to what Abbate calls 'pure music'. By assigning music a space very much of its own, the preludes and interludes might offer reinforcement to this argument. Neither the scenic nor the verbal discourses have any equivalent to this space because they are always accompanied by music or by each other. Only music is presented in isolation, and while this separation might be seen

[40] Wotan's despairing monologue in Act II of *Die Walküre* would suggest self-knowledge, and yet he continues to focus on the problem of ownership, as though keeping the ring out of Alberich's evil hands would somehow stave off the downfall that his own complicity has set in motion.

to entrust music with a dramatic, narrative function, it might also set it apart, as though there were something here that resisted any bridging with the stage, something unique to music. Put another way, the dominating presence of the leitmotifs within the preludes and interludes suggests a bridging function, but the very fact that their presence is felt so strongly here seems to imply that something about the leitmotifs is irreducibly 'musical', as though they gravitated *away* from the verbal and visual signifiers with which they have been associated during the staged scenes. It is as if here, in the absence of word or scene, they become their authentic selves, able to develop, vary, and interact with one another in ways that the staged scenes stifle in the interests of a theatrical, not musical, coherence.

Abbate's 'pure music' depends on an *imagined* liberation of the leitmotif, as though they *could* be freed from the stage, but in practice are not. This sense of an absolute music that is implied if never actually heard lies behind Dahlhaus's reading of the leitmotif:

The only appropriate kind of reception, as in the poetry of Stéphane Mallarmé, lies in a process which, to be sure, begins with the simple, linguistically expressible meanings of the motifs (in poetry it is the everyday meaning of the words), but which gradually, the more numerous and entangled the musical and musical-dramatic relationships between the motifs become, moves further and further away from the original tangible meaning, without, however, crossing the boundary where the linguistically and scenically conveyed meaning dissolved totally in the absolute musical one. The aesthetic goal, paradoxically expressed, consists in the path from illustrative to absolute music, whereby the starting point, being a crude simplification, is immediately crossed and the goal is never supposed to be reached.[41]

Like Abbate and Adorno, Dahlhaus configures the leitmotif in terms of a forced alliance between music and stage, an alliance that music gradually relinquishes once set free to 'be' music. But what is particularly interesting here is Dahlhaus's configuration of absolute music as a goal that is always implied rather than attained, as though it existed only as a kind of fantasised surplus that could never actually be heard. The suggestion is that music drama sets up an imaginary process of increasing musical independence that has as its conclusion an absolute Music. Perhaps, then, a 'pure' Music might be nothing more than an idea constructed when music drama *appears* to constrain music; it is the sense of surplus that the leitmotif establishes in a negative sense. This is surely what lies behind the preludes and interludes, where Wagner sets music apart, only to then limit it in a way that invites a projection of what might have been.

[41] Carl Dahlhaus, 'The Music', trans. Alfred Clayton, in Müller and Wapnewski (eds.), *Wagner Handbook*, p. 310.

All this has implications for the metaphysics of music. The effect here is surely not to cast music in negative terms as though it *lacked* meaning, but precisely to elevate it beyond the *mere* symbolic order of language and worldly affairs, to endow it with too much meaning (Adorno's characterisation of music as a 'language remote from meaning' is certainly not meant in a pejorative sense). Music is positioned as though it transcended the scenic and visual, but is then returned to the stage, leaving behind what Wagner had called in *The Artwork of the Future* the 'foreboding of the infinite'. Or, to use the language of the later Schopenhauerian essays, the stage offers visual and verbal explanations (or perhaps translations) of music's native metaphysical language.

In *The Birth of Tragedy* Nietzsche conveys a sense of the necessity of these explanations as counterweights to the Dionysian character of Wagner's music:

> To these genuine musicians I direct the question whether they can imagine a human being who would be able to perceive the third act of *Tristan und Isolde*, without any aid of word and image, purely as a tremendous symphonic movement, without expiring in a spasmodic unharnessing of all the wings of the soul.[42]

This sense of excess, of a pleasure that would overwhelm the subject, is captured in Lacan's concept of *jouissance*, a term he defines as 'painful pleasure'.[43] Like the death drive, *jouissance* is 'beyond the pleasure principle', beyond the regulation of pleasure that characterises the symbolic order. The excess that it represents threatens the sense of structure and strict limitation on which the symbolic order depends, and so it must be renounced if the subject is to function within the symbolic, within language. This prohibition is, in a sense, the price of language and subjectivity, but it also invites transgression. When the captivating – if illusory – images of the imaginary order give way to language, plenitude and sufficiency are replaced with difference and lack; the subject learns that it can have no real possession of the world around it, that it must separate itself off from objects, designating them with signifiers that stand in for those objects and that link with other signifiers in an endless chain.

But this exclusion and deferral never fully succeeds because the subject still partly holds on to the promise of full possession, the promise of an object that will bring all this lack to an end and prove to be the reason for or substance of *jouissance*. In other words, the process of limiting and excluding encourages an investment in, and idealisation of,

---

[42] Friedrich Nietzsche, *The Birth of Tragedy* (1872), in Kaufmann (ed. and trans.), *Basic Writings of Nietzsche*, pp. 126–7.
[43] Jacques Lacan, *The Seminar, Book VII: The Ethics of Psychoanalysis, 1959–1960*, trans. Dennis Porter (London: Routledge, 1992), p. 184.

that which is limited and excluded. It creates a space (a void) for a fantasy object that promises a pleasure excluded by the symbolic order. Lacan refers to the fantasy object as 'objet petit a', that is, an object with only a little otherness (Fr. 'autre'), one that is always bound up with our own ego, in contrast to the radical alterity of the Other. Never comfortably assimilated into the symbolic order, *objet petit a* has the value of a surplus-enjoyment that seems to highlight and point beyond the limiting function of the symbolic. This excluded space to which the *objet petit a* seems to point is termed by Lacan the real, and it becomes the third order, together with the imaginary and symbolic, in the Lacanian system. The real is that which cannot be symbolised, which the symbolic order must exclude because, in terms of signification, it is 'impossible'.[44] In this sense it bears some resemblance to Kristeva's semiotic, which can be seen to incorporate elements of both the real and the imaginary. The crucial difference, however, is that Kristeva positivises the void of the Lacanian real: 'Thus perhaps the notion of the semiotic allows us to speak of the real without simply saying that it's an emptiness or a blank; it allows us to further elaborate on it.'[45] As we have seen, of course, it is 'music' that serves to positivise that emptiness, a notion that can only be seen to reinforce the traditional isolation of music, and that diminishes the appeal of Kristeva's thought for a critical musicology.

But how is Lacan relevant to Wagner? In a remarkable study of the relationship between Lacanian thought and the traditions of nineteenth-century philosophical idealism, Slavoj Žižek compares the real to the Kantian *Ding-an-sich*. Both seem to occupy a place that we can posit but never actually access: the real is always beyond the reach of the symbolic, while the *Ding-an-sich* only becomes perceivable via the transcendental object, that is, the object of appearance. But Žižek draws a crucial distinction:

[T]he real designates a substantial hard kernel that precedes and resists symbolization and, simultaneously, it designates the left-over, which is posited or 'produced' by symbolization itself. However, what we must avoid at any price is conceiving of this left-over as simply secondary, as if we have *first* the substantial fullness of the real and *then* the process of symbolization which 'evacuates' *jouissance*, yet not entirely, leaving behind isolated reminders, islands of enjoyment, objets petit a. If we succumb to this notion, we lose the paradox of the Lacanian real: there is no substance without, prior to, the surplus of enjoyment. *The substance is a mirage retroactively invoked by the surplus.* The illusion that

[44] Jacques Lacan, *The Seminar, Book XI: The Four Fundamental Concepts of Psychoanalysis, 1964*, trans. Alan Sheridan (London: Hogarth Press and Institute of Psycho-Analysis, 1977), p. 167.
[45] Cited in Julia Kristeva, *The Kristeva Reader*, ed. Toril Moi (New York: Columbia University Press, 1986), p. 7.

pertains to *a* qua surplus-enjoyment is therefore the very illusion that, behind it, there is the lost substance of *jouissance*.[46]

Symbolisation, then, 'manufactures' the real by configuring *jouissance* as surplus, so that the real is perceived to be the pre-existent source of that *jouissance*. It is this illusion, Žižek suggests, that can be detected at the root of Kant's *Ding-an-sich*:

[W]hat Kant fails to notice is that *das Ding* is a mirage invoked by the transcendental object . . . all that 'actually exists' is the field of phenomena and its limitation, whereas *das Ding* is nothing but a phantasm which, subsequently, fills out the void of the transcendental object.[47]

The key for Žižek is Lacan's symbolic order, the 'intervention of the signifier' that divides an 'accessible, symbolically structured, reality'[48] from an apparently lost encounter with an object that would yield total satisfaction.

The same mirage might be detected as the root of Schopenhauer's metaphysics, where the inaccessible Thing becomes the Will:

The will as thing-in-itself is quite different from its phenomenon, and is entirely free from all the forms of the phenomenon into which it first passes when it appears, and which therefore concern only its objectivity, and are foreign to the will itself.[49]

But music offers a special access to the inaccessible:

[M]usic differs from all the other arts by the fact that it is not a copy of the phenomenon . . . but is directly a copy of the will itself, and therefore expresses the metaphysical to everything physical in the world, the thing-in-itself to every phenomenon.[50]

Words and scenery, then, copy the phenomena, the symbolic world of appearances, while music concerns itself with the higher reality of the Will that courses through the world:

For this reason the effect of music is so very much more powerful and penetrating than is that of the other arts, for these others speak only of the shadow, but music of the essence.[51]

The result in opera, argues Schopenhauer, is a certain imbalance in which word and scene, concerned with phenomena in all their particularity, stand as 'random examples' compared to the 'universal language of music'.[52] There is, in other words, an arbitrariness to the music–stage

[46] Slavoj Žižek, *Tarrying with the Negative* (Durham, N.C.: Duke University Press, 1993), p. 36.

[47] Ibid., p. 37. [48] Ibid.

[49] Arthur Schopenhauer, *The World as Will and Representation* (1818; 1859), trans. E. F. J. Payne, 2 vols. (New York: Dover Publications, 1969), vol. I, p. 112.

[50] Ibid., p. 262. [51] Ibid., p. 257. [52] Ibid., p. 263.

alliance in which words and images become exchangeable, even dispensable. Nietzsche's reading of the orchestra in *Tristan* echoes Schopenhauer here, and perhaps aligns itself with the Lacanian real even more closely by attributing to this music a dangerous quality that suggests the traumatic character of the real, 'the object of anxiety par excellence'.[53] If words and scenery constitute the symbolic order in this reading, music suggests an excess, a *jouissance*, that refuses to be contained by the symbolic. Music is the *objet petit a* that points in the direction of the unknowable real.

But what the preludes and interludes suggest is that music is very much *positioned* as surplus, as uncontainable. What they seem to uncover is the process by which Wagner aligns music with excess, *constructing* it as surplus-enjoyment. And as with *objet petit a*, the appeal of the musical fantasy-object consists in its very excessiveness and unattainability. This much is obvious from Nietzsche's 'what if' reading of *Tristan*, configuring the Dionysian power of the orchestral music as a pleasure beyond the limit, unbearable, and ultimately only to be fantasised, not experienced. And so music drama continues to anchor us in the world of appearances, reining music in, as it were. Here the stage represents the 'intervention of the signifier', dividing the symbolic from the lost *jouissance* of an unheard music.

There is a strong sense of this limitation as the prelude to *Das Rheingold* gives way to the opening scene: the surging orchestra, by now at full volume, is suddenly cut back, and the ascending scales for strings that had once threatened to 'throw off all restraint', as Adorno suggested of Schreker's music, are now reduced to accompaniment, allowed to echo their former power only intermittently. The effect is usually less abrupt, as in the interlude that introduces the Prologue scene between Siegfried and Brünnhilde in *Götterdämmerung*. Here again the orchestra reaches a climax, throwing off the gloomy restraint of the Norns scene and gathering momentum in a wave of sound that is at once a sunrise (stage directions indicate a growing light) and a monumental act of love-making of which only Teutonic heroes would be capable. See, for example, the inflated renditions of Siegfried's horn motif (the very sort of gesture that Strauss was to satirise in *Feuersnot*). By comparison, the appearance of Siegfried and Brünnhilde introduces an element of restraint, and it is some time before the lovers work up to the kind of intensity to which the orchestra has just abandoned itself so freely. And by the conclusion, when the pair have worked themselves into a frenzy of heroic-erotic zeal, there is a reverse effect: the music 'spills over' into

---

[53] Jacques Lacan, *The Seminar, Book II: The Ego in Freud's Theory and in the Technique of Psychoanalysis, 1954–1955*, trans. Sylvana Tomaselli (New York: Norton, 1988), p. 164.

Example 6.1   Wagner, *Siegfried*, Act III (p. 285)

the following interlude (the famous Rhine Journey), as if its accumulated energy could no longer be held by the scene and the increasingly
excited cries of 'Heil!' marked the limit of the voice's capacity to sing this
music. Cutting off the final cry is a full-brass arrangement of the horn
motif that seems to absorb the momentum and very gradually dispel
the energy, before the Rhine Journey inaugurates another orchestral
climax.

Nor is this effect simply about power or energy. The interlude preceding the final scene of *Siegfried* promises a great deal more than the scene
ever delivers. The extraordinary, ethereal melodic arch for unaccompanied violins (example 6.1), heard while Siegfried scales Brünnhilde's
rock amidst a 'fine rose-coloured mist', suggests an ineffable longing
that is cruelly dispelled by what is ultimately a raucous, ham-fisted
love scene in Wagner's most brutal style. And do the five hours of
Tristan really live up to what the prelude delivers in its super-
concentrated ten minutes? This is not to suggest, absurdly, that a polarisation is set up in which a musical intensity or immediacy is consistently associated with the orchestra (clearly the staged scenes offer
their own share), but rather that certain key sites such as these have
the effect of aligning music with a capacity that is beyond the stage, a
surplus. They place music in a position of excess, and in so doing contribute to the construction of that metaphysics of music that Wagner
propagated in his later writings and that emerges in Nietzsche's
Dionysian vision.

In one sense the regressive character of the preludes and interludes
seems to be countered by the concentrated presence of the leitmotif,
an appeal to the symbolic as against that imaginary experience likened
by Wagner and others to dreaming, narcosis, floating, sleeping, and
the 'retuning of the whole sensorium'. But in another sense Wagner's
theorising 'redeems' this experience by granting it a metaphysical benediction. That musical 'foreboding of the infinite' Wagner describes in

The Artwork of the Future or that 'inexpressible' with which the orchestra is associated in *Opera and Drama* already constitute a metaphysics of music. Wagner's argument in the Zurich essays, for example, that the 'limitless depths' of the musical ocean demanded word and scene to make sense of them – adjectives such as 'indefinite' and 'vague' are common in *Opera and Drama*[54] – compares with the later configurations in which the stage serves to ground music in ways that provide necessary limitations to its metaphysical meaning. But Schopenhauer's philosophy, that 'gift from heaven' as he described it to Liszt,[55] seems to provide Wagner with a means of articulating and justifying this metaphysics. Here those ocean depths become the very proof of music's transcendent value. Here it is precisely music's remoteness from the symbolic on which its power and fascination depend. And this is not presented as something regressive and presymbolic, as the ocean metaphors might have suggested. Rather, it is utterly beyond the grasp of language and the world of phenomena, a shadow of a higher reality.

Music, then, begins with the imaginary environment of the dream, but its goal is the real, completely passing over the symbolic towards that which defies symbolisation. Music drama utterly refuses to acknowledge its seductive means for what they are. It must idealise its 'world of dreams' as echoes of the Will, and impart 'infinite significance' to the 'waves' of sound that flood the audience. 'In the *Gesamtkunstwerk*,' writes Adorno, 'intoxication, ecstasy is an inescapable principle of style; a moment of reflection would suffice to shatter its illusion of ideal unity.'[56] But even in the preludes and interludes, where that intoxication seems to collide so transparently with metaphysical pretension, no trace of reflection emerges.

Schreker's operas pick up on this issue, presenting the relationship between music, dream, and idea as the 'distant sound' that is at once carnal and ephemeral, embodied and yet 'separated from empirical reality by a heaving abyss'. But, as we saw in *Der Schatzgräber*, Schreker renders the issue transparent; he is unwilling to align music with metaphysics without casting doubt, without exposing the idealisation lying beneath 'idea'. What Schreker's problematic also highlights is the question of sensuality, the recognition that the seductive means of operatic music rest on a visceral appeal to the body. For Adorno, Wagnerian music drama represents an attempt to breathe life into a metaphysics seriously eroded by positivism, a response to the 'disenchantment of the world' that is anything but enchanted:

---

54 Wagner, *Oper und Drama*, p. 189.
55 Wagner, letter to Franz Liszt, December 1854, in Kesting (ed.), *Richard Wagner Briefe*, p. 295.
56 Adorno, *In Search of Wagner*, pp. 104–5.

The totality of the music drama is an aggregate of all the reactions of the sense organs and this aggregate is founded not only on the absence of a valid style, but even more on the dissolution of metaphysics. The aim of the *Gesamtkunstwerk* is not so much to express such a metaphysics as to produce it.[57]

What we have, then, is a metaphysical vacuum which Wagner fills by constructing a metaphysics from very physical means. Running through Adorno's analysis is that same suspicion of sensuality we noted in his Schreker criticism. It is the same all too direct appeal to the body that he detects in the popular culture of the twentieth century, a connection he summarises when he sees in music drama the 'birth of film out of the spirit of music'.[58]

'A truly sensual pleasure'

What Adorno resists, Baudelaire embraces enthusiastically. Writing to Wagner after an 1860 Paris performance of excerpts from *Tannhäuser*, *Lohengrin*, and *Tristan*, he enthuses:

I frequently experienced a rather odd emotion, which could be described as the pride and pleasure [*jouissance*] of comprehension, of allowing myself to be penetrated and invaded – a truly sensual pleasure recalling that of floating through the air or rolling on the sea . . . Generally those deep harmonies seemed to me comparable to those stimulants that speed up the pulse of the imagination. Finally, I experienced in addition – and I beg you not to laugh – feelings that probably stem from my particular cast of mind and my frequent preoccupations. Your music is full of something both uplifted and uplifting, something that longs to climb higher, something excessive and superlative.[59]

Baudelaire's reaction echoes many of the themes that we have encountered before – the sea metaphor, narcosis, excess – but of particular interest here is his characterisation of Wagner's music as both a 'truly sensual pleasure' and something 'uplifted and uplifting'. Here Baudelaire seems, innocently, to confront Wagner with the very antithesis that music drama dare not name. This is not simply that sensual–spiritual struggle that Wagner explicitly thematicises in his music and libretti, and that Baudelaire was to identify as the meaning of the *Tannhäuser* prelude in his article 'Richard Wagner et *Tannhäuser* à Paris'. Baudelaire's concern in his letter is not so much with representation (that is, what Wagner's music sets out to trace or evoke) as with the ways in which it *affects* him. This is his stated purpose in writing the letter: 'Above all, I want to say that I am indebted to you for the greatest musical pleasure I've

---

[57] Ibid., p. 107.   [58] Ibid.
[59] Charles Baudelaire, letter to Wagner, 17 February 1860, trans. in Lacoue-Labarthe, *Musica ficta*, pp. 2–3.

ever experienced.'[60] While acknowledging the impression of sublimity, that 'longing to climb higher' which Wagner's music arouses in him, he does not hesitate to equate that sublimity with very down-to-earth effects. The impressions of the music never seem to be anything more than that for Baudelaire; he reads Wagner in performative terms as a music that sets out to achieve certain effects and succeeds, impressively, in achieving them. In this sense he falls far short of Wagner's claims for his music. To describe it in terms of the *effect* of something spiritual or metaphysical is very different from positing an *actual* transcendence whereby music touches on a reality beyond the scope of the finite, visible, embodied world.

We can get some idea of Wagner's attitude to music and the body by tracing his own use of the concept of sensuality (*Sinnlichkeit*), a term that has emerged repeatedly in this study. In *Opera and Drama* Wagner associates musical sensuality with 'tone painting', and particularly the music of Mendelssohn and Berlioz. He credits this music with having enriched the 'sensual power' of instrumental music, but adds that the 'tone painters' had failed to address what he calls 'the feeling' and had appealed only to the imagination. Had they done so, he argues, they would have avoided a certain 'coldness' that he detects in this music. (As we might expect, Wagner sees drama as the only possibility of introducing that appeal to 'feeling'.)[61] In *A Message to My Friends* (1851) he uses the term in a critique of his early operas, singling out *Das Liebesverbot* as the product of an 'impetuous, sensually stimulated perceptive faculty' (*Empfindungsvermögen*).[62] And later in the same essay he defines the sensual in a way that seems to anticipate the more overt metaphysical perspective of the later texts:

Humanity's sentient nature longs to escape from a wretched and dishonoured sensuality towards a noble sense of reality more in keeping with its nature.[63]

Clearly, even before his adoption of that Schopenhauerian 'gift from heaven', Wagner demonstrated, at least in theory, a deep suspicion of music as sensual experience. It is something incomplete, demanding justification or control or elevation.

With Schopenhauer Wagner seems to have discovered a means of articulating this idealism: an entire philosophical system built around the rejection of sensuality. Schopenhauer exalts the blissful state of the ascetic, in whom the Will is 'completely extinguished, except for the last glimmering spark that maintains the body and is extinguished with it'.[64] Schopenhauer expresses a disgust with the body and its Will to live and

[60] Ibid., p. 2.   [61] Wagner, *Oper und Drama*, p. 188.
[62] Wagner, *Eine Mitteilung an meiner Freunde*, p. 255.   [63] Ibid., p. 332.
[64] Schopenhauer, *The World as Will*, vol. I, p. 390.

reproduce, and the individual who strives to be free of the Will must be on guard against it:

His body, healthy and strong, expresses the sexual impulse through the genitals, but he denies the will, and gives the lie to the body.[65]

For those still ensnared by the Will, this Will-less existence is foreshadowed, if only temporarily, by the aesthetic experience, and particularly by music:

The inexpressible depth of all music, by virtue of which it floats past us as a paradise quite familiar and yet eternally remote, and is so easy to understand and yet so inexplicable, is due to the fact that it reproduces all the emotions of our innermost being, but entirely without reality and remote from its pain.[66]

If denial of the Will is a denial of the body, then music, by providing a glimpse of this existence, implies a similar resistance to the body and indeed to the material as a whole. Put another way, music enters the body while, in a sense, bypassing the body. In a letter of 1871 to an Italian admirer, Wagner aligns this sensual–ideal duality with national tendencies. The German, he writes, has always maintained a certain resistance to sensuality and appearance:

If this necessarily led us to an idealistic account of the world, it also protected us from the flaw of abandoning ourselves to it all too realistically. With us, music became less of a beautiful and more of a sublime art; and this sublimity seems to have a great magical effect, for those who have been transfixed by it have shown no inclination towards the seduction of more sensual beauty.[67]

In stark contrast to Baudelaire and his apparent innocence of Wagner's metaphysical pretensions, Nietzsche understood only too well what was at stake here. Having contributed in *The Birth of Tragedy* to the construction of the metaphysics of music drama, he proceeded to expose the scaffolding holding it up. In the Third Essay of the *Genealogy of Morals*, entitled 'What is the Meaning of Ascetic Ideals?', he wonders if the

sweetness and plenitude of the aesthetic state might be derived precisely from the ingredient of 'sensuality' . . . so that sensuality is not overcome by the appearance of the aesthetic condition, as Schopenhauer believed, but only transfigured and no longer enters consciousness as sexual excitement.[68]

It is a deconstruction that seems to anticipate the Freudian concept of sublimation, and it returns as a central critical thrust of *The Case of*

---

[65] Ibid., p. 380.   [66] Ibid., p. 264.
[67] Wagner, 'Brief an einen italienischen Freund über die Aufführung des *Lohengrin* in Bologna' (7 November 1871), *SSD*, vol. IX, pp. 290–1.
[68] Friedrich Nietzsche, *The Genealogy of Morals* (1887), in Kaufmann (ed. and trans.), *Basic Writings of Nietzsche*, p. 547.

Wagner. There he takes one sarcastic swipe after another at Wagnerian pretensions:

To elevate men one has to be sublime oneself. Let us walk on clouds, let us harangue the infinite, let us surround ourselves with symbols! . . . Let us never admit that music 'serves recreation'; that it 'exhilarates'; that it 'gives pleasure.' Let us never give pleasure! We are lost as soon as art is again thought of hedonistically.[69]

Unable to tolerate music as 'mere' pleasure, Wagner insists on puffing it up to become an experience of the sublime. But as we have seen, Nietzsche also sees Wagner as the 'artist of decadence', the actor, tyrant, and conjurer whose music acts like a stimulant on the nerves. This for Nietzsche is no longer a question of sensuality *per se*, but of a very calculated reduction of 'sound, movement, colour' to an elementary and styleless form that is interested only in effect.[70] Wagner, in other words, hollows out (polarises) a 'healthy' musical sensuality to become pathologically oriented effect clothed in the trappings of the sublime. At the root of this corruption and deception is theatre:

Wagner was not a musician by instinct. He showed this by abandoning all lawfulness and, more precisely, all style in music in order to turn it into what he required, theatrical rhetoric, a means of expression, of underscoring gestures, of suggestion, of the psychologically picturesque . . . Wagner's music, if not shielded by theatre taste, which is a very tolerant taste, is simply bad music, perhaps the worst ever made. When a musician can no longer count up to three he becomes 'dramatic', he becomes 'Wagnerian'.[71]

Nietzsche implies a fundamental incompatibility between 'good' music and theatre, and he is in no doubt as to where Wagner's talents lie. Nor is he reticent about his contempt for the theatre, which he describes as 'always only *beneath* art, always only something secondary, something made cruder'.[72] This resistance to the theatre had already emerged in the imaginary wordless, stageless *Tristan* of *The Birth of Tragedy*, but now Wagner's music holds out no promise of its own. Nietzsche can no longer imagine a music freed from the stage because he no longer believes in a Wagnerian 'music' as distinct from Wagnerian 'histrionics'; it is all tainted by the theatre.[73]

Nietzsche's definition of a healthy musical sensuality claims a middle ground, a pleasure that deconstructs metaphysics while remaining aloof from the theatre. It is a position that is vulnerable to some of the charges that Nietzsche levels against Wagner: Nietzsche, too, would seem to engage in a degree of idealisation, delimiting the aesthetic so as to exclude the 'crude' appeal of the theatre. But Nietzsche's seemingly

---

[69] Nietzsche, *The Case of Wagner*, pp. 624–5.   [70] Ibid., p. 629.   [71] Ibid., pp. 628–9.
[72] Ibid., p. 638.   [73] Ibid., p. 628.

excessive polarisations of Wagner's music never hide their polemical intent. Their purpose is to draw attention once again to the doubleness in music drama, to the lofty metaphysical claim that is actually everything it disavows.[74] Put another way, the more music drama gives the impression of transcending mundane reality, the more it relies on its sensual appeal to create that impression. And again, the preludes and interludes would seem to exemplify this doubleness. They depend on the pleasure of sound and of the absence of sight, and, if the accounts of the Bayreuth critics are anything to go by, this sightless sound holds considerable sensual appeal. When Twain describes the experience as something 'delicious' and 'exquisite', when Lavignac writes of being 'possessed' and 'transported', or when Hanslick likens the music to a 'mild opium jag', sensual experience is very much to the fore. This is why Nietzsche turns to parallels with 'physiological degeneration' and 'hystericism'.[75]

At the same time, the interludes represent a slippage away from the very direct physicality of the theatre; their sensual appeal is not that of theatre. It is a difference that hinges, as Weissmann realised, on the actor, on the sight and sound of the singing body. 'Whatever else music is "about",' writes Richard Leppert, 'it is inevitably about the body; music's aural and visual presence constitutes both a relation to and a representation of the body.'[76] Leppert's observation applies with particular force to opera, where the double physical demand of acting and singing places the body's stamina, control, and presence at the centre of attention and perhaps accounts for part of the fascination of being in the theatre and watching the performance. But, as Leppert recognises, Bayreuth problematises the issue by splitting sight from sound. The orchestral discourse is also performed by bodies, but there they remain hidden from view. When the singers are absent from the stage and everything depends on the orchestra, we are denied the pleasure of watching and feeling the presence of the performing body. Or should that be the *embarrassment* of watching?

Oh, I hate the thought of all those costumes and grease paint! When I think that characters like Kundry will now have to be dressed up, those dreadful artists' balls spring to mind![77]

---

[74] For a more detailed discussion of Nietzsche's polemical 'masks' and his attitude to the theatre, see my ' "Alienated from His Own Being": Nietzsche, Bayreuth and the Problem of Identity', *Journal of the Royal Musical Association*, forthcoming. Nietzsche's Wagner criticism demands readings that are open to the plurality of voices that run through his texts. For an astute handling of this question see Tambling, *Opera and the Culture of Fascism*, pp. 60–9.

[75] Nietzsche, *The Case of Wagner*, p. 625.   [76] Leppert, *The Sight of Sound*, p. xx.

[77] Cosima Wagner, diary entry for 23 September 1878, in Gregor-Dellin and Mack (eds.), *Cosima Wagner's Diaries*, p. 324.

Perhaps, then, the preludes and interludes testify to the same qualms about the theatre that underlie Nietzsche's criticism. Wagner, too, seeks refuge in music from the physicality of the theatre. The crucial point here is the contrast between a visible, embodied theatre and an invisible, seemingly disembodied music. Music is positioned as different because it distances itself from the more overt materiality of the stage. It is within the space of this *apparent* remoteness from the physicality of the theatre that the preludes and interludes contribute to the idealisation of music on which Wagner's metaphysics depends. But for Nietzsche Wagner's appeal to the ideal, to the magical, to the unknowable, only masks the all too vivid presence of the body at the heart of his music.

And as Gary Tomlinson observes, the contradiction is nowhere more apparent than in *Parsifal*, where so much of the stage imagery suggests a leaden, material quality – Tomlinson writes of a 'sinking heaviness' – that defies the metaphysical embrace of Wagner's orchestra.[78] *Parsifal*, he argues, sums up the late Wagner's quest to touch on magic, but it equally shows that this quest was always deeply rooted in the material world. This contradiction also surfaces in the handling of the leitmotifs, whose interchangeability has reached new proportions and whose transformations into one another connote mystery and magic. Here the symbolic economy with which we have associated the leitmotifs resembles increasingly the exchange value that Adorno identifies when he characterises the leitmotif in terms of the Marxian commodity. But Wagner's leitmotifs also insist on their individuality, drawing attention to what Tomlinson calls their 'autonomy and expressive self-sufficiency'.[79] They appear out of the musical ether and unfold ritualistically as though individually charged with the capacity to summon the spirit. This opposition between autonomy and interchangeability could be read as a dialectic in which the leitmotifs' individual objectification of religious magic happens only in the context of their absorption into the mystifying dissolution of exchange. But for Tomlinson Wagner reduces this dialectic to a mere 'dualism' in which 'literal' and 'objective' representation is redeemed into a much more 'ideal' form.[80] In other words, *Parsifal* strives towards a form of representation appropriate to its mystical content, just as the Symbolists would seek to redefine the nature of representation. Tomlinson concurs with Adorno on the 'truth value' of *Parsifal*, on its illumination of the nature of exchange and the parallels of this exchange process with the modern subject's search for autonomy in the face of its own commodification. But, he adds, this value depends on critical appropriation: 'Truth this may be, as Adorno

---

[78] Gary Tomlinson, *Metaphysical Song: An Essay on Opera* (Princeton: Princeton University Press, 1999), p. 141.
[79] Ibid., p. 140.   [80] Ibid., p. 141.

has it, a truth rescued from falsehood. But it is hardly the truth Wagner intended.'[81]

'The hashish dream of the ecstatic female'

By characterising the sensuality of Wagner's music in terms of hysteria, Nietzsche also invokes gender associations. Hysteria was considered the female symptom *par excellence* – the very term is derived from the Greek for 'womb' – and the late nineteenth century, seemingly fixated with the pathology of hysteria, only strengthened its associations with the feminine when female hysterics were presented before audiences of enquiring scientific minds, analysed in writing, and photographed to document its effects on the body. Is musical sensuality then also a musical hysteria, a feminised music in which the body asserts itself uncontrollably? Hanslick is in little doubt as to its effect and its appeal:

It is through its sensually fascinating magic that this music, as a direct nervous stimulant, works so powerfully on the audience and on the female audience particularly. The professional musician's part in this highly advanced orchestral technique also has a lot to do with how it is all accomplished. I underestimate neither the one nor the other; but neither is entitled to violent domination. Neither the technical gourmet interest of the conductor, nor the hashish dream of the ecstatic female, fulfils the nature and benediction of genuine musical composition.[82]

Here Wagner's music oscillates between an orchestral technique characterised by empty virtuosity (the charge that Adorno would level against Strauss) and a feminine appeal to the senses (Bellaigue's criticism of Massenet). It is women who respond to Wagner's musical 'stimulants' because it is women who identify with the condition of ecstasy that it generates. Nietzsche, for his part, writes of Wagner's 'success with nerves and consequently women' and of woman as 'embodying the cause of Wagner'.[83] (Wagner's own theorising may have provided reinforcement for gendered readings of this kind when he described woman as the 'essential embodiment of the purest sensual instinct' ('reinsten sinnlichen Unwillkür'), characterising the feminine in terms of a quality beyond woman's conscious control.)[84] Implied by Nietzsche and Hanslick, too, is the idea that male identification with this music might mean identification with a feminine position, with an ecstasy/hysteria/*jouissance* that is Other to the masculine aesthetic

---

[81] Ibid., p. 142.
[82] Hanslick, review in *Neue Freie Presse*, in Hartford (ed. and trans.), *Bayreuth: The Early Years*, p. 84.
[83] Nietzsche, *The Case of Wagner*, pp. 622, 641.
[84] Wagner, *Eine Mitteilung an meiner Freunde*, p. 302.

experience. Here Wagner's music is not only feminised but feminising, an issue to which we shall return later. It is also worth recalling the Lacanian thesis that man aligns woman with *jouissance*, with that excess which he 'must renounce' in order to establish (masculine) identity; woman's excess here becomes the Other that defines the limits of the self. Wagner's music, it seems, might pose a threat to those limits, seducing the male listener into letting down his guard against domination and against the feminised pleasures of the body. Baudelaire is unusual here, too, in that he enthuses about 'allowing myself to be penetrated and invaded' and 'a paroxysm of ecstasy' without any of the gender demarcations that so often accompany reactions of this kind.

The preludes and interludes would seem to epitomise masculinist concerns over Wagner's music, in the sense that their tendency towards the regressive might be seen, like Esclarmonde's island or Els's bedroom, as disempowering and feminising, while the position of excess they seem to occupy in relation to the stage might suggest a crossing of the limits of the masculine Word into Music's feminine night. Wagner sets up just such an impression in *Opera and Drama*, where masculine poetry finds fulfilment in the 'eternal feminine' of music. It is through melody, Wagner suggests, that music reaches out to greet poetry, as we can see in this passage partially quoted earlier:

Through the redeeming, loving kiss of that melody the poet is now initiated into the deep, endless mysteries of woman's nature: he sees with other eyes, and feels with other senses. To him the bottomless sea of harmony, from which that blissful vision rose to meet him, is no longer an object of dread, of fear, of terror – that strange and unknown element that had appeared in his imagination. Now, not only can he float on the waves of this ocean, but, endowed with new senses, he dives into its lowest depth. Up from the lonely, eerie reaches of her maternal home the woman had driven herself to await the approach of her beloved. Now the poet descends with his bride and truly learns the hidden wonders of the depths.[85]

Here the familiar sea metaphor is overlaid with gender imagery that echoes the familiar alignment of the feminine with the unknowable. And since it is above all the orchestra with which Wagner associates the harmonic 'depths',[86] a configuration is established in which the orchestra emerges as music's 'motherly home', a mysterious feminine space accessible only thanks to the mediating presence of melody and its coupling with the masculine Word. The combination of pleasure and horror resembles Elis's encounter with Els's 'unsettling' music, and it relates

[85] Wagner, *Oper und Drama*, pp. 146–7.
[86] Ibid., p. 165. On Wagner's gendered metaphors see Grey, *Wagner's Musical Prose*, pp. 130–80, and Jean-Jacques Nattiez, *Wagner Androgyne*, trans. Stewart Spencer (Princeton: Princeton University Press, 1993).

to our reading of the preludes and interludes as *objet petit a*. Here the fantasy object is an unknown feminine that invites phallic investment (implying knowledge and possession) while simultaneously raising the spectre of a castrating loss of control and authority. Pleasure is offered, but only at the price of submission.

Pleasure and horror re-emerge centrally in more recent accounts of this sightless encounter with the feminine, as Silverman has demonstrated. Silverman cites Michel Chion's theorisation of the voice in cinema, in which he invokes a fantasy of entrapment by the mother's voice:

In the beginning, in the uterine night, was the voice, that of the Mother. For the child after birth, the Mother is more an olfactory and vocal continuum than an image. One can imagine the voice of the Mother, which is woven around the child, and which originates from all points in space as her form enters and leaves the visual field, as a matrix of places to which we are tempted to give the name 'umbilical net'. A horrifying expression, since it evokes a cobweb – and in fact, this original vocal tie will remain ambivalent.[87]

Chion presents the mother's voice as a suffocating acoustic cloak, contrasting her discursive mastery with the child's complete domination. It is an unpleasurable, even paranoid fantasy and it surely echoes the 'lonely, fearsome reaches' of the 'motherly home' in Wagner's metaphor. We might also compare Chion's images of a 'uterine night' and the omnipresence of the mother's voice with the observations of the Bayreuth critics: the darkness that 'envelops the hall', the sounds that issue from the 'depths of the mystic abyss' and the 'mysterious heaving of the invisible orchestra'. The spectator, like the child in Chion's account, is surrounded by a sound that appears to come, mysteriously, from 'all points in space'. A very different reading of the mother's voice is to be found in the work of Guy Rosolato:

The maternal voice helps to constitute for the infant the pleasurable milieu which surrounds, sustains and cherishes him ... One could argue that it is the first model of auditory pleasure and that music finds its roots and its nostalgia in [this] original atmosphere, which might be called a sonorous womb, a murmuring house – or music of the spheres.[88]

Again the setting is very much in keeping with the kinds of images evoked in critical responses to the Wagnerian orchestra. Here we return to Kristeva's semiotic chora and its alignment of a now repressed 'music' with a maternal space, and again music is idealised. But Kristeva does not equate the semiotic simply with some irretrievably lost pleasure,

[87] Michel Chion, *La voix au cinéma* (Paris: Editions de l'Etoile, 1982), p. 57, trans. in Silverman, *The Acoustic Mirror*, p. 74.
[88] Rosolato, 'La voix: entre corps et langage', 81, trans. in Silverman, *The Acoustic Mirror*, pp. 84–5.

but rather the potentially unpleasurable activity of the drives *and* their regulation by the primary process acting in the name of the pleasure principle. The fantasy Rosolato outlines, by contrast, is an investment in undiluted pleasure, seeking to revive and embrace the maternal aura of sound as strongly as Chion's seeks to escape it. Both represent extremes, but perhaps they illustrate what is at stake in male fantasies of the musical-maternal. They suggest an extraordinary polarisation between images of pleasure and satisfaction on the one hand and of horror and entrapment on the other. And if Elis's acoustic fantasies are anything to go by, these images are never brought into any kind of compromising synthesis, oscillating instead between extremes. It is an instability that testifies to the function of this fantasised feminine: its very Otherness defines the masculine, but that Otherness can represent both a completion/fulfilment (i.e. what would mythically satisfy all desire) and a threatening difference that would collapse masculine identity.

In *Beethoven* this pleasure–horror duality re-emerges as part of Wagner's reading of Schopenhauer. It is above all through sound, he argues, that the workings of the Will become apparent, nowhere more directly than through the scream, 'the direct manifestation of the anguished Will'. The scream, source of every gentler form of cry, forms the foundation of aural comprehension.[89] Music, too, is a transfiguration of the scream, and Wagner asks how it is that music can be considered an art when, according to Schopenhauer, the creation and perception of art represents precisely a 'diversion of consciousness' from the Will.[90] Here Wagner aligns music with the pain and horror of the Will, an alignment that echoes the 'fear' and 'terror' of music's 'unknown' feminine domain. And there can be no mistaking the feminine connotations of Schopenhauer's Will, that elemental but unknowable force aligned with the body and sexuality. It is because of music's relationship to the Will, Wagner suggests, that 'aestheticians have resisted the idea that a true art could be derived from what seems to them a purely pathological element'.[91] But just as the masculine Word had rendered feminine mystery benign, so Schopenhauer's aesthetic theory provides Wagner with a means of redeeming music from the role of the Will's mouthpiece.

The key, Wagner argues, is the transformed relationship with the Will that the aesthetic state implies. Schopenhauer defines 'aesthetic pleasure' in terms of the deliverance of knowledge from the service of the Will, the forgetting of oneself as individual, and the enhancement of consciousness to the pure, Will-less, timeless subject of knowing that is independent of all relations.[92] The aesthetic state is tantamount to a temporary bracketing off of the Will and the world that objectifies it, so

---

[89] Wagner, *Beethoven*, pp. 69–70.　　[90] Ibid.　　[91] Ibid., p. 72.
[92] Schopenhauer, *The World as Will*, vol. I, p. 199.

that the subject 'knows' the Will without embodying it. Pleasure consists here in being able to perceive the Will, as it were, from the outside. But if, in the case of the visual and verbal arts, this knowledge amounts to a complete silencing of the Will, music, because of its direct relation to the Will, permits a whole new level of 'knowledge'. This is something Wagner repeatedly emphasises when he contrasts the 'purely disinterested perception of objects' in the visual arts with music's revelation of our oneness with the whole world, so that the 'universal Will' is brought to 'full self-consciousness'.[93] Music, in other words, enjoys the double advantage of expressing the Will while enabling an aesthetic withdrawal from its effects.

This is where Nietzsche's critique has such an impact. When he asks whether Wagner 'was a musician at all' – when he accuses him of catering only to pathological effect – Nietzsche judges Wagner according to the concept of aesthetic redemption on which Wagner's own theorising depends. Here Wagner fails by his own measure because his music never attains the aesthetic transformation that would redeem it from its origins in that 'pathological element'. In this sense, Wagner's music would never fully elude the trauma of the scream, a notion that Nietzsche clearly incorporates and sexualises when he invokes the term hysteria. But, as we have seen, Nietzsche appears to venture a step further and ask whether the aesthetic, as conceived by Schopenhauer, is not what it seems, whether, in fact, it is merely a sublimation of the kind of sensual, embodied experiences from which it seeks to distance itself. If Nietzsche's argument poses a direct challenge to the redemptive 'asceticism' of Wagner's theories, does it not also challenge the drama of sexual difference that underpins them? The answer, as always with Nietzsche, depends on the reading.

One particularly provocative statement is to be found in *Nietzsche kontra Wagner*, where the author seeks to come to terms with the all too obvious doubleness that he detects in Wagner's music. The problem with Wagner, he writes, is his

thirst for ecstatic sensuality and desensualization [*Sinnlichkeit und Entsinnlichung*] – this whole give and take of Wagner's regarding material, images, passion, and nerves clearly expresses the *spirit of his music* – given that this itself, like any music, would not know how to speak unambiguously about itself: for *music is a woman*.[94]

Nietzsche's claim that music is unable to speak about itself with any certainty suggests an impenetrability or opaqueness to analysis, to enquiry,

---

[93] Wagner, *Beethoven*, p. 72.

[94] Friedrich Nietzsche, *Nietzsche kontra Wagner* (1888), in Giorgio Colli and Mazzino Montinari (eds.), *Friedrich Nietzsche: Sämtliche Werke, Kritische Studienausgabe*, vol. VI (Munich: Deutsche Taschenbuch Verlag, 1980), p. 424.

to questioning. It is as if music simply 'is', that it refuses to name itself or to reveal where it came from, or even what it is about. It eludes Wagner, too, resisting his attempt to appropriate it for the theatre and replace its subtle treatment of cause and effect with an obvious and self-advertising arsenal of musical tricks calculated to unite the most carnal with the most ephemeral. Nietzsche's point is useful in that it undermines the kind of total control that Wagner claims for himself as artist-genius. But it is deeply problematic as a general observation on music in that it posits ambiguity as intrinsic to music, as though this were a generic trait that differentiated music from other forms of discourse. Here Nietzsche appears to reinforce – and none too subtly – the configuration of both music and woman in terms of an Otherness not unlike that which emerges so clearly in Wagner's music and theory.

And yet statements like this have often been cited to reinforce feminist readings of Nietzsche in which woman and music come to stand for a resistance to phallic discourse. Music and woman elude any attempt to inscribe them into the phallic economy, slipping away from containment under concepts. Their 'ambiguity', in other words, is an ambiguity that frustrates a normatively masculine discourse. But, we might ask, what is the cost of this resistance? Does it not merely reinforce the isolation from language and the symbolic order that we have witnessed repeatedly in configurations of music and the feminine? Denied any self-reflective capacity, music and woman are positioned outside discourse in a way that merely defines what they are not; they are presented as an ambiguity that is Other to Nietzsche's own discourse. But what if this self-reflective ambiguity is not intrinsic to music, but rather an attitude that music can assume? And what if it is an attitude that Wagner's music actually exploits? It is arguable, in fact, that in the preludes and interludes ambiguity becomes a defining feature, that this music 'would not *want* to speak unambiguously about itself'.

Central here is the question of the music's discursive origins (performers, implied narrators, authorial subjects), a question that music drama seems deliberately to problematise. Partly this stems from the invisible orchestra and its contrast with the voices of the singers. As Tomlinson's *Metaphysical Song* shows, the operatic voice raises many issues and problems of its own, but, if anything, the Wagnerian orchestra complicates matters further. While the music issuing from the mouths of the singers might be traced to them as imagined authorial subjects or as performers, the orchestral sound seems to emanate from nowhere. The orchestral performers are hidden and usually never revealed, and as a voice within the musical text the orchestral discourse occupies an utterly uncanny position. From where does its authority issue? It never aligns itself consistently with the dramatic characters in ways that might allow it to be weighed against other characters – to be usurped or silenced or dismissed. It can seem to come under the control of a character, only to slip back to a kind of meta-position (this was the effect in 'The Walk to the Paradise Garden' when the orchestral music seemed to come from Sali and Vreli, only to 'arrive' at the Paradise Garden before them). It is very much a part of the diegesis, and yet it repeatedly forms a frame that seems to define and exceed the limits of the diegesis. At times it is audible to the characters on stage (like the hunting horns in Act II of *Tristan*), at times fantasised (Brünnhilde's murmuring spring in the same scene), but usually it weaves around them seemingly undetected, announcing their fate and recalling their past without their knowledge.

A cinematic parallel is to be found in the disembodied voice-over, a subject that, to quote Silverman, 'sees without being seen, and speaks from an inaccessible vantage point'.[95] It occupies a privileged, superior position that cannot be questioned because it cannot be identified. 'Conversely,' Silverman adds, 'it loses power and authority with every corporeal encroachment', and when it is fully embodied and its source revealed, it becomes, as Pascal Bonitzer puts it, 'decrepit' and 'mortal'.[96] But even the voice-over always betrays, through the sound of the voice, an identifiable human agency. It suggests a single, centred point of origin that, if not visible, at least reveals an aural identity. Wagner's orchestral discourse might be imagined to stem from an authorial figure ('Wagner' himself) or from narrating subjects, but its goal ultimately seems to be a sort of transcendence in which no single identifiable – and therefore challengeable – subjectivity predominates. To associate the orchestra with something identifiable and locatable, with a finite and human source, would be to limit its absolute knowledge and authority, and expose the mystery of the 'mystic abyss'. It is a sense of mystery that certainly echoes Nietzsche's ambiguous, unknowable feminine music, a parallel Wagner reinforces when he likens the music emanating from the 'mystic abyss' to the 'vapours rising from the holy womb of Gaia'. Like Erda, Gaia is mother of the earth, and it is interesting to see how both this imagery and the depths of the 'motherly home' in *Opera and Drama* seem to come together in that first deep, 'primal' E flat of the prelude to *Das Rheingold*.

Indeed, the whole orchestral impression of transcendence would seem to find its apex in the preludes and interludes, in the sense that, when the invisible orchestra extends its domain to an invisible stage, we no longer see embodied subjects that can be imagined as a source of enunciation

---

[95] Silverman, *The Acoustic Mirror*, p. 51.
[96] Pascal Bonitzer, *Le regard et la voix* (Paris: Union Générale d'Editions, 1976), pp. 31–2, trans. in Silverman, *The Acoustic Mirror*, p. 49.

(recall, for example, Mohr's 'mysterious impression' dispersing across the closed curtain). One of the potential outcomes of this absence, as we have seen, is for the spectator to fill the void, to imagine that s/he is in fact the point of origin, and this is how the preludes and interludes facilitate fantasy. But, as we saw in the orchestral eulogies, this kind of internalisation is very much bound up with the construction of subjects whose ideal attributes encourage identification. Not that these ideal subjects are limited to the preludes and interludes, or even to the orchestra, but what is unique here is the slippage of identity, the sheer deception and disguise made possible by the deliberately amorphous form that the orchestra assumes in and around the diegesis. Who is imagined to eulogise Siegfried in the *Trauermarsch*? It could be Wotan, whose narratives earlier in the cycle already placed him in an authorial role of sorts. But it is interesting that his withdrawal from the action to assume an 'unseen god' role increasingly conflates him with the kind of meta-discursive position that we might imagine Wagner occupying. That conflation would seem to be sealed by the *Trauermarsch*, where the mourning of the absent father-god meets the extradiegetic commentary of the 'Greek chorus'. And of course the function of that chorus is to speak on behalf of the people, implying that, within all this slippage, the crucial point is that I, as spectator, come to regard *myself* as one of the authors of the eulogy. Here is music that 'speaks about itself' in profoundly ambiguous terms and depends on it for its effect.

Adorno relates effects of this sort to the idea of 'phantasmagoria', a term he uses in Marx's sense as an aspect of commodity fetishism. It is illusion designed to conceal the process of production, to create the impression of a product that is 'self-producing'. Music drama 'perfect[s] the illusion that the work of art is a reality *sui generis* that constitutes itself in the realm of the absolute without having to renounce its claim to image the world'.[97] The invisible orchestra is obviously central here, and Adorno cites several instances of the orchestra's deployment to create the 'acoustic delusion' of the 'distant sound' in which 'music pauses and is made spatial'.[98] Distances collapse and time is distorted so that years elapse in moments and moments seem eternal. Among Adorno's examples is the Transformation Music in Act I of *Parsifal*, and the dialogue that introduces it:

PARSIFAL: I hardly move,
                     yet seem already to have come far.
GURNEMANZ: You see, my son, here time becomes space.

For Adorno, it is a moment emblematic of the Wagnerian phantasmagoria and its desire to step out of the world: 'The characters cast off their

---

[97] Adorno, *In Search of Wagner*, p. 85.   [98] Ibid., p. 86.

Example 6.2   Wagner, *Parsifal*, Act I, Transformation Music (p. 66)

empirical being in time as soon as the ethereal kingdom of essences is entered.'[99]

Particularly relevant here is a seven-bar *espressivo* passage beginning with the change of key signature to two flats (example 6.2). Motivically, the passage centres on the descending chromatic motif associated with the suffering of Amfortas, juxtaposing it with the Monsalvat bell motif in the bass. It is the bell motif, with its cyclical, descending form and firmly diatonic character, that seems to determine the harmonic shape and chord structure of the first three bars, anchoring the chromatic and occasionally dissonant voice leading of the 'Amfortas' music in the upper voices with a chorale-like descending sequence of root-position chords. This solid, unambiguous effect is quickly dispelled, however, when the bass assumes the same chromatic character as the upper voices. Gone is the solid foundation, replaced by semitonal steps that seem to follow, rather than underpin, the lengthy, almost weary ascending melodic sequence. Certainly the chorale-like harmonic rhythm is maintained and each chord can be analysed in familiar functional terms, but the overall impression is one of sliding and meandering. It is as if a firm tread had given way to a kind of fluidity, and it acts as a perfect musical representation of the disorienting effect that Parsifal describes. It also recalls the regressive sensations described by the Bayreuth critics, and Nietzsche's

---

[99] Ibid., p. 88.

sense of floating in Wagner's music. Gurnemanz's phrase might indeed apply to the whole experience of the interludes and the sense of magic and removal (one thinks of the *Entrücktheit* that Bekker perceived in *Die Rose*) that they promote. Adorno's phantasmagoria suggests that at the root here is the desire to locate music drama as a whole in a 'mystic abyss', to encourage a loss of footing that allows the work of art to appear as 'imperceptibly' (to use Wagner's term) as the columns of the Gralsburg.

It was suggested earlier that images such as 'loss of self' and 'floating' in the critical responses to Wagner's music might recall Freud's 'oceanic feeling', and that this concept might be related to a pleasure in the Lacanian 'fragmented body'. This implies a pleasure in the loss of a centred self, a pleasure in letting down the armour of the ego. It suggests a music that sweeps its listeners along in a way that suppresses both the ego's defences and the demand those defences might generate to 'know' how it works. Writing on the final moments of *Götterdämmerung*, Hanslick marvels at the way Wagner 'releases all the demons of the orchestra and so overwhelms us that we are hardly capable even of admiring the technique with which it is all accomplished'.[100] Knowledge and rational explanation, it would seem, become powerless when confronted with the bursting banks of the Rhine. Even the post-rift Nietzsche is forced to acknowledge moments when Wagner's music creates a disturbing, even subversive effect:

He knows a sound for those canny-uncanny midnights of the soul, where cause and effect seem to have come off their hinges, and, at any moment, something can emerge out of nothing.[101]

Almost recalling the kind of Dionysian experience he had once extolled in *Tristan*, Nietzsche evokes a pleasure in a loss of bearing, a release from reason and understanding. Both he and Hanslick imply a liberation that is submissive, echoing Baudelaire's 'allowing myself to be penetrated and invaded' or Lavignac's 'taking possession of your whole being'. And this is where the gender associations of Wagner's music begin to unravel, for if ambiguity is to be equated with woman, then Wagner's self-concealing music actually masks a desire to dominate, an attitude that in fact assumes a phallic role in relation to the listener. Wagner's ambiguous orchestra reduces the listener to the role of passive

100 Hanslick, review in *Neue Freie Presse*, in Hartford (ed. and trans.), *Bayreuth: The Early Years*, p. 82.
101 Nietzsche, *Nietzsche kontra Wagner*, in Colli and Montinari (eds.), *Friedrich Nietzsche: Sämtliche Werke*, vol. VI, p. 417, trans. in Susan Bernstein, 'Fear of Music? Nietzsche's Double Vision of the "Musical Feminine"', in Peter J. Burgard (ed.), *Nietzsche and the Feminine* (Charlottesville: University Press of Virginia, 1994), p. 111.

recipient, assaulting and ultimately dismantling the fortifications of the ego. It understands only one attitude on the part of its audience: submission.

At issue here is the acknowledgement of pleasure in this domination, and the anxiety that this generates in the male ego. One defence is to trace this pleasure to a feminised source, a move that, while raising the spectre of feminine empowerment, also frames and marginalises the experience as Other. In Nietzsche's characterisation of music as woman, musical 'ambiguity' is configured as something that would resist any attempt by Wagner (or any composer) to appropriate it. But we can compare this to *The Case of Wagner*, where Wagner is described as a figure 'distinguished by every ambiguity, every double sense, everything quite generally that persuades those who are uncertain without making them aware of what they have been persuaded. Thus Wagner is a seducer on a large scale.'[102] Here we have the same sense of an obscurity and resistance to rational enquiry, but now ambiguity becomes a deliberate and effective tool in Wagner's 'persuasive' arsenal. Taken together, these observations might articulate a masculinist response to Wagner's music, one in which its dominating effects would be ascribed to a feminine refusal to 'speak about itself'. At the heart of this position is a disavowal that comes to terms with the disarming effects of Wagner's music by locating their origins 'outside' masculine experience. The same sort of slippage comes through in responses to the sensuality of Wagner's music. Wagner is hypnotist and tyrant – he assumes, in other words, the position of the Master. But his success rests on 'stimulation', on his appeal to the senses and to the nerves. He mobilises 'all that trembles and is effusive, all the feminisms from the *idioticon* of happiness!'[103] Here his ability to dominate assumes a different character, not unlike Hanslick's 'hashish dream of the ecstatic female'. He is part Titurel and part Kundry. But Nietzsche sums up this double identity by likening him to Klingsor, hysterical magician and emasculated Master.[104] In this circle of male fantasies (which Nietzsche seems at times to reinforce and at others to ridicule), desire, fear, and disgust constantly collapse into one another.

Wagner, of course, is fully caught up in a similar kind of defensive slippage, as we saw in his Schopenhauerian theorisation of an all-embracing (feminine) Music that is contained through aesthetic experience. And with this in mind, we might look again at the 'death drive' that seems to underpin the regressive character of the preludes and interludes. Freud suggested in his articulation of the death drive that 'we have unwittingly steered ourselves into the harbour of Schopenhauer's

[102] Nietzsche, *The Case of Wagner*, p. 639.   [103] Ibid., p. 640.   [104] Ibid.

philosophy',[105] and we have detected in the preludes and interludes a convergence of Freud and Schopenhauer. The desire for death is central for Schopenhauer – it is a desire to escape the body and its ensnarement by the Will. To the extent that the preludes and interludes represent an imaginary release from the body, they might be seen to trace this desire, but where the gender implications of Schopenhauer's disgust for the body are never made explicit, Wagner offers a more vivid picture. We saw in the *Parsifal* Transformation Music a regressive quality that seemed to parallel the world-withdrawal represented by Monsalvat and its death-haunted initiates. But this withdrawal is also a withdrawal from woman and the contamination of her sexuality. It is a withdrawal into the asceticism and chastity that Schopenhauer presents as resistance to the Will (although the issue is complicated in *Parsifal* by the vivid homoerotic connotations of the grail brotherhood, and Schopenhauer, unequivocal about the need to renounce heterosexual relations, is more ambiguous on the question of homosexuality).[106] Embodied in Kundry, woman becomes the focal point for an astonishing concentration of disgust, hatred, fear, and pity, and it is telling that Kundry's final weary utterances in Act I ('Schlafen, schlafen, ich muß!') seem to recede, vocally and orchestrally, into nothing just before the first bell-like motifs ('Slow and solemn') announce the beginning of the journey to the Gralsburg. In this sense, to enter Monsalvat is to enter a Music from which Kundry is excluded, leaving her to the torment of 'sleep without rest', a fate that suggests the endless striving of the Will. Monsalvat stands for death as that 'endless sleep' for which Kundry longs – it is redemption, defined as a release from sexuality and the body. Act II ensures that we understand the feminine foundations of sexual desire – flower maidens, Kundry as seductress, Klingsor the emasculated magician – and it is only when Parsifal has confronted and spurned that desire that Kundry can be cleansed and allowed to enter Monsalvat, where she finds the death she has sought.

In the *Ring* we encounter an altogether different form of withdrawal. We have seen how the 'elemental' quality of the musical material in the orchestral nature portraits (a combination of the static and the repetitive) might suggest the death drive as a desire to regress and withdraw into nature. But, as the figure of Erda makes clear, nature in the *Ring* is clearly encoded as feminine-maternal, an impression reinforced by Wagner's theoretical associations of the orchestra with the depths of the 'maternal home' and Gaia's 'womb'. The Forest Murmurs enfold Siegfried in a way that suggests Rosolato's 'sonorous womb', and Siegfried's reverie

---

[105] Freud, *Beyond the Pleasure Principle*, pp. 43–4.
[106] Schopenhauer, *The World as Will*, vol. II, pp. 560, 567.

on the identity of the mother he never knew evokes all the nostalgia of that image.

With the Rhinemaidens we seem to encounter an eroticised counterpart to this feminine nature. 'Siegfried's Rhine Journey' begins with 'symphonic' material based on Siegfried's horn theme, but the material is literally swept away by Rhine music familiar from *Das Rheingold*. Siegfried's theme, however, resurfaces as counterpoint to the Rhinemaidens' wave motifs, weaving seamlessly into the Rhine music texture. It is as though his music had found a home in this element, a symbol of complete and pleasurable immersion in nature (Cosima wrote of the Rhinemaidens being 'glad of [Siegfried's] arrival').[107] In a less obvious way, Brünnhilde's ring of fire represents nature as eroticised feminine. In an anticipation of *Feuersnot*, the soaring, unaccompanied string melody that precedes Siegfried's approach to the sleeping Brünnhilde provides an arch of intensely sensual sound that maps the magic fire onto the libidinal fire burning in Siegfried. Sustained for twenty-six bars in slow tempo without a single rest, and unaccompanied, save for a brief quotation of the 'Fate' motif, it seems to capture Siegfried's total fixation on the object of desire that has been promised by the woodbird.

Do these immersions in nature not then represent an embracing, perhaps even an exaltation, of the maternal and feminine? The problem is that the 'feminine' celebrated by Wagner is the 'eternal feminine', a concept that, as Žižek observes, has traditionally served merely to reinforce the actual subjugation of women.[108] It is the classic realisation of the fantasised woman, here configured not as the threatening Other, but as the mythical and idealised answer to all male lack:

To the isolated being not all things are possible; there is need of more than one, and it is woman, suffering and willing to sacrifice herself, who becomes at last the real, conscious redeemer: for what is love itself but the 'eternal feminine'?[109]

Woman here is nothing more than the negative space of the male, a missing component in the process of his self-realisation. And Wagner's construction of the maternal is central here because it reinforces the notion of woman as the figure who nurtures and sustains, sacrificing to enable the realisation of man's goals. How ironic that Siegfried seeks to know his mother as *Menschenweib*, a mortal, flesh-and-blood woman rather

---

[107] Diary entry for 5 February 1870, in Gregor-Dellin and Mack (eds.), *Cosima Wagner's Diaries*, p. 49.

[108] Slavoj Žižek, 'There Is No Sexual Relationship', in Renata Salecl and Slavoj Žižek (eds.), *Gaze and Voice as Love Objects* (Durham, N. C., and London: Duke University Press, 1996), p. 228.

[109] Wagner, letter to Röckel, 25 January 1854, in Kesting (ed.), *Richard Wagner Briefe*, p. 283.

than a mere idea. Even when she did appear before our eyes, Sieglinde was little more than fantasy object of Siegmund's desire, something his own words make clear:

> All that I longed for I see in you.
> I find in you all that I lacked.

Menschenweib is the last thing Wagner would ever be able to grant Siegfried. Instead, the 'maternal' realm of the orchestra relocates the feminine into myth, as far removed as possible from the all too sobering figure of historically grounded, socially determined woman.

Conclusion: 'innocence among opposites'

A feminine music that is both idealistic redemption and embodiment of shame and disgust; a sensuality that refuses to acknowledge itself, cloaked in the trappings of metaphysics; an affirmation, through the leit-motif, of music's reciprocity with language that simultaneously posits music as beyond linguistic signification – what are we to make of these contradictions? Nietzsche sees them as signs of Wagner's modernity:

Such *innocence* among opposites, such a 'good conscience' in a lie is actually *modern par excellence*, it almost defines modernity. Biologically, modern man represents a *contradiction of values*; he sits between two chairs, he says Yes and No in the same breath. Is it any wonder that precisely in our times falsehood has become flesh and even genius? that *Wagner* 'dwelled among us'?[1]

For Nietzsche, Wagner sums up modernity, offering the 'most instructive case' of the doubleness that he sees as its characteristic symptom. And as his own attitude towards the feminine suggests, Nietzsche's diagnosis is also a self-diagnosis:

But all of us have, unconsciously, involuntarily in our bodies values, words, for-mulas, moralities of *opposite* descent – we are, physiologically considered, *false*.[2]

Part of what Nietzsche identifies here is the modern subject's need both to challenge and to affirm the autonomy and centredness of the ego. Modernity unleashes the social and cultural forces capable of question-ing the limits and definition of the self, but it treats this decentring as exceptional, as a loss or gap from which the ego should recover and re-establish itself. It is precisely this loss of 'self-possession' that Nietzsche has in mind when he likens the experience of Wagner's music to immersion in the sea.

The contradictions we have identified in music drama might be viewed in terms of this double movement that opens the ego up to a loss of bearing, but then responds to the experience by framing it,

---

[1] Nietzsche, *The Case of Wagner*, p. 648.   [2] Ibid.

recontaining it with appeals to metaphysics, idealism, and patriarchal authority. Wagner's preludes and interludes offer a particularly vivid manifestation of this doubleness in the sense that whatever they open the spectator up to is always framed, either literally, by the staged action, or figuratively, by a recovery. This sense of containment can be seen to license qualities, such as regressiveness, that are less easily assimilated into the staged scenes. In other words, the frame around the interludes becomes a buffer that allows for both the release and the suppression of decentring and disempowering experiences. This is the effect we witnessed in the *Esclarmonde scène d'amour*, with its fantasy of seduction and feminine empowerment, while in *Pelléas* the interludes seemed to stand for a resistance both to the conscious (traces of the raw dream work) and to the symbolic (infractions of the Kristevan semiotic). But the framing of these experiences can also be detected *within* the interludes. The fantasies of fragmentation that we identified in *Die Rose vom Liebesgarten* and *Wozzeck* suggest a temporary collapse of what Lacan terms 'the armour called ego', and a manipulation of the desire for wholeness. It is a music that, like the Lacanian imaginary, embraces an illusory immediacy and fullness of self-possession, unleashing but then compensating for a sense of loss and fragmentation.

Equally relevant to Nietzsche's sense of modern 'doubleness' is the role the interludes seem to assume in defining the identity of music itself. The debate over the 'spiritualisation' of opera and the concomitant fears over the corruption of music's 'essence' speak precisely to the contradictory impulses identified by Nietzsche. On the one hand the interludes bracket music off from the theatre and potentially address the concern over its subservience to the stage and its entanglement in the brute materiality of the theatre. But on the other hand they draw instrumental music into a narrative, representational (and therefore 'extramusical') role in ways that played to contemporary critical preoccupations with questions of musical illustration, nervous stimulation, emotional excess, overrefinement of musical language – not to mention the challenge to opera as a vocal and implicitly *melodic* genre.[3] For all the shifts in critical language – from Bellaigue's concerns over the 'debasement of the musician's ideal' to Niemann's talk of 'impressionism' to Weissmann's warnings of 'degeneration' – the problem repeatedly returns to the all-important issue of musical meaning, to the nature of music's autonomy, to its relationship with language, image, and the body. And repeatedly it is Wagnerian music drama, and its own unresolved contradictions, that proves to be a point of reference (both negative and positive) for these controversies. Yet, as Nietzsche implies

---

[3] Niemann, for example, complains that when the voice should be front and centre, 'the tireless great mill of the orchestra grinds on'. Niemann, *Die Musik der Gegenwart*, pp. 65–6.

with the term 'innocence', there is a strong sense that Wagner genuinely fails to recognise the contradiction between his metaphysical claims and his material means. This is an innocence that returns in post-Wagnerian opera, evident in the contrast between the vivid, sumptuous score of *Die Rose vom Liebesgarten* and the austerity of Pfitzner's *Wort-Ton-Verhältnis*, and in Delius's rejection of the musical 'physicality' that courses so strongly through 'The Walk to the Paradise Garden'. At the same time, the contradiction loses its innocence in that it becomes the focus of critical debate, and in this more conscious, polemical form it finds its way into the *Feuersnot Liebesszene*, where it articulates a position both post and contra Wagner: Strauss defines himself in relation to both the metaphysics and the realism that he detects in the Wagnerian inheritance. It is this duality, reconfigured as a conflict between idealism and sensuality, that we detected in Schreker's *Liebesszene*, but now, two decades after *Feuersnot* and nearly half a century after the first Bayreuth festival, another characteristic of music drama proves untenable.

Clearly one of the impulses behind the interludes in Wagnerian music drama is the maintenance of a musical continuum, the avoidance of any gap that might threaten the totality of music drama and rudely awaken the spectator from that dream-like state that is the goal of Bayreuth. Such a gap might amount to a moment of reflection, and that, as Adorno argued, would 'shatter [the] illusion of ideal unity'.[4] Of course, the interludes are also characterised by difference: they potentially frame the stage action in a way that assumes an extradiegetic function, distancing the here and now of an orchestral narrator from the recited 'story' of the stage. This is the effect Wagner has in mind when he likens his *Trauermarsch* to a Greek chorus, and we can detect a similar effect in the narrative intrusions of 'The Walk to the Paradise Garden' and in the orchestral eulogies of Pfitzner and Berg. But, as we have seen, whatever difference is asserted here is also smoothed over. Rather than separate themselves off from the surrounding orchestral discourse, they emerge from and return to it seamlessly. They are both 'about' the action and very much 'of' the action. The effect is to foster an ambiguity that only heightens the dream-like effects characteristic of music drama and strengthens the impression of something *sui generis*. (Berg's eulogy is exceptional in that it emphasises its difference, but here the goal is precisely to establish the kind of Wagnerian 'immersion' that has so far been resisted, and, as we have seen, it depends for its effect on a highly calculated ambiguity of its own.)

The interludes offer a point of entry 'into' the work, a position of identification that seems to open up in the absence of stage characters or of any definite extradiegetic position. Through them, music

---

[4] Adorno, *In Search of Wagner*, pp. 104–5.

drama delineates the parameters of its own reception, building audience response into itself. What is resisted in each case is any sense of a definite distancing, one that might serve to recontextualise or perhaps even iro-nise the staged action. Instead the interludes serve to immerse the au-dience in the vapours of the 'mystic abyss' so that everything serves the goal of a unified, totalised effect. This is one possible reading of those mo-ments in *Pelléas* when the uncanny effects suggestive of the Kristevan semiotic might have pointed to a release from symbolic subjectivity, but ultimately seem to function only as components in the persuasive post-Wagnerian arsenal of illusion. In other words, orchestral interludes of this kind testify to the assertion of the deceptive wholeness charac-teristic of the Lacanian imaginary over the radical plurality connoted by Kristeva's semiotic. Potentially sites of difference and heterogeneity, they ultimately ensure that these qualities are contained within singular-ity and an imaginary wholeness. Rather than confront their audiences with re-evaluation, they reinforce identification with alluring ego im-ages. It is this issue with which the *Schatzgräber Liebesszene* seems to wrestle, bringing to the fore that transparency of illusion that Bekker detected as a defining feature of Schreker's operas. Its gesture is one of subtle unmasking from the inside, and it signals a loss in the abil-ity or willingness to invest in this defining feature of post-Wagnerian modernism.

The outward signs of a reaction against post-Wagnerian opera from the mid-1920s are not difficult to detect: in place of large orches-tral resources and huge through-composed structures with elaborate thematic/motivic webs we see the emergence of smaller, 'neoclassical' or jazz-based ensembles and an adoption of the conventions of closed numbers. Part of a larger trend towards a conscious allusion to and manipulation of styles and genres, it suggests a detached, ironic stance towards music and an out-and-out rejection of the metaphysics and to-tal illusion of post-Wagnerian opera. It marks a phase of modernism in which an often radical attitude towards musical material would be countered by a deliberate, at times reactionary restraint towards what was seen as 'emotionalism' and 'narcotic' effects[5] – in which, indeed, the whole question of subjectivity was somehow to be bracketed.

It is here that we encounter the heart of the issue and it is here that the orchestral interlude proves to be representative of profound and far-reaching cultural phenomena that exceed mere style history. The inter-lude *per se* proved adaptable to the new trends in the sense that it could return to its closed-number, *entr'acte* roots, while its potential for dis-tancing and framing the staged action could be exploited to new effect.

---

[5] Bertolt Brecht, 'On the Use of Music in an Epic Theatre' (1935), in John Willett (ed. and trans.), *Brecht on Theatre* (London: Methuen, 1964), p. 89.

But the roles we have analysed in interludes from the *Ring* to *Wozzeck* surely stand for something quintessentially Wagnerian. The fact that they can unleash experiences so Other to the staged action and stand apart so clearly from its visual and verbal means, yet remain so utterly integrated into the total experience, testifies to the post-Wagnerian desire for all-embracing illusion. The goal here is nothing less than a complete involvement that excludes reflection and detachment. The latter half of the twentieth century perhaps confirmed the post-Wagnerian generation in at least one important sense: the combination of a music unapologetically immersed in subjective experience with an environment dedicated to total illusion is something that Western (and many non-Western) audiences continue to embrace wholeheartedly. The proof is to be found in popular cinema and the continued success of its appeals (through both form and technology) to a total and self-forgetful immersion 'in' the film. Like Bayreuth, Hollywood promotes complete audience identification and an unabashedly subjective experience. Wagner's darkened auditorium proved entirely prophetic, while the invisible pit has found a successor in 'surround sound' speakers. That so much film music preserves the language, timbre, and leitmotivic organisation of music drama only makes the connection explicit. The classic Hollywood sound owes its origins to émigré composers in the central European, post-Wagnerian tradition, but perhaps more telling is the more recent success of film scores that are not so much *post-Wagnerian* as consciously and openly *Wagnerian*. While Wagnerian singing, embodied in the image of the portly pigtailed soprano, has become an object of ridicule in popular culture, the Wagnerian orchestra continues to reach numbers that even Wagner could hardly have imagined. The success of the *Star Wars* films seems unthinkable without John Williams's music, and Danny Elfman's *Batman* scores linger longer in the memory than the films to which they belong.

For Adorno, the relationship between Wagnerian music drama and cinema only confirms their joint complicity in mass culture and its tendency towards stupefaction and domination. The representation of subjectivity in music drama, he suggests, is a craft that Wagner refined to the point where we can speak of a 'technification of the inward'.[6] But the idea that expression might be bound up with technique is anathema to music drama and its goal of immediacy, and Adorno relates this contradiction to the doubleness outlined in *The Case of Wagner*:

Nietzsche had an inkling of this when he taxed Wagner, that tamer of expression, with hypocrisy, without perceiving that this was not a matter of psychology but of a historical tendency. The transformation of expressive content from an

---

[6] Theodor W. Adorno, *Minima moralia* (1951), trans. E. F. N. Jephcott (London: Verso, 1978), p. 214.

undirected impulse into material for manipulation makes it palpable, ex-hibitable, saleable.[7]

What is at the root of this subjectivism for Adorno, then, is commodifi-cation, a process in which art prepares itself for the market. So Wagnerian and post-Wagnerian opera, by cultivating the expression of inner experience, pave the way for some of the highly marketable forms of entertainment in mass culture, and Adorno is clear as to the primary beneficiary:

[T]he hostility to art of film, which passes in administrative review all materials and emotions in order to sell them most effectively to the public . . . has its source in art, in the growing domination over inner nature.[8]

What emerges here is a dialectic in which film (as mass culture) opposes art by cultivating subjective experiences for their commodity value, experiences that were in fact developed in art in the first place. But Adorno's argument loses its dialectic rigour when he takes music drama as film's model. His reading of music drama suggests that it only ever masqueraded as art, that it always lent itself to commodification in ways that, though authentic to its historical situation, were inauthentic as art. In other words, art, as Adorno understands it, would not be touched upon here, except to reinforce its privileged status by negation: the debt of film to music drama merely demonstrates what the *debased* forms of art might lead to. Typical here is Adorno's position on Schreker, who is shown to touch far too closely on subjective experiences redolent of mass culture.

Both post-Wagnerian opera and popular film are seen to fall short of the characteristics and social roles that define authentic art for Adorno, a position that invites us to question the aestheticised ideology that draws a sharp dividing line between the rarefied domain of art and the debased realm that lies outside. The images of pleasure and self-alienation that we have encountered repeatedly throughout this study – Delius's 'throb-bing, swelling' music, Schreker's 'wild consuming flames', Baudelaire's *jouissance*, the reactions of the Bayreuth critics – surely need to be seen as expressions of a legitimate, grounded, embodied, material experience, and not merely as symptoms of debasement and manipulation. If cin-ema audiences continue to submit to that Wagnerian 'retuning of the whole sensorium', it is a submission that demands to be understood not only in terms of ideology critique: it is a *pleasurable* investment in an illu-sory environment that, like the Lacanian imaginary, always beckons the subject away from an alienating reality. To the extent that they celebrate these quasi-cinematic experiences, the orchestral interludes characterise the post-Wagnerian phase of modernism (in contrast to the 'objectivity' and high modernist 'restraint' that displaced it) in terms of an openness to sensual, overwhelming, self-forgetful pleasure.

Of course, as the interludes in *Esclarmonde* and *Feuersnot* remind us, any recourse to the idea of pleasure needs to ask 'Whose pleasure?' In this sense any uncritical celebration of operatic and filmic experience would amount to an ideological gesture in itself. And as Adorno demonstrates, the self-alienated state of total immersion can facilitate persuasion: the rhetorical, even manipulative, strategies evident in *Die Rose vom Liebesgarten* and *Wozzeck* are just the sort of characteristics that allowed film to become such a propaganda tool in the twentieth century. In this sense post-Wagnerian opera shares with film the capacity to embrace and reinforce both the pleasures and problems of modernity. Where opera differs is in its ability to lay claim to an idealised aesthetic heritage, something that has been much more problematic for film. The operas investigated in this study mobilise quasi-cinematic experiences while simultaneously seeking to transfigure and redeem them as something more noble, uplifting, even metaphysical. This is the attitude that seems to underpin so many of the interludes when their fantasmatic effects coincide with an idealistic appeal to Music's difference and transcendence. Here music not only holds on to the lofty perch that the nineteenth century had granted it, but offers to elevate the tawdry effects of the theatre into its wordless, sightless domain. Applied to cinema, this metaphysics of music would mean repeatedly fading the screen to black while the film score continued in the darkness.

BIBLIOGRAPHY

Scores

Alban Berg, *Wozzeck*, piano-vocal score, Vienna: Universal Edition, 1925.

Claude Debussy, *Pelléas et Mélisande*, piano-vocal score, Paris: Durand, 1907; full score, Paris: Fromont, 1904.

Frederick Delius, *A Village Romeo and Juliet*, piano-vocal score, Vienna: Universal Edition, 1920.

Jules Massenet, *Esclarmonde*, piano-vocal score, Paris: Georges Hartmann, 1889.

Hans Pfitzner, *Die Rose vom Liebesgarten*, piano-vocal score, Leipzig: Brockhaus, 1901; full score, Lörrach: Brockhaus, 1905.

Franz Schreker, *Der Schatzgräber*, piano-vocal score, Vienna: Universal Edition, 1919; full score, Vienna: Universal Edition, 1918.

Richard Strauss, *Feuersnot*, piano-vocal score, Berlin: Adolph Fürstner, 1901; full score, Berlin: Adolph Fürstner, 1901.

Richard Wagner, *Siegfried*, piano-vocal score, New York: G. Schirmer, 1904.

Richard Wagner, *Parsifal*, piano-vocal score, New York: G. Schirmer, 1904.

Literature

Abbate, Carolyn, 'Tristan in the Composition of *Pelléas*', *Nineteenth-Century Music* 5 (1981), 117–41.

Unsung Voices: Opera and Musical Narrative in the Nineteenth Century, Princeton: Princeton University Press, 1991.

'Opera; or, the Envoicing of Women', in Ruth A. Solie (ed.), *Musicology and Difference: Gender and Sexuality in Musical Scholarship*, Berkeley: University of California Press, 1993, pp. 225–58.

Adany, Bernhard (ed.), *Hans Pfitzner: Briefe*, Tutzing: Hans Schneider, 1991.

Adorno, Theodor W., *Adorno–Benjamin: Complete Correspondence 1928–1940*, ed. Henri Lonitz, trans. Nicholas Walker, Cambridge: Polity Press, 1999.

The Philosophy of Modern Music (1949), trans. Anne G. Mitchell and Wesley V. Blomster, New York: Seabury Press, 1973.

Minima moralia (1951), trans. E. F. N. Jephcott, London: Verso, 1978.

In Search of Wagner (1952), trans. Rodney Livingstone, London: Verso, 1981.

Quasi una fantasia (1963), trans. Rodney Livingstone, London: Verso, 1992.

The Culture Industry, ed. J. M. Bernstein, trans. Andrew Arato and Eike Gebhardt, London: Routledge, 1991.

Beecham, Thomas, *A Mingled Chime*, New York: G. P. Putnam's Sons, 1943.

Bekker, Paul, *'Die Rose vom Liebesgarten'*, *Neue Musikzeitung* 31 (1910), 249–55.

Franz Schreker: Studie zur Kritik der modernen Oper, Berlin: Schuster and Loeffler, 1919.

Klang und Eros, Stuttgart and Berlin: Deutsche Verlags-Anstalt, 1922.

'Schreker und das Theater', *Anbruch* 6/2 (February 1924), 50–3.

'Irrelohe', *Anbruch* 6/4 (April 1924), 131–8.

Bellaigue, Camille, 'Revue musicale', *Revue des Deux Mondes* 83 (June 1889), 698–706.

'L'opéra symphonique', *Revue des Deux Mondes* 103 (June 1909), 165–87.

Benjamin, Walter, 'The Work of Art in the Age of Mechanical Reproduction' (1935), in Hannah Arendt (ed.), *Illuminations*, trans. Harry Zohn, New York: Schocken Books, 1969, pp. 217–54.

Bergeron, Katherine, 'The Echo, the Cry, the Death of Lovers', *Nineteenth-Century Music* 18/2 (1994), 136–51.

'Mélisande's Hair, or the Trouble in Allemonde: A Postmodern Allegory at the Opéra-Comique', in Mary Ann Smart (ed.), *Siren Songs: Representations of Gender and Sexuality in Opera*, Princeton and Oxford: Princeton University Press, 2000, pp. 160–85.

Bergson, Henri, *Time and Free Will: An Essay on the Immediate Data of Consciousness* (1889), trans. F. L. Pogson, London: George Allen and Unwin, 1910.

Matter and Memory (1896), trans. Nancy Margaret Paul and W. Scott Palmer, London: Swan Sonnenschein, 1911.

'Dreams' (1901), in his *Mind-Energy*, trans. H. Wildon Carr, London: Macmillan, 1920, pp. 84–108.

Blaukopf, Herta (ed.), *Gustav Mahler–Richard Strauss: Correspondence 1888–1911*, trans. Edmund Jephcott, London: Faber and Faber, 1984.

Blunden, Allan (ed. and trans.), *Thomas Mann: Pro and Contra Wagner*, London: Faber and Faber, 1985.

Brancour, René, *Massenet*, Paris: Libraire Félix Alcan, 1922.

Brand, Juliane, Hailey, Christopher, and Harris, Donald (eds. and trans.), *The Berg–Schoenberg Correspondence: Selected Letters*, New York: W. W. Norton, 1987.

Brzoska, Matthias, *Franz Schrekers Oper 'Der Schatzgräber'*, Stuttgart: Franz Steiner Verlag Wiesbaden, 1988.

Burgard, Peter J. (ed.), *Nietzsche and the Feminine*, Charlottesville: University Press of Virginia, 1994.

Caughie, John, and Kuhn, Annette (eds.), *The Sexual Subject: A 'Screen' Reader in Sexuality*, London: Routledge, 1992.

Charlton, David, *Grétry and the Growth of Opéra-Comique*, Cambridge: Cambridge University Press, 1990.

French Opera 1730–1830: Meaning and Media, Aldershot: Ashgate, 2000.

Chua, Daniel, *Absolute Music and the Construction of Meaning*, Cambridge: Cambridge University Press, 1999.

Dahlhaus, Carl, *Nineteenth-Century Music*, trans. J. Bradford Robinson, Berkeley and Los Angeles: University of California Press, 1989.

The Idea of Absolute Music, trans. Roger Lustig, Chicago: University of Chicago Press, 1991.

Darcy, Warren, 'Creatio ex nihilo: The Genesis, Structure, and Meaning of the *Rheingold* Prelude', *Nineteenth-Century Music* 13/2 (1989), 79–100.

Dijkstra, Bram, *Idols of Perversity: Fantasies of Feminine Evil in Fin-de-Siècle Culture*, Oxford: Oxford University Press, 1986.

Durkheim, Emile, *The Elementary Forms of the Religious Life* (1912), trans. Joseph Ward Swain, London: George Allen and Unwin, 1915.

Ellenberger, Henri F., *The Discovery of the Unconscious: The History and Evolution of Dynamic Psychiatry*, London: Allen Lane, 1970.

Emmanuel, Maurice, *Pelléas et Mélisande: Etude historique et critique*, Paris: Mellottée, 1926.

Ennemoser, Joseph, *Der Magnetismus in Verhältnisse zur Natur und Religion*, Stuttgart and Tübingen: Cotta, 1842.

Finck, Henry, *Massenet and His Operas*, New York: John Lane Company, 1910.

Franklin, Peter, 'Distant Sounds – Fallen Music: *Der ferne Klang* as "Woman's Opera"?', *Cambridge Opera Journal* 3 (1991), 159–72.

Freud, Sigmund, *The Interpretation of Dreams* (1900), trans. James Strachey, New York: Avon Books, 1965.

'On Narcissism: An Introduction' (1914), in Strachey (ed. and trans.), *The Standard Edition*, vol. xii, pp. 67–104.

Introductory Lectures on Psycho-Analysis (1916–17), in Strachey (ed. and trans.), *The Standard Edition*, vol. xv.

Beyond the Pleasure Principle (1920), trans. James Strachey, New York: Norton, 1961.

'Group Psychology and the Analysis of the Ego' (1921), in Strachey (ed. and trans.), *The Standard Edition*, vol. xiv, pp. 64–144.

Civilization and Its Discontents (1930), trans. James Strachey, New York: Norton, 1961.

Gable, David, and Morgan, Robert (eds.), *Alban Berg: Historical and Analytical Perspectives*, Oxford: Clarendon Press, 1991.

Gay, Peter, *The Bourgeois Experience*, vol. i: *Education of the Senses*, Oxford: Oxford University Press, 1984.

Freud: A Life for Our Time, New York: Doubleday, 1989.

Gilliam, Bryan (ed.), *Richard Strauss and His World*, Princeton: Princeton University Press, 1992.

Richard Strauss: New Perspectives on the Composer and His Work, Durham, N.C.: Duke University Press, 1992.

Grayson, David A., 'The Interludes of *Pelléas et Mélisande*', *Cahiers Debussy* 1988–9, 100–22.

Gregor-Dellin, Martin, and Mack, Dietrich (eds.), *Cosima Wagner's Diaries: An Abridgement*, trans. Geoffrey Skelton, New Haven: Yale University Press, 1994.

Grey, Thomas S., *Wagner's Musical Prose: Texts and Contexts*, Cambridge: Cambridge University Press, 1995.

Groos, Arthur, and Parker, Roger (eds.), *Reading Opera*, Princeton: Princeton University Press, 1988.

Großmann-Vendrey, Susanna (ed.), *Bayreuth in der deutschen Presse: Rezeptionsgeschichte Richard Wagners und seiner Festspiele*, vol. i, Regensburg: Gustav Bosse Verlag, 1977.

Hailey, Christopher, *Franz Schreker, 1878–1934: A Cultural Biography*, Cambridge: Cambridge University Press, 1993.

Hartford, Robert (ed. and trans.), *Bayreuth: The Early Years*, London: Victor Gollancz, 1980.

Heath, Stephen, *The Sexual Fix*, London: Macmillan, 1982.

Heidegger, Martin, *Nietzsche*, trans. David Farrell Krell, 2 vols., New York: Harper and Row, 1979.

Hemmings, Frederic, *Theatre and State in France, 1760–1905*, Cambridge: Cambridge University Press, 1994.

Holloway, Robin, *Debussy and Wagner*, London: Eulenburg, 1979.

Howard, Patricia (ed. and trans.), *Gluck: An Eighteenth-Century Portrait in Letters and Documents*, Oxford: Oxford University Press, 1995.

Huebner, Steven, 'Massenet and Wagner: Bridling the Influence', *Cambridge Opera Journal* 5 (1993), 223–38.

Huret, Jules, *Enquête sur l'évolution littéraire*, Paris : Bibliothèque-Charpentier, 1901.

Irvine, Demar, *Massenet: A Chronicle of His Life and Times*, Portland: Amadeus Press, 1994.

Jacobs, Arthur, 'An Expectation Fulfilled', *Musical Times* 93 (March 1952), 127.

Janet, Pierre, *Autobiography*, in Carl Murchison (ed.), *History of Psychology in Autobiography*, vol. I, Worcester, Mass.: Clark University Press, 1930.

Jarman, Douglas (ed.), *Alban Berg: 'Wozzeck'*, Cambridge: Cambridge University Press, 1989.

Jelavich, Peter, *Munich and Theatrical Modernism*, Cambridge, Mass.: Harvard University Press, 1985.

Johnson, James H., *Listening in Paris: A Cultural History*, Berkeley and Los Angeles: University of California Press, 1995.

Kaiser, Georg (ed.), *Sämtliche Schriften von Carl Maria von Weber*, Berlin and Leipzig: Schuster and Loeffler, 1908.

Kaufmann, Walter (ed. and trans.), *Basic Writings of Nietzsche*, New York: Random House, 1966.

Kerman, Joseph, *Opera as Drama*, New York: Alfred A. Knopf, 1956; rev. ed. Berkeley: University of California Press, 1988.

Kesting, Hanjo (ed.), *Richard Wagner Briefe*, Munich and Zurich: Piper Verlag, 1983.

Kittler, Friedrich, 'World-Breath: On Wagner's Media Technology', in David Levin (ed.), *Opera through Other Eyes*, Stanford: Stanford University Press, 1993, pp. 215–35.

Klose, Friedrich, *Meine Lehrjahre bei Bruckner: Erinnerungen und Betrachtungen*, Regensburg: Gustav Bosse Verlag, 1927.

Kramer, Lawrence, *Music as Cultural Practice, 1800–1900*, Berkeley: University of California Press, 1990.

'Culture and Musical Hermeneutics: The Salome Complex', *Cambridge Opera Journal* 2 (1990), 269–94.

Classical Music and Postmodern Knowledge, Berkeley: University of California Press, 1995.

Kristeva, Julia, *Revolution in Poetic Language*, trans. Margaret Waller, New York: Columbia University Press, 1984.

The Kristeva Reader, ed. Toril Moi, New York: Columbia University Press, 1986.

Lacan, Jacques, *The Seminar, Book II: The Ego in Freud's Theory and in the Technique of Psychoanalysis, 1954–1955*, trans. Sylvana Tomaselli, New York: Norton, 1988.

Le séminaire, livre IV: La relation de l'objet, 1956–1957, ed. Jacques-Alain Miller, Paris: Seuil, 1994.

The Seminar, Book VII: The Ethics of Psychoanalysis, 1959–1960, trans. Dennis Porter, London: Routledge, 1992.

The Seminar, Book XI: The Four Fundamental Concepts of Psychoanalysis, 1964, trans. Alan Sheridan, London: Hogarth Press and Institute of Psycho-Analysis, 1977.

'Ecrits': A Selection, trans. Alan Sheridan, New York: W. W. Norton, 1977.

Les complexes familiaux dans la formation de l'individu: Essai d'analyse d'une fonction en psychologie, Paris: Navarin, 1984.

Lacoue-Labarthe, Philippe, *Musica ficta (Figures of Wagner)*, trans. Felicia McCarren, Stanford: Stanford University Press, 1994.

Langham Smith, Richard (ed. and trans.), *Debussy on Music*, New York: Alfred A. Knopf, 1977.

Laplanche, Jean, and Pontalis, Jean-Bertrand, *The Language of Psycho-Analysis*, trans. Donald Nicholson-Smith, New York: Norton, 1973.

Leppert, Richard, *The Sight of Sound: Music, Representation, and the History of the Body*, Berkeley: University of California Press, 1993.

Lesure, François (ed.), *Claude Debussy: Correspondance 1884–1918*, Paris: Hermann, 1993.

Lockspeiser, Edward, *Debussy: His Life and Mind*, 2 vols., London: Cassell, 1965.

Louis, Rudolf, *Die Deutsche Musik der Gegenwart*, Munich and Leipzig: Georg Müller, 1909.

Maeterlinck, Maurice, *The Treasure of the Humble* (1896), trans. Alfred Sutro, London: George Allen, 1905.

Le temple enseveli, Paris: Fasquelle, 1902.

The Unknown Guest, trans. Alexander Teixeira de Mattos, New York: Dodd Mead, 1916.

Mallarmé, Stéphane, 'Théâtre', *National Observer*, 1 July 1893, in Henri Mondor and G. Jean-Aubry (eds.), *Oeuvres complètes*, Paris: Gallimard, 1945, pp. 328–30.

Mann, Thomas, *Reflections of a Nonpolitical Man* (1918), trans. Walter D. Morris, New York: Frederick Ungar, 1983.

'Richard Wagner und der *Ring des Nibelungen*' (1938), in *Thomas Mann: Gesammelte Werke*, vol. IX, Berlin: Aufbau-Verlag, 1955, pp. 502–27.

'Schopenhauer' (1938), in Hermann Kurzke and Stephan Stachorski (eds.), *Essays*, vol. IV, Frankfurt: S. Fischer Verlag, 1995, pp. 253–303.

Mann, William, *Richard Strauss: A Critical Study of the Operas*, London: Cassell, 1964.

McClary, Susan, *Feminine Endings: Music, Gender, and Sexuality*, Minnesota and London: University of Minnesota Press, 1991.

Messmer, Franzpeter, *Kritiken zu den Uraufführungen der Bühnenwerke von Richard Strauss*, Pfaffenhofen: W. Ludwig Verlag, 1989.

Metz, Christian, *The Imaginary Signifier: Psychoanalysis and the Cinema*, trans. Celia Britton, Annwyl Williams, Ben Brewster, and Alfred Guzzetti, Bloomington: Indiana University Press, 1977.

Morgenstern, Soma, *Alban Berg und seine Idole: Erinnerungen und Briefe*, Lüneburg: zu Klampen, 1995.

Müller, Ulrich, and Wapnewski, Peter (eds.), *Wagner Handbook*, translation edited by John Deathridge, Cambridge, Mass.: Harvard University Press, 1992.

Nattiez, Jean-Jacques, *Wagner Androgyne*, trans. Stewart Spencer, Princeton: Princeton University Press, 1993.

Newman, Ernest, *Wagner as Man and Artist*, New York: Alfred A. Knopf, 1924.

Nichols, Roger, and Langham Smith, Richard, *Claude Debussy: 'Pelléas et Mélisande'*, Cambridge: Cambridge University Press, 1989.

Niemann, Walter, *Die Musik der Gegenwart*, Berlin and Leipzig: Schuster and Loeffler, 1921.

Nietzsche, Friedrich, *The Birth of Tragedy* (1872), in Kaufmann (ed. and trans.), *Basic Writings of Nietzsche*.

Untimely Meditations (1876), trans. R. J. Hollingdale, Cambridge: Cambridge University Press, 1983.

Human, All Too Human (1886), trans. R. J. Hollingdale, Cambridge: Cambridge University Press, 1986.

The Genealogy of Morals (1887), in Kaufmann (ed. and trans.), *Basic Writings of Nietzsche*.

The Case of Wagner (1888), in Kaufmann (ed. and trans.), *Basic Writings of Nietzsche*.

Nietzsche kontra Wagner (1888), in Giorgio Colli and Mazzino Montinari (eds.), *Friedrich Nietzsche: Sämtliche Werke, Kritische Studienausgabe*, vol. VI, Munich: Deutsche Taschenbuch Verlag, 1980.

The Will to Power (1901), trans. Walter Kaufmann and R. J. Hollingdale, New York: Alfred A. Knopf, 1968.

Pfitzner, Hans, *Gesammelte Schriften*, vol. II, Augsburg: Benno Filser, 1926.

Sämtliche Schriften, vol. IV, Tutzing: Hans Schneider, 1987.

Redwood, Christopher (ed.), *A Delius Companion*, London: John Calder, 1976.

Reich, Willi, *Alban Berg*, trans. Cornelius Cardew, New York: Vienna House, 1974.

Rose, Jacqueline, *Sexuality in the Field of Vision*, London: Verso, 1986.

Rosolato, Guy, 'La voix: entre corps et langage', *Revue Française de Psychanalyse* 38/1 (1974), 75–94.

Rushton, Julian, *Berlioz: 'Roméo et Juliette'*, Cambridge: Cambridge University Press, 1994.

Schmidt, Leopold, *Aus dem Musikleben der Gegenwart*, Berlin: A. Hofmann and Co., 1909.

Schopenhauer, Arthur, *The World as Will and Representation* (1818; 1859), trans. E. F. J. Payne, 2 vols., New York: Dover Publications, 1969.

'Essay on Spirit Seeing and Everything Connected Therewith', in *Parerga and Paralipomena* (1851), trans. E. F. J. Payne, Oxford: Clarendon Press, 1974, vol. I, pp. 247–58.

Schubert, Gotthilf von, *Die Symbolik des Traumes*, Bamberg: Kunz, 1814.

Schuh, Willi (ed.), *Richard Strauss: Briefe an die Eltern*, Berlin: Atlantis Verlag, 1954.

Betrachtungen und Erinnerungen, 2nd edn, Zurich: Atlantis, 1957.

Segal, Lynne, and McIntosh, Mary (eds.), *Sex Exposed: Sexuality and the Pornography Debate*, London: Virago Press, 1992.

Showalter, Elaine, *Sexual Anarchy: Gender and Culture at the Fin de Siècle*, New York: Viking, 1990.

Silverman, Kaja, *The Acoustic Mirror: The Female Voice in Psychoanalysis and Cinema*, Bloomington and Indianapolis: Indiana University Press, 1988.

Solenière, Eugène de, *Massenet: Etude critique et documentaire*, Paris: Bibliothèque d'Art de la Critique, 1897.

Sternfeld, Richard, and Wolzogen, Hans von (eds.), *Richard Wagner: Sämtliche Schriften und Dichtungen*, Leipzig: Breitkopf und Härtel, 1916.

Stevens, Miriam, *Turn-of-the-Century Cabaret*, London: Routledge, 1989.

Strachey, James (ed. and trans.), *The Standard Edition of the Complete Psychological Works of Sigmund Freud*, London: Hogarth Press, 1953–74.

Strunk, Oliver (ed. and trans.), *Source Readings in Music History: The Romantic Era*, New York: W. W. Norton, 1965.

Tambling, Jeremy, *Opera and the Culture of Fascism*, Oxford: Clarendon Press, 1996.

Threlfall, Robert, *Frederick Delius: A Supplementary Catalogue*, London: Delius Trust, 1986.

Tomlinson, Gary, *Metaphysical Song: An Essay on Opera*, Princeton: Princeton University Press, 1999.

Trenner, Franz, 'Richard Strauss und Ernst von Wolzogen', *Richard Strauss Jahrbuch*, 1953, 110–21.

Trillig, Johannes, *Untersuchungen zur Rezeption Claude Debussys in der Zeitgenössischen Musikkritik*, Tutzing: Hans Schneider, 1983.

Wagner, Richard, *Das Kunstwerk der Zukunft* (1849), in Richard Sternfeld and Hans von Wolzogen (eds.), *Richard Wagner: Sämtliche Schriften und Dichtungen*, Leipzig: Breitkopf und Härtel, 1916 (*SSD*), vol. III.

Oper und Drama (1851), *SSD*, vols. III–IV.

Eine Mitteilung an meine Freunde (1851), *SSD*, vol. IV.

Zukunftsmusik (1860), *SSD*, vol. VIII.

Programme note to *Tristan und Isolde*: Prelude (1860), *SSD*, vol. XII, pp. 346–7.

Beethoven (1870), *SSD*, vol. IX.

'Das Bühnenfestspielhaus zu Bayreuth' (1873), *SSD*, vol. IX, pp. 322–44.

'Das Bühnenweihfestspiel in Bayreuth 1882' (1882), *SSD*, vol. X, pp. 297–308.

Briefe, ed. Hanjo Kesting, Munich and Zurich: Piper Verlag, 1983.

Warlock, Peter, *Frederick Delius*, London: The Bodley Head, 1923.

Weininger, Otto, *Sex and Character*, trans. unidentified, London: Heinemann, 1944.

Weissmann, Adolf, *Musik in der Weltkrise*, Stuttgart and Berlin: Deutsche Verlags-Anstalt, 1922.

Whitman, Walt, *Leaves of Grass*, ed. Bradley Sculley and Harold Blodgett, New York: W. W. Norton and Co., 1973.

Willett, John (ed. and trans.), *Brecht on Theatre*, London: Methuen, 1964.

Williamson, John, *The Music of Hans Pfitzner*, Oxford: Clarendon Press, 1992.

Winston, Richard, and Winston, Clara (eds. and trans.), *Letters of Thomas Mann, 1889–1955*, New York: Alfred A. Knopf, 1971.

Wolzogen, Ernst von, *Wie ich mich ums Leben brachte: Erinnerungen und Erfahrungen*, Brunswick and Hamburg: Westermann, 1922.

Žižek, Slavoj, *Tarrying with the Negative*, Durham, N.C.: Duke University Press, 1993.

'There Is No Sexual Relationship', in Renata Salecl and Slavoj Žižek (eds.), *Gaze and Voice as Love Objects*, Durham, N.C., and London: Duke University Press, 1996, pp. 208–49.

INDEX

216

Index

217